MW01170938

I Am Woman

Natasha Bostic Baymon

J. Elyse Publishing, LLC

Copyright © 2023 by Natasha Bostic Baymon

Library of Congress Control Number: 2023903785

All rights reserved.

No portion of this book may be reproduced in any form without written permission from the publisher or author, except as permitted by U.S. copyright law.

Contents

Chapter 1

THE STEPFATHER

I was walking into a large room that reminded me of a high school gymnasium. In this dim room there appeared to be hundreds of people asleep, either on the floor or on cots. As I looked around the room for my daughter, I thought I spotted her asleep with her father, asleep right next to her. I could tell her father was moving back and forth as if he was having *sex* with our daughter. They were both lying on their left sides and her back was towards him. I immediately started walking towards them so I would know for sure what I thought I saw, as it was dark, and the only light was a glimmer from under the closed door into the hallway.

I was screaming to myself, "he'd better not be messing with my child!" I did not want to make any assumptions, so I figured once I got to where they were I would pull her father off and I would check to see if his penis was wet. When I got close enough and could see it looked like he *was* having sex with our daughter, I grabbed him off her and felt that his penis *was* wet!! My MAMA BEAR instincts rose inside me, and I got so much strength that I literally grabbed his penis with my right hand and yanked it out of its socket, right from his body! I then flung his penis all the way to the wall and blood splattered everywhere! My heart was beating so fast out of my chest. I did not realize what I had done, or where this strength came from. Then I woke up; sweating profusely, panting uncontrollably and realized... it was just a dream, Tasha... breathe. It was just a dream.

In April 2006, shortly after my divorce from Charles, my child's father, I decided I would visit my stepfather, James Garner, who was in the Lakeland Correctional Facility outside Grand Rapids, Michigan. Charles never thought it was a good idea to visit James when we were married.

"What are you expecting to get from him, an apology?" he'd ask with cynicism. Charles never supported me anyway, except in small endeavors, but nothing too challenging, so I was not surprised at his response. As soon as I separated from Charles, I decided to move forward with this plan.

James had been convicted - a LIFE sentence without parole - for a Homicide/Felony Murder charge. I was having a conversation with my Auntie Terri, who helped me find him on the prisoners' website. I then called and spoke to the warden of that prison and she gave me instructions on how to go about paying my stepfather a visit. I was told I would need to write him a letter and request he add me to his visitor's list. Since the divorce between him and my mother had been finalized almost 30 years ago, I was technically not considered a family member, and as a former stepdaughter, I would not be allowed to visit without his permission.

I did what she advised me to do and wrote him a letter telling him I would be in town looking at some real estate in the area and would love to see him. I was a real estate agent and had been investing in real estate for several years at this point in my life. James quickly wrote me back in a matter of a week telling me how happy he would be to see 'his daughter' again, and he sent me the application to fill out in order to be added to the visitor's list, which I immediately sent back completed. About a week or so later I received a letter from the prison warden stating I was cleared to visit James, and giving me the days and hours of visitation.

On the same day I received that letter, without hesitation, I booked a flight to Grand Rapids, Michigan, to visit my former stepfather. I booked a hotel, rented a car, and the next day I was on my way to the Gerald R. Ford International airport. I would only plan to stay for one night.

On Friday, April 7th, 2006, at about 9 a.m. in the morning, I checked into the Holiday Inn and Suites in Grand Rapids. I did not bother to unpack anything from my suitcase and spent the majority of my time there going over the conversations in my head, and pumping myself up to have enough courage to do what I came here to do.

On the hour and a half long drive from Grand Rapids to Lakeland Correctional Facility, I wondered if I had made the right decision. I had not seen James since I was about ten years old, well after he and my mother finally divorced when I was about seven years old, almost 25 years ago. I also had never been to visit anyone in prison, so this would be a first. The prison was located well off the beaten path and I suspect if someone did find a way to escape, they would have a long way to go to reach civilization, and they would probably be apprehended by then.

As I drove up to the prison gates, it reminded me of the prisons I had seen on television, tall wired gates with barbed wires at the top. I wondered if those wires could electrocute a prisoner to keep him from escaping? I surely was not planning on finding out! After parking the car, I started to feel a little bit of anxiety, so I began to pray. I prayed that God would give me the courage to do what I set out to do and then decided to call my grandmother to let her know where I was. I also called three of my aunts, Terri, De-De, and Nita. I informed them I was at the prison to see James to have this much-needed conversation. They encouraged me to carry out my plans which gave me the confidence to continue this journey I had embarked upon, knowing each of them had their own experiences with the likes of James.

I finally got out of the rental car, closed the door, took a couple of deep breaths, and began slowly walking towards the front door of the prison. I took a moment to look around the parking lot and did not see a single person walking, no car was moving, no birds chirping. It was like everything was at a standstill for an entire five seconds. *I* even appeared to be walking in slow motion! Everything except my breathing, that is! I began to pray again as I felt like I was having heart palpitations. "God, I know you are with me, I know that you have called me to stand up and do what is right, even when it is an extremely difficult thing to do. Not just for myself, but for others who have come before me, and those who will come after me. I'm here now, God! I showed up, and I need you to take it from here."

I then noticed people walking, having conversations, cars were moving again, and birds were chirping. I even noticed the sky was blue with no clouds, the sun was shining bright, and the air was crisp and clean. "These deep breaths will do me some good," I said to myself. I walked into the prison. I was screened and given a locker to put my personal items in, along with a visitor's badge. The locker room was damp with a hint of mildew and the stench of anxiety in the air from all the visitors. Whether we were there to visit a loved one, or a not-so-loved one, the tension in the air was evident. We were then directed into a room that resembled a high school cafeteria. The walls were cinder block and painted a dingy off-white color. The room was filled with guards at each station and there were cafeteria tables throughout the room. Some of the prisoners wore orange jumpsuits and others wore street clothes. I had no idea how they chose who could wear street clothes or not, or if they even had options. The room smelled of musk and was filled with anticipation. Most prisoners looked excited to see their visitors. Most visitors appeared burdened and worried. The tables were angled in such a way that each guard at each post was able to watch the prisoners' every move. All prisoners had to sit facing a guard at all times. The inside of this prison was nothing like I had imagined. I thought there was going to be a plexiglass between us, and I would have to pick up the phone to talk to this man while he was on the other side of the plexiglass. I probably would have felt much safer, but hey, I'm here now. This facility seemed extremely relaxed compared to what I've seen on television. Housing convicted murderers and all; but then again, television is the only experience I had to compare it to.

I stood around waiting for about 15 minutes while they went to retrieve the prisoner. Observing the passersby, I wondered what this or that prisoner may have done to get here, and what type of burden his family carried for him to have to visit him. Palms sweating, heart-pounding, yet feeling a level of achievement I had never felt before. I was grateful I had even made it this far.

James was escorted into the cafeteria by a guard, in handcuffs. He wore his street clothes which consisted of a nice button-down shirt with animal prints, and a pair of black slacks with black dress shoes. It looked like he was going to Bible study or something; I guess he dressed up for the occasion, I do not know why though. He was looking like a sneakin' deacon! Whereas I came in my jeans and tennis shoes, ready to 'tho' down!' James stood about 5ft 8in, 225 pounds, medium build, with a dark brown complexion. He was not a very attractive man at all, with his wide nose stretched across his face and extra full lips. Most people would say he was 'strong in the face!' Not that there is anything wrong with a wide nose and big lips, as some of the most beautiful black people have such features, but on his face, nothing would be a compliment. He possessed these shifty eyes as if he was always up to no-good. He had the kind of coarse hair that his mama would have to put a straightening comb through, just to be able to comb it when he was younger. I swear he looked just like 'them Stricklands,' which is what my family would always say about him and his family.

Once inside the room, the guard removed the handcuffs and directed us to one of the cafeteria tables where James had to sit facing a guard, as those were the rules.

James started in on the small talk while I just listened. While strolling down memory lane, he reminisced about how we were the perfect little family, and how he really missed having his family in his life. He particularly spoke about how adorable I was as a child and how I was such a *good* little girl who never gave him any problems. He looked at me, leaned in, and spoke as if he was just catching up with an old friend, reminiscing, shooting the breeze. I just stared at him, mean mugging, not even believing the audacity that he pompously attempted to paint this perfect picture of my childhood; when the truth is, it could not have been further from the truth. As he continued the small talk, I realized he was wearing cologne. He actually wore cologne! A nasty, smelly, moldy, funky, musk cologne from the early 90's. I guess he had not had a chance to update his collection since he had been in prison. I am surprised I did not notice the smell earlier, as I am usually very sensitive to odors. Perhaps it was the words that were spewing out of his mouth that made me nauseated, or perhaps just the look on his face. He was probably wondering why I was here, or maybe he was just happy anybody would come to visit him. I was still trying to muster up enough courage to just say what I needed to say. However, for now, I would allow him to chat me up to buy me some time.

"I remember when you were just a little girl, you were nothing like the other kids," James began.

He had a light, high voice for a man which I never noticed as a child. When young, any voice coming out of a man seemed big and boisterous. But today, he sounded like a little girl! I do not know if his voice was always this high, or if it got this high since he had been in prison. I guess he bent over and picked up the soap! (Hint, Hint).

"You never liked to go outside and play in the dirt because you never wanted to get your clothes dirty," he went on. "You always wanted to wear dresses to daycare and look pretty. You did not like anybody messing up your clothes or your toys, and your hair always had to be combed before you would even go outside to play. The other kids were rough with their toys, and always tearing up their clothes and breaking things, but you, no, you were the only one who was *very particular* about yourself and your things."

Wow! He was actually right. When I was growing up, I did feel like I was different from my other siblings. I almost felt like I did not belong to this family. Maybe I was adopted? I liked things one way; they liked things another way. I liked things neat and clean, like my room. They kept their rooms messy and dirty. My little sister Punkin and I shared a room, and her side of the room always resembled a pig pen. She was Messy Marvin's sister! I also had an older and a younger brother.

I liked to do certain things, like reading books and playing school, while they liked to do certain other things, like playing in the dirt and climbing trees. We were like oil and water and just never seemed to mix. To sit here and listen to James confirm who I am and apparently who I always was even as a little child, was both enlightening and torture! Why should I sit here and let him scurry down memory lane while tormenting me with the memories of the past, all with a smirk on his face? If he wants to have small talk, then by all means, I will be more than happy to oblige....my way!

I started out by asking him, "So what were you convicted for?" Of course, I had already done the research, so I knew why he was in prison. But he was talking way too much, and I was determined to get the purpose of my visit back on track.

He hesitated before answering. "Well, what had happened was......" the notorious chatter people do when they are about to lie... "it was really self-defense," he stammered.

"But you're not in prison for self-defense. I asked what were you convicted for?" I'm pretty sure I would have made a good attorney as I am great at drilling people with questions.

"Murder," he finally said, hesitantly. "But I am appealing the conviction of life without parole because the police officers tampered with the evidence."

The sad part is, I knew there was a possibility he was telling the truth, at least the part about the police tampering with evidence, especially when dealing with convicting a black man. Why were they always trying to take out the 'Black Man?' Why did they feel a need to tear down the 'Black Family structure?' This has been going on indeed since slavery, and is deemed a form of systemic racism. It is a known fact many black men have been arrested for no apparent reason and convicted for crimes they did *not* commit. Black men pulled over by the cops, gunned down in the streets, shot in the back, wrestled down to the ground, tased until paralyzed, knees on neck, and cries of, "*I Can't Breathe!*"

Life sentences and death penalties for crimes they did *not* commit, all because the police *tampered* with evidence. Additionally, a black man with a prior criminal record won't stand a chance. However, I also knew *this* man, James, was more than likely guilty of the crimes he was convicted of because I had experienced his level of violence first hand, and knew what he was capable of. No, he did not need the police to destroy him and his family; he was successful at doing that all by himself, with no assistance from the cops. Matter of fact, he was probably finally paying for some shit he had previously gotten away with.

"So, who did you kill?" I asked very matter-of-factly.

"My girlfriend's uncle. But this was in self-defense, which is the reason why I feel like I have a chance to appeal."

"How was it self-defense?" In all actuality, I could care less why he was in prison for life without parole. I was merely warming up the conversation, trying to keep my emotions under control.

"My girlfriend and I were having a domestic dispute."

"Of course," I thought.

"And she left and went to her uncle's house. I came over there asking to speak to her so that we could work out our differences. The situation got physical and the uncle went to get his gun. He pulled his gun out on me, so I had no choice but to fire my weapon. Unfortunately, he died and that is how I got here. He threatened my life first, and I had no other option but to defend myself."

Hmmm-mmm. James had been in prison before and did a 10-year sentence for the same type of incident. He was reportedly in a domestic dispute and shot someone who was trying to help the woman, when a police officer was caught in the line of fire. The police officer was shot, but survived the gunshot wound. James was no stranger to domestic violence; this seemed to be his forte. His relationship with my mother lasted all of seven years. The worst seven years of my life, full of nothing but violence and abuse.

My mother and James had gotten married after only knowing each other for a few weeks. James was home on military leave from the United States Army, and was on his way back to the base. I am not quite sure where they met, but I would assume it was at a local bar. My mother was 18 years old with two infant children. My older brother, Lewis, was 18 months old, and I was literally only a couple of months old when they were married. James was stationed outside Tacoma, Washington, and that is where we lived for the first two years of my life. My sister, Punkin, was born there. My mother experienced a lot of physical, mental, and emotional abuse from this man throughout the entire marriage. He was 'rotten to the core.'

I was tirelessly listening to his stories as they bore a resemblance to me watching a Charlie Brown cartoon, wha-wha-wha-wha-wha... "Your lips are moving, but you just ain't saying nothing," I said to myself.

"Let me interrupt you so that I can get to the reason why I'm here," I boldly said. "About a month ago I was watching this movie called The Antwone Fisher story. This movie was based on a true story about a young man who was mentally, emotionally, and physically violated by his foster family and needed to confront them about what they had done to him when he was a child. I am here for the same reason, to confront you about molesting me when I was a child." I am pretty sure I got all that out in one breath.

When James repeatedly molested me, he would sneak into the bedroom, careful to not wake my little sister, as we shared a twin bed. He would carry me out of the room into the hallway on those creaky wood floors and then to the kitchen.

"Where am I going?" I would ask half asleep.

"Shut up!" he'd reply in a mean whisper.

James would lay me on the kitchen table, pull my gown up and pull down my panties to my ankles. He would cock open my thighs and begin to rub his hands up and down my body. I became numb, paralyzed, at the act of him touching me. It would be like scorpions crawling up and down your body from head to toe. Frozen. Dead. Silenced. Then I began to hear noises, sounds, awkward moans coming from his voice, as if he was delighting in the torture he bestowed upon me. He would begin to kiss my inner thighs up and down my legs, then into my vagina. I did everything I could to keep myself from throwing up. I did not move, I did not open my eyes, I did not make a sound. As he used the tip of his tongue to lick my private parts until he was good and satisfied, I attempted to hold my breath until this heinous act was over. Until he had had enough.

I slowly began to open my eyes to see if he was done with his business. As he was getting up from the kitchen table, wiping his mouth, he snatched my panties from around my feet, put them up to his nose and began to inhale my scent with his eyes closed. He then put my panties back on me and stood me up on the floor. My body was limp as a rag doll and my head was spinning from holding my breath.

"Now you make sure you keep your mouth shut. If you ever breathe a word of this to anybody, you know what will happen, right?" he would say while grabbing both my arms and shaking me.

"Y-y-yes." I would reply, whimpering. I knew what he would do to my mother. He would beat her bloody and try to kill her, like he had done so many times before. And what happens when he succeeds?

"You don't want your mother to die, do you? Do you?" Once he stopped shaking me, he stood up and hugged me, pressing my face against his *hard* penis.

"N-no," squeezing the tears from my eyes and turning my face away. He finally released me to return to my bedroom.

That's the one thing I remember the most as a child, that I didn't want my mother to die. It wasn't the molestation, the violation, the abuse. I just did not want to be responsible for him killing my mother. It was a massive burden to bear.

The thought of James killing my mother haunted me for years. Because of him, I could only see my mother in this light:

Black eyes, bruises, arm in sling, swollen jaw, busted lip, cries through the night, forced smile, sadness, depression, no friends, scared, trampled over, low self-esteem, no self-love. I often wondered if my mother thought that if James killed her, would she be better off? I never understood why she would not fight back, not even try. Almost as if she had given up before the fight started. Now, I may not win every fight, but you best believe you would know you have been in a fight with me!

"Oh no!" James exclaimed. "You were really young when I was married to your mother. You were too young to remember anything like that. I don't know where you're getting this from."

Although he tried to sound surprised that he was being accused of such a thing, he was not fooling me! I believe he knew why I had come to see him, but he was hoping it was not true. I bet he was up all night rehearsing his lines, just like I was! Sounding all robotic and whatnot! It was now about to be curtain time for this stage play called *This is Your Life*!

He was right about one thing; I was very young when the molestation took place, between the ages of 3-7 years old. I remember because I was in a Head Start Program from 3-5 years old. During the latter time in this program, I can recall an incident where I had gradually become extremely reclusive when it came to socializing with the other kids. One day, I overheard the owner of the daycare speaking to one of the staff members and they were talking about me and the possibility that someone may have been "messing" with me at home.

"Have you noticed anything different about Tasha in the past few weeks?"

"I have. She's no longer playing with her friends, not even with her favorite toys."

"Yeah, normally she's the first one to grab the little black baby doll with the long hair, but it's still sitting on the shelf."

"She won't even agree to read when I call on her anymore, she just stares at me with tears in her eyes. When I ask her if anything is wrong, she just shakes her head with a firm NO!"

"I think something is going on at home. I think somebody's 'messing' with her."

"I think you're right, but what can we do?"

"I have tried to call her mother, left her several messages. I even drove by their house one day and left a note on the door, since the Daycare van picks her up and drops her off at home every day, we never get to see her mother."

"Did her mother ever call you back?"

"It's been two weeks and I'm still waiting."

"Damn shame."

"Damn shame, indeed."

I wanted so badly to speak up at the time, but could not because I was afraid James would kill my mother. Of course, I believed him because he did not hesitate to physically abuse her right in front of my siblings and me. Did I really want my mother's blood on my hands? No! I would never let that happen! So I remained silent, in exchange for the burden I would carry for my mother, until this moment, when I was able to release it.

Since my mother married James when my brother was a toddler, and I was just a newborn baby, we always *assumed* he was our father. I am not sure if my mother wanted us to believe that he was, but James *surely* wanted us to know he was *not* our real father. My mother never made mention of our real father. James is the one who told me my father's name for the first time. I guess he thought it was not as bad if I was being molested by my *stepfather* instead of my *real father*. Also, to slightly ease his guilty conscience, he would give me a dollar to put under my pillow after each violation.

"Here, take this," he would say, handing me a $1 bill. "Put this under your pillow and you better not tell nobody where you got it from, you hear me?"

"Yes," I'd say shamefully on my way back to my room. I honestly did not know what to call what was happening to me. All I know is, I felt filthy, dirty, grimy….unclean. I stopped by the bathroom and closed the door as I took some toilet paper from the roll and wiped between my legs. The tissue was wet, I mean really wet and I threw the tissue in the toilet and flushed it. "Yuck!" I then ran to my room and closed the door. I jumped in the bed with my little sister who was still sound asleep. I curled up in a fetal position and began to cry myself back to sleep. I hated feeling dirty…unclean!

Either James thought he was paying for my silence, or he thought he could buy my silence with a dollar. Regardless, I could not risk my mother's life by telling anyone. So this $1 bill would have to do, what other options did I have?

My mother would sometimes ask me, "Tasha, where did you get that money?"

"I found it." Yes, I had learned to lie at a very early age; the stakes were far too high not to. I would take that dollar when we went to the store and buy myself some candy, and not share it with my other siblings. "They don't want this dirty candy, bought with this dirty dollar," I would think to myself. I needed to keep them at bay, as far away from this dilemma of mine as possible. Just like me, they had enough to worry about. I am sure I had managed to acquire over $100 throughout this time period prior to reaching the first grade. One hundred filthy, dirty, nasty, disgusting one-dollar bills! How dreadful!

I continued to press the issue with James, no matter how much he resisted. "We lived in that white house near the railroad tracks on Willow Road in Kankakee, IL. When Mama was working the graveyard shift at A.O. Smith, you would come to me and my sister's room and get me out of bed."

"No, you are mistaken!" he was on the defense.

"You would carry me into the kitchen and lay me on the table under this low-hanging chandelier," I continued.

"I'm telling you, that was not..." James attempted to cut me off.

"I remember because the bright light in my face would awaken me each time you did it," I continued.

"No, that wasn't me, I would never do that!"

"On that metal kitchen table, with that light in my face, spreading my legs with your face between my thighs..."

"You're confused," he tried to silence my voice yet again, but I was relentless.

"No, I am not confused; you were just banking on me not remembering because I was 'so young.' I always pretended to be asleep, but you would sneak into our room and pick me up out of bed, carrying me into the kitchen and lay me on that kitchen table. You molested me! As you stroked my baby clit with your grown-ass, manish-ass, nasty-ass tongue!"

I refused to let up. Once I got started, it was hard to stop.

In my mind, I would pretend I was outside playing hopscotch, or jumping rope somewhere out in an open field with the sun shining down on me, and the wind in my face to keep myself from being present during these periods of violation.

"Month in, month out, year-end, year out, for four years until my mother finally divorced yo' sorry ass! No, I'm not confused, I'm well aware of what happened. I was there! I was put in a position of fear and shame! I was a helpless, vulnerable baby girl with no voice, because of your threats on my mother's life! I have had to carry that burden all of my life because of you!"

I was really getting emotional and raising my voice until I saw the guard look over at me to pipe it down. I reminded myself again, "Deep breaths, Tasha, deep breaths."

James appeared to be shocked, but not really, because he had to play out his scene. "I'm telling you that couldn't have been me because I never lived with you all in that house near the railroad tracks." He attempted to defend his position. I guess he had to try to come up with something. "Me and your mother were already separated. You may be thinking about my brother, Weetie. People always said we looked just alike and your mother was cheating on me with him. That had to have been him because it was not me!"

Perpetrators will *ALWAYS* try to place the blame on someone else. They will do anything to not have to take some responsibility for their actions. I definitely was not expecting James to come clean with me and confess the truth. Why would he? He's a liar, abuser, molester, and murderer, among other things. If he did, he would also have to offer up an explanation, which there would never be an explanation good enough to cover such heinous actions, right? Some people will never be able to accept the truth of their wrongdoing. My purpose for being here was not to coax him into apologizing for what he had done. My purpose was to face the hardcore facts about my experience with him and to look him square in the eyes as I did it, so that *I* could be *free*. I deserved that!

I was on a mission! Now it was time for me to fire my backup bullets!

"Not only did you molest me, but I have had conversations with three of my aunts who said you also either molested or attempted to rape them, too. My grandmother has even expressed that when we were living with them when my grandfather was at work, you came and slipped into *her* bed one night, trying to rub up on *her*, pretending to be my grandfather! So you mean to tell me they were all too young to remember, too? Could they possibly have thought that it was somebody other than you, like your brother, Weetie? I think not!"

Yes, I had his ass cornered now! I had punched him in the jugular, and had him right by the balls!

So he thought all these years had passed and the women in my family would have never shared our stories with one another? Never shared our pain? Our fears? Clearly, he was banking on that, but this was not the case. Not with the Bostic women!

He pathetically looked down towards the floor, sadly, as I stared right at him with ultimate disgust. Not even batting an eye. I didn't know if this melancholy demeanor was authentic or not, but I honestly did not care. I would let God be the judge of that. We sat there in silence for moments until he finally spoke.

"Well, if you feel like I've done something to you that hurt you, then I apologize for that," he stated reluctantly, in his high, girly voice. While he looked despondent, with solemn eyes, shoulders humped over and head hung low, his energy gave me manipulative vibes. These are his rehearsed lines for the stage play as he had been awaiting my arrival. He had played out in his head all the different ways this could go. His last resort was to apologize if he could not get me to budge. He was playing checkers, not chess, and he had one last man on the board and it was not a King.

"I am not here for your apology, and especially not the lame one you are trying to give. If I feel like you hurt me? What kind of statement is that? My purpose for being here is to look you in your face and let you know that you *did* hurt me, you *did* violate me, you *did* molest me as a child, yet you did *not* destroy me. You must live with the sins you have committed against me, my mother, and my entire family. This life sentence you are serving is not just because you murdered, you abused, you controlled and manipulated, but you have violated every woman in my family and you will pay for it as you rot in your prison cell for the rest of your life! You and your violent acts have not been able to steal my joy, my confidence in ME, or my ability to strive to bring about healing to my family, and to other women in this world. I am a survivor! I have survived you and I will continue to elevate myself above my experiences until I breathe my last breath! Now you shut up!"

Ha! Umph, I guess I told him!

So many years of suppressed anger, emotions, hurt, pain, and devastation was unleashed onto James at this moment, but with dignity and a smidge of class. I would not give him the satisfaction of seeing tears flow from these eyes, or seeing that little girl, afraid with no voice. Yes, when I first arrived, I may have been nervous and scared, but TODAY my courage more than outweighed my fear of him. I refused to give him the authority to control my emotions! No, I was not about to do that! He had controlled enough of my life up to this point, but the buck stops here! What James was experiencing was the grown woman who came to visit him in prison and sucker-punched him dead in the throat, with the most powerful uppercut that I had been building up the strength for over the past 30 years! He got what he deserved. I got what I came for. My inner child that he had instilled such fear in, had to be put on the back burner. The fear that James would kill my mother, the fear that if I ever spoke of the molestation my mother's blood would be on my hands. No, no, no, not today! Today, I mustered up just enough courage, put my 'Big Girl Panties' on, got my emotions in check, and SLAYED!

Looking dumbfounded, James could not say a word and obviously did not know what to say. As I stood up to walk towards the exit door, he stood up along with me, and I happened to glance downward and noticed his ass had a *HARD ON*!

"Really? You damn pervert!" I begin to walk quickly towards the exit to get away from him. Can you believe this nasty bastard was "getting off" on the conversation of me describing the molestation to him! Motherfucka!!!

The guard was following us to the exit and watching us very closely at this point.

Since he knew he was being watched, James finally stated, "Well I hope when you're in town again you'll come by for another visit." At this point his voice was reminiscent of Mickey Mouse.

"The hell!" I thought. He must be hard up for some company, nasty bastard! "You don't ever have to worry about me coming for another visit." *Period!*

Oh! My! God! I exited out of that cafeteria room and had to take a couple more deep breaths. I felt like I had been holding my breath the entire time with anticipation. But now that I have had an opportunity to release all that pent-up energy, it was time for me to exhale. Grinning from ear to ear, almost laughing out loud, I ran outside to the parking lot to get back into my rental car, with my shoulders back and my head held high; that is exactly what I did... exhaled. The wind was now blowing through my hair, the air was now nippier as the tears flowed down my face. Not tears of joy, not tears of sadness, but tears of relief! Tears of mental and emotional freedom! Suddenly, life seemed bearable, brighter, easier. I felt like I could conquer the world! I was so proud of myself! I was proud I was able to face my perpetrator. Courage is the ability to do something even when it frightens you. Trust me, I was scared shitless to face this man, but I did it anyway. Through all the fear, I did it! Courage is not a given. You have to fight through some demons in order to obtain it. I was able to muster up enough courage to put this demon to rest, in order to bring closure to that chapter in my life. I was immensely proud of myself! Proud of the brave woman who lived inside of ME!

Who Will Cry?

Who will cry for the little girl?
Lost and all alone
Who will cry for the little girl?
Abandoned without her own
Who will cry for the little girl?
She cried herself to sleep
Who will cry for the little girl?
She never had for keeps
Who will cry for the little girl?
She walked the burning sands
Who will cry for the little girl?
The girl inside the woman
Who will cry for the little girl?
Who knows well, hurt and pain
Who will cry for the little girl?
She died again and again
Who will cry for the little girl?
A good girl she tried to be
Who will cry for the little girl?
Who cries inside of me

This is my rendition of the poem from the Antwone Fisher story and the response is, "I will cry for that little girl."

Chapter 2

TO FORGIVE OR NOT TO FORGIVE

F orgiveness. Easier said than done. What does it really mean? From the root word, **forgive**: *stop feeling angry or resentful toward (someone) for an offense, flaw, or mistake.*

In other words, if someone told me to *"stop feeling angry or resentful"* towards James for molesting me, I would probably curse them out or slap them in the face. Or here is another good one from the Bible that states, *if you forgive other people, God will forgive you.* As a person who believes in the Bible, I happen to know that no one is capable or willing to do everything the Bible says we should do. However, I do want to be forgiven by God, right? So, if I do not forgive James, does that mean God will not forgive me for *my* wrongdoings? Is God putting conditions on His forgiveness? If so, I'm fresh out of luck!

Some synonyms to the word forgive are:

pardon, excuse, exonerate, absolve, acquit, let off, grant an amnesty to, amnesty, make allowances for, stop feeling resentful toward, feel no resentment toward, stop feeling malice toward, feel no malice toward, harbor no grudge against, bury the hatchet with, let bygones be bygones, let someone off the hook, go easy on, exculpate.

After researching this definition, the only thing I can say is, "Well that's not what happens in real life!"

Forgiveness is absolutely a process, and although most of us will never obtain the goal of these definitions, it took me over 30 years to realize that forgiveness is not about letting James 'off the hook' as much as it is about letting myself 'off the hook.'

God knew exactly what He was doing when He made me and I believe God met me where I was. However, it took me quite a bit of time to get where I needed to be and He gave me that time. There was no rushing, no pushing, no forcing. There was nothing but LOVE.

Why would I pardon James? Excuse, exonerate, absolve, acquit, or grant him amnesty? He did not deserve it; he had not even admitted to his wrongdoing. Why would I not harbor a grudge against him? Why would I bury the hatchet, let bygones be bygones, let him off the hook?

I came to realize I never did let James 'off the hook.' However, when I came to a place where I could let myself 'off the hook,' by default, he was then let 'off the hook.' I released myself from the emotional chains that he bound me with. After all, this was about me, and no longer about him. I had to release myself so I could move on. The molestation held me hostage when it came to my intimate relationships. As the song goes, "*Your body's here with me, but your mind is on the other side of town...*" While I was there physically, my mind was always somewhere else...caged, shackled, bound up, and the man in my head was my stepfather. Still controlling me, still tormenting me, and keeping me in fear, holding me hostage. Fear of what? Fear of letting go and liking it?

For many years to come, in my head, I would hear that train from those railroad tracks behind that little white house we used to live in. I can't stand to make love with the lights on and God forbid any man tries to put me on top of a kitchen table! A little Post Traumatic Stress Disorder goes a long way!

I personally would blank out when I should be enjoying my man 'going down on me,' 'going downtown,' or oral sex performance. Instead, I would feel nothing at all, because that is what I programmed myself to do from when I was a little girl. I would literally have to talk myself into enjoying the moment, being present in that moment. It was extremely difficult to do, with failed attempts many times over.

Now I am a 50+ year-old woman, and I still have conversations in my head during sexual intimacy.

"It's okay, Natasha, to live in the moment. You chose to be here this time; this is for you. Enjoy this moment!"

A little self-encouragement goes a long way. The journey to forgiveness was a challenging process, but once I realized it would benefit *me* to forgive, is when the definition of forgiveness began to make more sense in my situation. I did not focus on forgiving James for him, but I put all of my energy into forgiving James for myself. I owed it to myself to have a normal, emotionally healthy, and intimate relationship. It is what I have always wanted, and just like any other goal, I would do whatever it took to reach it. I was not about to slight my own life because of something that someone else did *to me*; violating my rights as a child, as a woman, as a human being. I couldn't let James win! He did not deserve to win. I deserved normalcy in my life, and I would do anything to achieve that. *Nothing but death would keep me from it.*

I chose to face my perpetrator and confront the issue directly when I was in my mid 30's. This was my therapy. Others perhaps will need to talk to family members, a spouse, a confidant, a pastor, or a counselor/psychiatrist/therapist. A little intuitive reading can also help. Do not knock it til you try it! I decided to take whatever avenues were available to me to attain my result. Some people are just able to put it aside and leave the past in the past. For me, the best way to get beyond it was to expose it and take back my voice. I have a voice and I deserve to be heard! And so do YOU! I prefer to get control of it before it can get control of me. Trust me, this experience ran its course in my life, but I decided to take back that power. The power that belongs to me, not anyone else.

For help with sexual abuse or if you or someone you know are in need of help call 800-656-HOPE.

Chapter 3

NO BLOOD ON MY HANDS

I can recall at the age of five or six, my mother and James got into a major argument. Not as if all the other arguments were not major, but this one tends to stick out so much more. Whenever they argued, James was more than comfortable letting us kids know what he was willing to do to my mother, as he feared no consequences. He would slap her in the face, punch her in the face, throw her across the room, call her all kinds of bad names, and shed her blood right before our very eyes. Kids, crying all the time, scared... ALL the time, to speak, to breathe, to ask questions, and God forbid we ask for anything. The price our mother had to pay for the times we were disobedient or broke something in the house, or just because we were alive or present. I never could figure out why James was so angry, so mean, so abusive, so hurt. He was always willing to hurt his wife, my mother, with no remorse.

It was reminiscent of scenes that I saw from movies where the slave master would beat the person in front of his or her family just to continue to instill an astronomical level of fear. We lived in fear of James. On this day, our cousin Benny was babysitting us until the parents made it home from work. My mother worked in a factory and James was a seamstress. *How ironic! A short, nasty, violating, abusive, murdering, ugly, seamstress, with a high voice!*

I digress....

Benny had already left the house prior to the start of this argument but apparently, he had forgotten something and came back to the house. All four of us kids were crying in a corner-hugging each other begging James to stop beating my mother. We just knew he would kill her someday. He didn't care! He was going to prove his point if it was the last thing he did. No matter how much we begged and pleaded, he would not stop beating her, taunting her, making her feel like less of a human being.

Once Benny got back to the house and heard all the commotion, he busted in the door and started fist-fighting James while my mother lay limp on the floor in a fetal position, holding her stomach, bleeding, crying, then bleeding some more as we kids tried our best to console her. Benny was a little bigger than James and was handling his 'family duties.' You mess with one of us, you mess with all of us! He punched James so hard that he went flying back into the huge living room window. Glass shattered everywhere and I was hoping that James was dead. I had seen those horror movies before where evil didn't die easily, and this was a prime example.

Although James had been punched pretty hard and went flying through the now broken palladium glass window, he got a crowbar from the backyard where he had been working on a car. Punks never fight fairly. They only fight people they know they can beat, and they always use weapons. James came back into the house, and while Benny was trying to gather us all together to get us out of the house, he hit Benny in the head with that crowbar. By this time the neighbors had called the police and the police had sent for an ambulance. Once the police arrived, the neighbors were all outside and took us kids in with them. James was taken off to jail, and my mother and Benny, who had a big hole in the top of his head and was bleeding, were both taken to the hospital. We must have stayed up all night frightened, crying, worried about our mother and cousin. All four of us were traumatized. It was my older brother, Lewis, me, my younger sister, and brother, Punkin and Adrian. Adrian had to have been around a year old at the time. He was still in diapers and barely walking.

We all slept on the floor in the living room that night at the neighbor's house, Ms. Pittman. She lived right across the street from us in a very nice looking, yellow house with an immaculate lawn. Ms. Pittman was an older woman, much older than my mother, and probably closer to my grandmother's age. She was pleasant, calm, warm, and poised, and she was always there for us. This would not be the first time Ms. Pittman had to call the police and come get us and take us to her house. We would have to run to Ms. Pittman's at least on a bi-weekly basis; it was a part of our routine.

I could imagine Ms. Pittman asking this about my mother, "Why won't she leave this fool alone?" I repeatedly asked myself the same question and to this day, the answer remains unknown. My mother was a young 25 year old, uneducated, broken woman, with four small children. James had convinced her that no man would want to take on all the baggage she brought to the table. Her self-esteem was already low, and he just beat her down even more.

Low self-esteem + lack of self-love = a recipe for disaster.

There were countless times when James was beating my mother and Ms. Pittman had to call the police in order to get us out of there. It's no wonder we were not taken into foster care. It's no wonder we all got out of there alive, especially my mother. It is no wonder that James never put a gun to his own head, since he was obviously 'crazy and missing a few screws,' as my grandmother would say. It's no wonder he didn't kill all of us. Or did he? He instilled such a level of fear in us that he killed a part of who we were, who we are, and perhaps even who we were meant to be. Mentally and emotionally we were dead at times, drowning in the sorrows of this thing called life. I recall being like a walking zombie, walking on eggshells, and even though they hurt my feet, never to make a whimpering sound. If James ever caught wind of that whimpering sound, he would take it out on my mother. We knew not to ever cross him because if we did, there would be another beating for my mother that she did not deserve.

Even as young as we were, I carried the burden of my mother's life on my shoulders. I could never let the death of my mother be because I said something or because I did something wrong. I was very careful to not get in trouble at school, no bad report cards were coming my way. If James said to do it, I did it. If he said jump, I asked how high. If my mother had to die at the hands of James, it definitely was not going to be because of me.

After attempting to escape from James a number of times, nothing ever seemed to work. My mother would pack us up in the middle of the night to steal away to one of her girlfriend's houses, and she would just be dragged right back to the house by James. We tried escaping multiple times while he was at work, but somehow, he would find out where she was, and drag her right back to the house with four kids in tow, kicking and screaming. This is the same white house on Willow Road near the railroad tracks. The one James claimed he never lived in when I went to visit him in prison. The lies!

A couple of years after that incident, when I was about seven years old, in the first grade, my mother came to pick my older brother Lewis and me up from school early. I knew something was happening because she would never pick us up from school, let alone early, as we always rode the school bus. We grabbed our book bags and hurried back to the car. Benny was already in the car, and I was so happy to see him. We then went to the daycare to pick up my younger brother and sister. To my mother's surprise, they had already been picked up by their father, James. I could tell my mother was in a panic, hence letting us know there was danger ahead.

"What's going on Mama?" I asked.

"Nothing," she snapped. "Just don't ask me any questions right now."

We were never allowed to ask any questions as a child. We just had to wait and let the situation unfold and stomach whatever life brought us.

I sensed my mother was nervous as she drove the car in full throttle; barely stopping at stop signs and screeching the wheels at every turn. Benny was on the passenger side being ultra-cool. He may have already smoked some weed that day and knew this was coming.

We finally pulled up to my younger sister and brother's grandparents' house, *'Them Stricklands,'* who were also James' parents. My mother hurriedly parked the car, jumped out and slammed the door.

"Stay in the car, I'll be right back!" she said to Lewis and me in a quivering voice as she struggled to stay calm.

Lewis and I watched her with anticipation as my mother ran up the steps into the house and disappeared from our sight.

"Don't worry, about it, it's gon' be alright," my cousin Benny tried to sound reassuring.

My mother quickly came out of the house carrying my little brother Adrian and almost dragging my sister Punkin by the arm. As soon as we saw her, James pulled up right behind us in his car screeching his brakes. My mother was now running even faster with my younger brother and sister. She somehow managed to throw them into the back seat and was trying to get in the car on the driver's side when James ran up to the car and grabbed her by the hair.

The car was still running and Benny was trying to put the car in drive so that we could pull away. Although he managed to shift gears into drive, James was already pulling my mother by her afro, through the driver-side car window.

Benny kept hollering at my mother, "Punch on the accelerator, give it some gas, give it some gas!"

As James forcibly had my mother by her afro trying to pull her out of a moving car, we kids were in the backseat using every muscle in our little fists to try to hit his hand as hard as we could so he would let her go.

"Let my mama go! Leave my mama alone!" We all cried as loud as our lungs would allow. Our little fists may not have been doing much good, but we were not about to let him drag my mother out of this moving car without a fight!

My mother was finally able to get her foot down on the accelerator and Benny's left foot was also on the accelerator as they both tried to 'punch the gas' while steering the car as my mother's limp body was halfway out of the car. The car began to speed up, James tried running with the car, but he could not keep up. He eventually had to let go of my mother's hair and we were off.....off to freedom, wherever that was.

We were all totally exhausted as if we had just been in a fight with Muhammad Ali. No one said a word, not even my 3-year-old baby brother dared to cry. We had no idea if James was going to try to follow us. We had no idea if he would try to run us off the road. We had no idea if he would find us and drag us back to that white house near the railroad tracks, where we would be right back in the prison we were so desperately trying to escape. I could tell we were on our way out to the country, to Beaverville, Illinois, where my grandparents lived, less than an hour away. I never knew why we did not try to run away to my grandparents' house sooner, but I assume my mother had her reasons. We rode with the windows down, and the wind in our faces. Tear drops dried on cheeks, runny noses, emotionally drained, confused, shaken to the core.

But now, we are going to live with my grandparents! A new outlook. New hope for us. A new life. Finally, a sense of security, peace, love, protection, comfort, calmness, and all the things children need from a family. Once my grandfather was involved in this situation, he will be damned if James will put another hand on his daughter. When I saw we were going to our grandparent's house, there was a great sense of relief. We *will* be safe now, I was sure of it, because *my* grandaddy did not play!

My grandmother, mother, and aunts were always reluctant to tell my grandfather about these ordeals. They would rather keep it hidden than expose the fact they were in trouble, in an abusive relationship with a man. My grandmother would always say, "Okay, we'll figure this out, but don't tell your Daddy, because you know how he is!"

My grandfather, whom we reverenced as Lil' Daddy, was a natural-born protector of his family. A Capricorn, the Earth sign, grounded, sturdy and stable minded. He stood about 5'9" and was a little stout, and was about 10 years older than my grandmother. He and my grandmother, whom we called Lil' Mama, had seven girls and no boys. Lil' Mama was an only child and her mother was also an only child; therefore, there were no men in the family at all. Lil' Daddy was raised by his grandparents and had been estranged from his family, so we had no connections to them. Lil' Daddy was the ultimate provider and protector. Although my mother knew he would protect her from James, she lived by Lil' Mama's suggestion of "don't tell your Daddy, because you know how he is." My grandmother was always afraid that my grandfather would kill somebody for messing with his daughters and as the only man in our family, our protector and provider, he might end up in jail or worse, dead.

Lil' Daddy sat in his wide, comfortable, recliner chair that was centered with the TV, smoking Phillip Morris cigarettes and watching baseball all day before work. (He was a huge Chicago Cubs fan.) He was a non-talkative man with a mysterious quiet strength about him. Lil' Daddy and Lil' Mama both shared all the household duties, cooked meals for all the grandkids, and made sure we got off to school on time. They both had outside jobs. Lil' Mama worked as a cook in the Riverside Hospital cafeteria, and Lil' Daddy worked as a janitor at A.O. Smith, the same place where my mother worked. They both loved all of us unconditionally. To this day, I had no idea how they were able to feed us all and keep a roof over our heads. Although money was scarce, somehow, they made it work.

After leaving James for the last time, we had nothing, just the clothes on our backs and whatever school supplies were in our book bags when my mother picked us up from school early that day. That was it. My grandmother would wash our clothes every single night so we could wear them to school the next day. We did not have much, but at least we were clean! We didn't care as long as we were away from Crazy!

One day, James called my grandfather and asked if he could bring our school clothes over to their house. Lil' Daddy reluctantly agreed because he knew we needed clothes for school. I personally would have been fine wearing the same clothes every day for the rest of the year, even while being talked about by the other school kids, so long as I did not have to deal with James. My grandfather was not afraid of James, so I don't think he thought anything of it. My gut was telling me that nothing good was going to come from letting James into this house, but who was I? I was just a kid.

I was in the kitchen helping Lil' Mama cook. We were making homemade cornbread when James arrived with three large black garbage bags full of our clothes. Lil' Daddy welcomed him in and thanked him for bringing the clothes by. James then requested he be able to have a conversation with my mother. He stated he already had come to terms with the fact that this marriage was over, and just needed to finalize some things with her. My grandfather allowed James to go to the backroom to talk to my mother. The backroom was the 4th bedroom in the house being used as a den. It had a sofa, record player, small TV, and so on. I started to get very nervous when I witnessed this as James was not inclined to just 'have a conversation with my mother.' We were always taught to not get in grown folks' business, so I did not say a word. Oh, but we were already deep into these grown folks' business. Unfortunately.

Lil' Daddy did not seem to be moved by James. He sat back down in his recliner chair and continued watching television. I, on the other hand, was nervous out of my mind! Lil' Daddy has never witnessed the physical abuse and beating this man had put on my mama all these years. These times will forever be engraved in my mind. After about 20 minutes or so I thought I heard my mother scream.

"Did y'all hear that?" I asked. I was still stirring the cornbread batter.

"Hear what?" my grandmother asked.

"I thought I heard some noise coming from the backroom," my heart started pounding.

I was used to hearing my mother scream in the middle of the night, during the day, and even if she wasn't there. It was a sound that would be forever embedded in my head, ringing in my ears. Maybe my mind is playing tricks on me. Then a few minutes later, I thought I heard the scream again.

"Y'all didn't hear that?" I was more sure that I heard it this time than I was the last time.

"Hear what, child?" This time Lil' Mama walked over to me. "Are you afraid for your mama?"

"Yes, ma'am." I began to cry.

She hugged me and said, "Don't worry, he's not gon' try nothing with your granddaddy sitting right here."

A few minutes later, we ALL heard the third scream from my mother.

"See there, I did hear my mother's scream! I did hear it!"

My grandfather leaped from his recliner chair and headed to the bedroom closet. We all knew what was in that bedroom closet, and James was in for a rude awakening! My Auntie Terri who was barely a teenager at this time, ran down the hall to the back room and tried to open the door which was locked. She then started banging on the door telling James to unlock it. By the time my grandfather retrieved his gun and ran down the hall to the back room, he shot the lock off the door in order to get it open. I could hear my mother crying in the back room as I was still in the kitchen with my grandmother's arms protecting me.

"He was choking me, Daddy!" my mother screamed. "He said he was going to kill me for leaving him and taking his family away!"

The next thing I saw was Lil' Daddy dragging James down the hallway in a headlock with the gun up to his head! I thought for sure he would be a goner that day.

"If you ever put your motherfuckin' hands on my daughter again, and if you ever step foot on my goddamn property again, I will blow your fuckin' brains out!" Lil' Daddy had a full, deep voice that echoed throughout the house. He also was a man of very few words. But when he spoke, everyone listened.

We never had any trouble from James again after that day and my mother was able to finally move on with her life. We lived with our grandparents for several years after that. James had reportedly remarried and now had other children. Supposedly he was a reformed husband and family man trying to do the right thing.

Several years later, he called my grandfather to request if he could pick us up and take us toy shopping. Poor kids always wanted new toys because we were not privy to much throughout our childhood. My mother was not living with us at the time, so my grandfather allowed James to come, but he was not allowed inside the house. I was very reluctant to go, but went anyway to be with my other siblings and to get a toy! He did buy us a toy and a McDonald's Happy Meal, then dropped us back off at my grandparents' house. He would request to pick us up and take us toy shopping periodically in the months to come, but I decided I would never go again. The stares, the way he tried to pay me extra attention, the uncomfortable energy in the air, none of this was worth a toy to even the poorest of little girls. My other siblings would go because they were none the wiser. So be it, I was better off being left out.

"I wonder why Tasha didn't want to go toy shopping with James and the rest of the kids?" I was eavesdropping on my Auntie Terri and Auntie De-De as they were in the bathroom getting ready for their dates.

"You think he did something to her?" asked Auntie Terri.

" I don't know. Probably," was Auntie De-De's reply.

Everything in me wanted to burst into the bathroom and tell them exactly what happened with James. But then I heard that voice in my head saying, "If you ever told a soul, I will kill your mother. You don't want her blood on your hands do you?"

Even though my mother had divorced James, he still could find her and kill her as he had always promised. Lil' Daddy could not be everywhere to protect her. If I told my aunts, what would they do? Would they tell Lil' Daddy? Would he then kill James and go to jail like my grandmother always feared. I was only 9 or 10 years old at this time and was incapable of making these types of decisions. I opted to live in silence to not get anyone killed or put in jail.

I especially did not want anything bad to happen to my grandfather on my account.

When I was about 12 years old, Lil' Daddy died of lung cancer. Smoking a pack of cigarettes a day is what ultimately ended his life. I saw him go from a husky, strong, stout man, to an 85lb thin, frail man in a matter of months. There was no reversal of lung cancer, and he did not adhere to any type of radiation. Lil' Mama took care of him until he could not fight for his life any longer. It was a sad day in the Bostic family, March of 1984, when we lost Lil' Daddy. He was our protector and provider. He taught us kids how to fight for ourselves and how to "take up" for each other. It was a tough world to live in, but he prepared us nonetheless, as best he could. At least he had gotten James out of our lives well before he got sick. That's one less demon we had to fight.

Once I became an adult, I started sharing with my aunts and my grandmother how James had molested me. My aunts also shared with me how they would be babysitting us when my mother and James lived in Chicago, and James had molested them or repeatedly attempted to. They had tried to tell my mother numerous times, but she pretended to not believe them. After a while, they stopped babysitting us for fear they would be violated by James.

After I went to confront James, I saw my mother a couple of months later when visiting our hometown of Kankakee, IL. I mentioned to her that I visited James in prison.

"What did you do that for?" she asked.

" I visited him to confront him about molesting me when I was a child."

"What!" she seemed surprised.

"Did you know that James was sexually molesting me between the ages of 3-7?"

"What? No! You know I would have never let him do anything to you!" She almost seemed offended that I would ask this question.

"Really Mama? You were so afraid of him, what could you have done?"

"Well, I know I would have done something!"

My mother was notorious for not elaborating on her feelings and for not being honest with herself. This brings me back to the dream I had where I saw my child's father having sex with her and I ripped his penis out of its socket and flung it into the wall. My child's father represented James, my child represented me when I was a child being molested, and I represented the mother I never had. I would never let anybody touch my child as there would be hell to pay. While my mother was docile, low self-esteem, careless, and either unable or unwilling to protect her cubs; I, on the other hand, am Mama Bear! I will rise with the strength of a Super Hero to protect my cub. Ripping dicks from bodies and slinging dicks and all, if need be. Whatever it takes. I was destined to be the mother I never had. A mother that my child could always depend on.

I always wondered if the spirit of James lived in that little white house near the railroad tracks.

I used to be concerned about the other little girls whose families occupied it years after we left. My heart goes out to anyone who had to endure what I had to endure in that house.

Just recently, in July 2022, I was visiting Kankakee, and decided to drive past that house on Willow Road. Lo and behold, the train was running just like old times, but the house was no longer there! Either the house was burned down or demolished, but the land is now vacant.

"Good!" I thought. "The house is gone; the memories of this house are gone. The spirit of James can no longer live here! Now everybody can be FREE of him! Now we can ALL *unsilence* our voices!"

Chapter 4

THE MEETING

L iving with my grandparents in the small town of Beaverville, IL was the best! The country was exactly what it was, country. The huge yard is where we played Hopscotch, Red Light-Green Light, Duck, Duck, Goose, kickball, and dodgeball. We never had to worry about locking our doors at night back then. We loved it out there! We were free! It was secure and safe, and we had no worries. In the summers, we would sleep with the windows open and take in all that fresh air. Trees were everywhere for maximum oxygen, but those mosquitoes were a beast!

At that time, I attended Ida L. Bush Elementary school for the third grade. My third-grade teacher, Mrs. Parker, was probably the best teacher I have ever had in my life. She was like everybody's grandmother. She baked us gingerbread cookies and cakes, she spent all the extra time with us that we needed, celebrating each of our birthdays as if we were the only child in class (from a total of about 25 kids), and she taught us math and grammar like nobody's business! She was patient with us, but she was also a disciplinarian. More importantly, she really cared about her students.

Mrs. Parker was an older woman. She wore her gray hair in a bun towards the back of her head, always wore pearls around her neck, and eye glasses that dangled towards the tip of her nose. Of course, she had the chain that held the arms of the eye glasses behind her ears, so when she had to take them off to look at you, you knew she was not playing! Every step she took was with care and precision. Every move she made was intentional as far as our lives were concerned. Like most teachers in those days, and in that area, she did not spare the rod when it came to disciplining her class.

I recall incidents when a kid would get caught talking during class or during a test or quiet time, she would make that kid come to the front of the class.

"Joseph Thorpe!" she called out.

"Huh?" Joseph was always getting into trouble.

"What did you say?" Mrs. Parker would look at him as if to say, "Who do you think you're talking to?"

"I mean, yes?" Joseph would try to correct himself.

"Yes, what?" Mrs. Parker was not about to let him get away with anything.

"Yes, ma'am." Joseph finally got it right.

"Have you been talking in my class, Joseph, when you are supposed to be taking a test?"

"Uhhh... n-n-n-o ma'am."

"Are you sure about that, Joseph?"

"Uhh...n-n-n-o ma'am." Joseph clearly wasn't one of the brightest of the bunch.

"Well, you know what to do don't you?" Mrs. Parker always spoke very calmly. "I saw you talking when I walked back into the classroom, and I see you have not finished your test. So put your leg up here on this crate and raise that pant leg. Raise it up high."

Joseph obeyed as he did not have a choice. Mrs. Parker would take her ruler and pop him on that naked, ashy leg several times until he screamed.

"Ouch! Ouch!" The rest of the class would jump and gasp for breath while in our seats, grateful it was not us who got caught talking.

After Mrs. Parker gave him a few licks, she then would make him go back to his seat and finish the test. And he had better finish on time, too!

Back in the 1970's when you got in trouble in school, the teacher also called your parents and you would be in trouble, again. That was double jeopardy at its best! Consequently, we were of the mindset that it took a village to raise a child. Parents and teachers respected one another and worked together on behalf of the child. Nothing at all like today's society.

Yes, Mrs. Parker was hard on us students. Making us learn things that were not even in the textbooks, she taught us to go beyond what people expected of us. Growing up in an impoverished area, we were already struck with multiple disadvantages of being black and poor; she dare not add being ignorant. Mrs. Parker meant business. And if you had the privilege of being a student in her class, you would learn to raise your expectations of life,

EXPEDITIOUSLY! As in the voice of Principal Joe Clark, played by Morgan Freeman from the late 1980's movie, *Lean on Me.*

I learned so much from Mrs. Parker, especially about discipline and hard work. Although I was pretty smart despite the environment I grew up in, I always knew if I was disciplined and worked hard, this could be my ticket out of poverty. When kids were playing outside after school, throwing rocks in the ditch across the road, climbing trees, and playing hopscotch in the dirt; I would be inside reading a book, studying my times tables, and making up math problems. I knew even at a young age, there had to be some advantage to working harder than other people were willing to. I was hopeful that someday, that hard work would pay off.

I had a couple of aunts before me who were also in Mrs. Parker's class in prior years. Since we all carried my grandfather's last name, *Bostic*, we were particularly popular in this small town. Very often, even as a new student, Mrs. Parker would call on me, "Bostic, get up and say your times tables in front of the class and show them how it's done." So, I would get up and say my times tables to the class and 'show them how it was done.' Shoot, I had been practicing my multiplications nearly all my life! I was always prepared for the challenge of reciting them, as math was my forte. I do not know if I had a little bit of favor with Mrs. Parker just because she knew the Bostics already; but as a new girl in class, I was extremely proud she would be able to call on me and I would actually be able to deliver.

When she said to study those multiplications, you knew to study! At that time in the third grade, we were going all the way up to the 12-times tables and it kind of went like this, "12 times 1 is 12, 12 times 2 is 24, 12 times 3 is 36, 12 times 4 is 48, 12 times 5 is 60, and so on. It was simpler if you put it into a song version! There would be no stopping, no pausing, no stammering, no counting on fingers to get the next answer. You had better know it like the back of your hand, or you would need to do more studying and practicing when you got home.

"No playing outside when you go home today! You *need* to know your time tables and the only way you will learn them is to study, study, and study some more!" Mrs. Parker would say to the class, very often.

One day, the girl who sat behind me, went home, and told her mother there was a new girl in class and the teacher was always calling on her. Her mother, of course, asked, "Well, what's the girl's name?"

"Tasha Bostic."

And then her mom said, "Well, I know the Bostics, and come to think of it, I went to school with Arlene Bostic, who is her mother. Matter of fact, we were both pregnant in high school... by the same guy! It seemed like about a month before she had her baby, I found out I was pregnant with you. So that would mean she's your sister because you two have the same daddy!"

The girl who sat behind me in class, Tabula, came to school that day and told me about the conversation she had with her mother about me. But before that, Tabula began to drill me.

"What's your daddy's name?" she asked in her little third grader's voice.

Of course, I really didn't *know* my daddy's name because I didn't *know* my daddy. However, I had heard from my stepfather James, that his name was Floy Murrell.

I hesitated with uncertainty, "Uhmmm, Floy Murrell." I wasn't too sure about the pronunciation of his name, since my mother never spoke of him, but I said it anyway.

She said, "Do you mean, Fl-o-y-d (*enunciating the "d"*) Murrell?" She made sure she corrected me.

"Uh....Okay," I said embarrassingly and just kind of shook my head and shrugged my shoulders because I really *wasn't* sure of his name. She more than likely knew better than I did.

Then she showed me a picture and said, "Is this him?"

I looked at the picture and I honestly did not know if that was him or not, because I had never seen the man before. Only in my mind had I seen him and apparently conjured up what he might look like. I just looked at her again and I shrugged awkwardly, "I-I-don't know."

Then she says, "Well, I went home and told my Mama about you and how the teacher always calls on you and she told me that my daddy and your daddy are the same person, so that would make us sisters!" She seemed to be totally excited about this!

I was shocked I was having this conversation in the third grade with another girl in the third grade, which means we were only maybe eight years old, and she was telling me we have the same father and that she was my sister! Oh my God! My heart was beating out of my chest as I stared at the picture, admiring every facial feature, and looking into his eyes. It was like having a new boyfriend, or in my case, having a boyfriend for the first time.

Tabula then said, "Do you want to keep the picture? You can take it home if you want to. My mama told me I could give it to you."

"Okay." I was still attempting to gather my thoughts. I did not know exactly what I was feeling, or just could not put this tingling feeling that ran through my body into words at the time. I could not take my eyes off this picture and I was so grateful that this girl who sat behind me in Mrs. Parker's class, my sister; was willing to let me have it, that I just held on to it for dear life! Wow! This day could not have gotten any better!

I studied that picture the rest of the day. This was my father? For real? I almost had to pinch myself to make sure I wasn't dreaming. He had a nice big afro, as the picture was taken in the 1970's. He wore this burgundy-colored vest with matching tight bell bottom pants, and a long-sleeve psychedelic shirt with a wide collar that spread from shoulder to shoulder. The smile on his face was just as wide as that collar. Boy! It kind of reminded me of those dancers going down the Soul Train Line or trying to unscramble the puzzle on the newest music artist! I could see myself in this picture, not the big afro, but the light caramel skin complexion, the round face, those smile lines, and the squinted eyes.

Lil' Mama used to call me her little China Doll when I was younger because when I smiled, I looked like a Chinese baby doll. He also had very nice teeth, which I unfortunately was not blessed with, but later in life I would get that problem corrected with braces. I could visualize myself in this picture with my father. Daddy and daughter.

As I rode the school bus home, I could not wait to get off the bus and tell my grandmother what happened. The bus barely came to a complete stop and I was off to the races, running as fast as my legs could carry me down that gravel driveway, speeding past the dusty lawn and into the front door.

"Lil' Mama! Lil' Mama!" I was almost out of breath. "Look at what I got!"

"Wait a minute, just slow down, slow down!" My grandmother was in the kitchen as usual when she got off work, cooking dinner and cleaning.

I told my grandmother what happened in school that day.

"Let me see that picture," my grandmother said. I gave it to her and she looked closely at it. "Mmmmm-hmmmm," she said, in that typical older black woman's voice. "That's him alright," as she handed the picture right back to me.

Lil' Mama did not seem too impressed with this picture, nor did she share in my enthusiasm of finding out about my father and wanting to know more. But I... I felt like I was in love for the first time. Or at least infatuated! I was literally on cloud nine, floating on air! This picture might as well have said, *"Will you go with me? Yes, or No?"* My answer was a resounding YES! My father was my Prince Charming! Of course, he had not done anything to deserve this title, it just was. It's how I reverenced him in my mind. He would be my Superhero someday... hopefully. Yes, I was known to believe in fairytales, as it was so much better than real life.

I had thought about my father hundreds of times before, when James told me he was not my real father. But now...now I can put a face with an imagination for the first time in my life! I was ecstatic! He was dream worthy, for sure!

I went to the bedroom I shared with my aunt, sister, and baby cousin. Closing the door, I laid on the bed while clutching this picture of my father close to my chest. I tried desperately to decipher my feelings. I closed my eyes tightly and began to take deep breaths. I attempted to take it all in, but suddenly, I had this overwhelming feeling of anxiety and these knots began to form in the pit of my stomach.

No matter what the situation was, I always yearned to have my father in my life. I needed to know who he was and I had so many questions about this man. Like, why did he abandon us? Why didn't he ever come to see us? Why was my first time knowing what he looks like from a picture from a girl in my third grade class? Why were we not living with him? Just so many questions I had in my heart, and yet at the same time, I loved this man unconditionally, or at least the idea of him. A man that I had never met, a man who I knew nothing about, but in my *mind*, my life would have been so much better with him than it was without him.

I knew he and my mother were still in high school when Lewis and I were born, but they were adults now, and they should take the responsibility of an adult.

If only he knew what type of daughter I was, that I was a very good girl. I rarely got into any trouble. I made straight A's, and I was a hard worker. I was the responsible kid. When I was told to do something, I made sure it got done. Adults did not have to ask me twice or check up on me in any way. I do not know if any of that would have mattered, but in my mind, if only I had the opportunity to tell him or to show him who I was and what he was missing in me, his child. I just feel like my life would have been so different, so much better than it was... If only he knew. I always hoped one day I would get the opportunity to meet him, to talk to him, and he would see what a loving person I was and he might want me. Then, he would want to be a father, *my* father, and would want to be a part of my life. I was sure of it!

That night and for many nights to come, I slept with the picture of my father under my pillow. I carried the picture with me everywhere I went. It was always in my bookbag, tucked away safely in the back of a notebook, so I would always know where it was when I wanted to just daydream about the man in this picture. I thought, just maybe if I kept it close enough, I could feel his presence. And somehow, miraculously, he would feel mine. I prayed to God that one day he would come for me, and be a part of my life. That he would show up and save me from the hell hole I was accustomed to living in with my mother, and give me a better chance at life than I had previously experienced. Right now I was living with my grandparents and this would have to do. But ultimately, what child would not want to be with her actual parents?

I never knew if this dream of mine would ever come true, or if this was just some wishful thinking I had conjured up in my mind. Well, at least I had a sister who was actually very involved with our father. Over the years I would learn things about him through Tabula, living vicariously through her. Even though Tabula and I became very good friends, there was still a sense of jealousy and envy I had towards her because she had the father I never had, but someday hoped to have.

What was so special about Tabula? Why did our father love her and not me? Why was she able to go to visit him for spring break, Christmas break, and go on summer vacations with him? What was it about her that made him want to be her father and not mine? Consequently, these questions haunted me for years as I strived to maintain a good relationship with my newly found-out sister, hoping maybe I could feel some sense of closeness to our father through her. Maybe she will be the bridge that connects us one day. Maybe....

Tabula and I were also in the same fourth-grade class, with Mrs. Hemphill, and then in the same fifth-grade class, with Ms. Shelton at Lorenzo R. Smith school in Pembroke, IL. This was a middle school from 4th-8th grades. All these small towns were just minutes away from each other and about 1-1 ½ hours south of Chicago IL. Of course, in small towns, being in the same class with someone every grade is quite common. I recall that in the fifth grade, Ms. Shelton's class, we had to fill out the emergency contact cards with our mother's name and phone number, and our father's name and phone number. When the class was over and the bell rang, Ms. Shelton stopped us.

"Wait a minute. You, you, and you, have a seat." She pointed to me, Tabula, and another kid in the class named Ron.

"Get up and close that door, Ron."

Ron got up and closed the door as we were all wondering what this could be about. Were we in trouble or something? Did we do something wrong?

Ms. Shelton was known for being a straight shooter.

"Do all y'all know y'all got the same father?" Looking a bit perplexed, Ms. Shelton spoke with a very high pitched, country voice. "Now, how do I have three kids in the same classroom with the same father and y'all all the same age! And... you all have different mothers! Jesus Christ Almighty!"

You just gotta laugh.

I knew Tabula and I had the same father because she told me in the third grade, but I did not know Ron had the same father, too! I learned later that Tabula and Ron knew about each other in the first grade, that they had the same father. Yes, this was the epitome of *Papa Was a Rolling Stone,* a song recorded by the Temptations in 1972.

After Ms. Shelton took some time to stare at each of us like specimens, we all just kind of looked around the classroom with smiles or smirks on our faces, and it was like, okay, I got *two* siblings in the same classroom, that is awesome! To have siblings who are the exact same age as you, in the exact same classes where we all go through the exact same things at the same time was amazing! Now, how many people can say this has ever happened to them? Ms. Shelton observed us as if we were going down in the Guinness Book of World Records! We all hung together like the three stooges in middle school. We were thick as thieves and anybody who messed with one of us had to mess with all of us; and that is the way it has always been, even 40 plus years later.

Ron and I were even nominated as May Day King and Queen of the fifth grade class! It was cool to be nominated and crowned with my own brother!

We grew to become extremely protective of one another and we went to bat for each other, always having each other's backs, and that was the best part of this siblingship. So, while my father created this type of division among us, by acknowledging Tabula, but not acknowledging Ron or myself, it did put some strain on our relationship over the years, but somehow, we managed to get through it all.

Chapter 5

DR. JEKYLL AND MR. HYDE

Several years after living with our grandparents, my mother had established a new relationship with a man named Eugene Johnson. Gene, as they called him, lived in Hopkins Park, IL, just a few miles from Beaverville.

Gene lived in a rather big house compared to the little white house we used to live in with James. I later learned the previous owners had a fire at this house and since Gene was a construction worker, he had done the renovations on the house himself. Or shall we say, he tried his best. Basically everything was "nigga rigged," but it worked!

There was a sidewalk leading up to the house with a long narrow covered porch, just enough to keep you dry from the rain. Upon entering the front door was the kitchen with this atrocious wallpaper, yellow I believe, with all different colored flowers. Then there it was, the legendary canary yellow rotary phone with the spiraling cord hanging on the wall near the front door. This would be the only house phone, the one we would run to every time the phone rang to see who could get to it first.

The living room, dining room, hall, and bedrooms all had that dark brown paneling on the walls. I guess you would not have to worry about painting the walls with this paneling. It created a dark, yet cozy feeling in the house, although the floors had no carpet, they were all linoleum; so the house seemingly stayed cool in the summer, but freezing in the winter.

I am not sure where Mama and Gene met, but when she came to my grandparents' house to get us and move us into Gene's house, I was thinking, "Here we go again!" How well did she even know this man? Who were his people? Did he have a criminal record? Did she even ask or check on these things before moving her four children in with him?

Oh right... my mother was a divorced woman with four children, no money, no assets, and no place to live. I am sure she did not ask this man any questions! Plus, who was I kidding? Gene was a tall, attractive man with a Steve Harvey style mustache and smile to go with it. He had kind eyes and was very welcoming to us kids. He had three children of his own from a previous marriage, two boys and a girl. The boys were a little older, but the girl was closer to Lewis and my age. They all lived with their mother and visited us only on occasion.

We learned much later that Gene did have a criminal record and had been in jail when he was younger, as did many black men. As the story goes, he had shot and killed his father for beating his mother and was sent to Juvenile Detention as a result of the incident. Violence, abuse, and poverty tends to run in a cycle where we're from, so this too, was very common.

Everybody had a past. I did not know anyone who did not have one. Not that all people used drugs, sold drugs, or killed someone and had to do jail time; but everybody experienced something they may have been ashamed of and may not be willing to share with others. Most people may not be willing to be transparent about their past, but the past is still there, nonetheless. Things we are proud of, and other things we are not so proud of; it is still all there. So, who was I to hold Gene's past against him? After the loser my Mama recently divorced, we were bound to be on the 'come up' with Gene. At least I was still hopeful.

Gene seemed to be a suitable man for my mother, from what I could tell. At least he was not at the bottom of the totem pole. I mean, he was at the top-bottom, but not the low-bottom. He at least was taking care of the household bills; he could make repairs when something broke down since he was very handy around the house, and he made sure we had food on the table. We even got multiple toys for Christmas when we lived with Gene. Everything seemed to be going well in the beginning.

Gene had a very decent paying job as a construction worker. He got paid every Friday and he also got drunk every Friday. Normally, Gene did not have much conversation with us except when he was drunk on Fridays. Drunk Gene was the best! He would come home from work and offer to take us kids to the Dairy Queen for ice cream.

"Hey, Family!" He would stumble into the house in a very good mood with a brown paper bag around a Crown Royal liquor bottle in his right hand. "How my family doing today?"

"Fine!" We would all gather around as we could sense when this was a good drunk day!

"Guess what?"

"What?" we'd recite.

"Chicken Butt!" We'd all bust out laughing as this was a regular routine leading up to one thing.

"Knock, knock."

"Who's there?"

"You?"

"You, who?"

"You all wanna go get some ice cream?"

"Yessss!" We all jumped up and down knowing exactly how this routine would play out. We were always excited about it, and always pretended to be surprised as if we did not know what the outcome would be.

My mother would intervene. "You can't be driving as drunk as you are."

"W-e-l-l how do you t-t-think I got h-home from work?" Gene stammered over his words.

"Gene, give me those keys!" She tried to snatch the car keys from his hands. "I ain't given you s-h-i-t!"

"I'll drive the kids to get some ice cream, myself."

"No you w-won't either, c-c-cause you ain't invited.

"You will not be driving my kids drunk!"

"I d-didn't say I w-was driving. I'm g-gonna let *the kids* d-drive."

"Yes!" my brother Lewis and I jumped for joy. "Can we Mama? Please! We already know how to drive because Lil' Daddy lets us drive all the time!"

Lil' Daddy had been teaching Lewis and me to drive for over a year now. Anytime we would come from going to the grocery store in Kankakee, once we hit that long stretch, Lil' Daddy would pull the car over and let Lewis and me take turns driving us home to Beaverville. We were no strangers to the road!

Since we had Drunk Gene riding in the car with us, and he would not let Mama go, we were okay with being the responsible parties in this situation. Plus, since we rarely got to go anywhere, this was always a treat! But better than that, Gene let us drive his recently purchased brand new 1980 red hot Monte Carlo with white leather interior seats! I was only 10 years old at the time, but anybody who grew up in the country had been driving illegally basically all our lives.

Gene would let me drive all the way there, and Lewis all the way back, just in case we got caught by the street lights at dusk dark. Although Gene attempted to sober up, we knew we had a better handle on the wheel than he did, I will tell you that much! I remember my legs were not long enough to reach the gas and brake pedals, and the seat would not come up far enough; so, I made do and just sat up close to the steering wheel without trying to lean my back against the seat. Seat belts were not required back then and we never drove past a police car. No worries there!

Once at the Dairy Queen, we were always hoping to see one of our classmates from school so we could show off, but we never bumped into anyone we knew, ever.

We loved Drunk Gene! He was nice, funny, playful, and generous! Until one Friday, the whole atmosphere changed. We realized there was another side to Drunk Gene. A mean side. This Drunk Gene came in like a hurricane, ripping shit apart and turning the family against each other!

Gene stumbled through the front door with liquor on his breath and evidence of Crown Royal in the brown paper bag. This is when we realized there was a difference between Dr. Jekyll and Mr. Hyde. We had been experiencing Mr. Hyde all along, now here comes the infamous Dr. Jekyll!

"Arlene, how many times I keep telling you to stop doing this shit! Stop treating Tasha better than you treat Punkin!" he'd come out of nowhere.

"What, what are you talking about?" my mother would say looking up from the straightening comb where she had been pressing the back of my hair.

Many times I can remember my mother would have to wash and press our hair with the straightening comb at the kitchen stove. In our house, whoever "called" it first would get their hair done first. When Mama asked who wants to get her hair washed first and who wants to get her hair straightened first, I usually beat my little sister to the punch. "Me! I do!" And that was that.

"Every time I come home, I see it and I need to call it out! You always treat Tasha better than you treat Punkin!" Gene was adamant about pressing his issue.

"Oh, please! You're talking nonsense, Gene!" My mother was known to deflect, but never tried to correct the man.

"No I'm not, I see it happening all the time!" he said drunkenly.

Gene did not know what he was talking about, but he was always assuming he knew. Sometimes Punkin did not even want to get her hair done first, so I would go first. Sometimes she *did* want to go first, but I had already "called" it, so I got to go first. Whatever the case was, why was it of any concern to a drunk man coming home from work? Why was he making such a big deal out of nothing? I always thought Gene had something against me because he was always calling out some issue where I was the main point of interest. Clearly my mother was accustomed to putting her man before *all* her children, hands down. I have never seen any favoritism at all. Ever! Not towards *any* of her children. Including myself!

It's funny how this would be the main source of his arguments on Dr. Jekyll Fridays; how my mother favored me over Punkin. However, Gene never made mention of all the times Punkin "called" first before me, and Mama would do her hair first. Since I was older, I was bound to be quicker than she, but not every single time. Plus, I would let her win on purpose sometimes, just so I would not have to hear his mouth! After a while, he was *always* fussing at my mother, complaining about something or other!

"Wait a minute!" I tried to explain to Gene. I raised my head slightly and Mama accidentally burned the back of my neck with the straightening comb. "Ouch!" I grabbed the back of my neck knowing there would be a burn mark on it later. "That's not even what happened."

"You shut up, you lil' heifer, ain't nobody talkin' to you anyway!" Gene was still bull dozing his point, but now was more upset that I had challenged him.

"You don't tell me to shut up, you ain't none of my daddy!" I stood up as if I was giving him the business. Even though I was a shy child, having to take up for my mother my whole life was starting to turn me into a tough little cookie!

"You right, I ain't yo' daddy, cause you ain't got no daddy!" Gene said viciously. He was getting angrier at the fact I stood up to him.

I looked at my mother, knowing she was not going to say anything about her man calling me out of my name and saying I had no daddy. In tears, I ran to my room and slammed the door, heartbroken. I never liked it when these men argued with my mother.

I hated it even more when she would not stand up for herself. I despised it even more that I felt a need to do something about it.

Gene was always going to have the last word, well into the wee-hours of the morning. "You never listen to me do you? Are you hard of hearing? They say you can't teach an old dog new tricks! I guess they were right. You just as ignorant as they come! I ain't never met nobody as stupid as you. And you ugly too! No good for nothin'... I wish you would just get out of my house and never come back!"

My mother spent those hours trying to 'hush' him to lower his voice to not wake us, but we were never asleep. Who could sleep in all this chaos? We rarely had any problems with him when he was sober. But I did realize that Dr. Jekyll didn't sleep at night, all he did was argue, which means we didn't sleep much either. Many tumultuous arguments went on between my mother and Gene when he was drinking.

When things were good, they were good. If we got Mr. Hyde on payday Fridays, he tended to stick around the entire weekend. But when we got Dr. Jekyll on payday Fridays, that beast liked to linger into the following week. There was very emotional, verbal, and physical abuse going on, but at least I can say I never saw Gene beat my mother in front of us. That is probably why we were not as afraid of him as we were James.

I recall being part of a writing class in the sixth grade at Lorenzo R. Smith School where we had to write our first play. I had no idea how to write a play, so I wrote about my family life with Mama and Gene, but changed the characters' names. The teacher was so enthusiastic about my writing style and the realization of the characters and tone, he said, "This feels so real! It's like you took a real life situation and put it on paper!"

I thought, "That's because it is real!" I learned that I never needed to make up any stories to create any drama. I was living it every day of my life! I did not have to think of what to write next, I can just recall last night's fight or argument, and that would suffice.

During the summers, Mama and Gene would often go to Kankakee and literally stay all day. He did not work on the weekends and she was only working part time at the jewelry department at Kmart, so we were typically at home being bored all day with nothing to do.

When Gene renovated this house, he put linoleum floors in the kitchen, dining room, living room, bedrooms, and hallway. Since we would be home alone all by ourselves on the weekend for hours on end, we decided to create our own fun! We filled up these gallons of water and poured the water down the hallway floors and created a slide. We would run and slide down the halls, splashing water all over the place! We would have so much fun! Weekend after weekend, we could not wait to be home alone so we could create our customized indoor water slides! This was the most fun we had in this house other than the few and far between "Mr. Hyde" Fridays. We could always figure out how to make the best of a situation.

You know how everything can be going south, but there is always at least one thing to look forward to? That light at the end of the tunnel? The rainbow after the thunderstorm? That was Bible Witness Camp for us! We discovered Bible Witness Camp through some neighbors. The kids from the school bus mentioned it to us and we asked Mama if we could start going.

"How much does it cost, and how are you going to get there and back?" my mother would say as this was her only concern.

"It's free and the bus will come pick us up and bring us home!" we'd reply.

FREE was the magic word in our house, and a *FREE* ride? Shoot! We could do pretty much anything if it included the word *FREE*!

Bible Witness Camp (BWC) is a faith-based ministry that has been around since the 1950's. They are committed to serving our underprivileged areas around Hopkins Park and Pembroke, IL. where there is almost 90% African Americans residing in these areas. Being black and poor did not lend many opportunities to do something different with our lives, but Bible Witness Camp created these opportunities.

BWC was owned and operated by this white family, the Williams. They were true Christians as I learned later what a true Christian was. I did not know whose heart God put it on to help the poor black folks, but I for one am grateful for it! They loved us kids and they were there to teach us things we may not have otherwise learned at home.

For instance, I did not grow up in church. My grandmother, as loving as she was, took us to church only on Easter Sunday. My mother would take us to church every blue moon when she was married to James, but I did not see how it did any good to pray to a God while you let your husband go upside your head every night. I was thinking, as it pertains to my mama and James, shouldn't God give you the strength to knock his ass out??? Isn't He the Almighty??? I just could not make it make any sense to me.

Bible Witness Camp, on the other hand, was just the opposite. They taught us about self-love, and about God's love for us. They taught us mostly about God's grace. They were kind, gentle, and patient with us. We learned Bible verses and there was a reward for learning these Bible verses. This was the best part for me! All I had to do was memorize some Bible verses, get points, or what they called 'shares,' which was like Monopoly money. At the end of each month, the Camp Store would open and we could spend this money on candy and toys. I swear I was on a mission to rack up those shares every single month! In addition, every year, if you had enough points, you would be allowed to go to Overnight Camp and Specials Week.

This was the first time I experienced riding on a helicopter, going to the Chicago Museum, and the St. Louis Arch. We did many fun things poor kids just could not afford to do. Although I was good at memorizing these Bible verses, I had no real clue about what they meant until later in life when I accepted Christ as my Savior; then those Bible verses came back to my memory and life began to make more sense.

Bible Witness Camp also kept us grounded. We learned how to be competitive, but in a good way. We were divided up into teams when we played sports and other physical activities. We had to learn to depend on our teammates in order to win the prize. Bible Witness Camp kept us busy and productive, which means they kept us out of trouble. We had something to do every Wednesday night and every Sunday morning since they would pick us up for Sunday morning service, too. They were faithful and never missed a beat.

The Camp taught me discipline and that there was more to life than I was privy to. If I worked hard and remained loyal to the cause, I would find the life I was searching for. My main goal was to stay on track, stay the course, and become a successful adult someday.

Since Mama and Gene rarely took us anywhere except the occasional drive to the Dairy Queen, we could hardly wait until Wednesdays rolled around and Mark Williams would pull up in our driveway in the blue Camp van. Mark and Mary Williams were twins of Mr. and Mrs. Williams, who ran the camp. They would be like an Aunt and Uncle's age and treated us as such.

I was so appreciative of the time and efforts they took with us, and it really made a difference in my life! Just having something to look forward to, getting out of the house, having something positive to focus on.

We were so tired of the arguing at home, the Dr. Jekyll and Mr. Hyde episodes. We did not know if we were coming or going, not knowing what kind of day it was going to be. Sometimes we would get lucky, and other times not so much.

On one Saturday, Mama and Gene were gone all day as usual, and we had just finished mopping up the homemade indoor waterslide when they got back home.

"Kids, come and meet us in the dining room, we have something to tell you!"

They never really talked to us much, so we did not know what this could be about.

Gene spoke first, "Your mother and I love each other and we just wanna let you know…"

"Ya'll getting married!" I blurted out.

"Well, we're already married." my mother said.

I didn't see that coming, but okay. We had already been living with Gene for the past two years and he was not *that* bad. At least he was not as bad as James, and we did truly like him… Sometimes. If only he could get that drinking under control. The only problem is, uncontrollable drinking is called alcoholism, and alcoholism is a disease and most people cannot control it on their own. The only way to help a person who drinks too much is to get them to acknowledge the fact that they have a problem. If they do not believe they have a problem, there is no way to help them. Gene would have had to commit to a rehabilitation program to help his situation, and that was never going to happen!

My mother and Gene also smoked weed, and lots of it. Marijuana was the hottest thing on the market in the late 1970's to early 1980's. Plus, this was all they could afford to smoke, apparently. One time we found a large grocery bag full of weed behind the sofa. Hmmmm, wonder who will be smoking all that?

One day, we were all in our rooms and Gene was at work. The phone rang once, twice, then I started running towards the kitchen, and Lewis started running towards the kitchen from the opposite direction, reaching the kitchen phone at the exact same time. Yes, that canary yellow rotary phone that hung on the kitchen wall on the flowery wallpaper.

"I got it!" My hand was on the phone first.

"No, I got it!" My brother Lewis snatched the phone out of my hand because he was stronger. "Hello…okay…one moment, who's calling?" Lewis covered the mouthpiece of the phone with his left hand as he held the receiver with his right hand. "Mama!" he hollered to the living room, "It's Azzarelli."

My mother came rushing into the kitchen. The energy shifted suddenly to a level of anxiety. "Azzarelli, why would they be calling?"

Azzarelli Construction was the company Gene worked for. She grabbed the phone apprehensively and spoke, "Uh h-hello. Yes, this is her. Say what? He what?"

My mother is a soft spoken person, yet her voice somehow kept getting louder and louder until…

"What! No! No! No! No!" She started screaming and crying at the top of her lungs. "No! No! This can't be happening! No! No! Lord! No!" She still had the receiver portion of the phone in her hand and was holding on to that spiraling telephone cord as she slid down the kitchen wall clawing the flowered wallpaper as if digging her fingernails into a chalkboard. She beat the wall with her hands until I thought for sure she would punch a hole in the sheetrock.

"Mama, what happened? What happened to Gene?"

By this time Punkin and Adrian had run into the kitchen to see what all the commotion was about. Anytime we saw our Mama crying it was an automatic tear bath as the whole family joined in. I even saw Lewis who lived under the old adages of "boys don't cry," "suck it up," "be a man," shed a tear too.

While we attempted to console our mother as she cried, screamed, and wailed throughout the house, I was thinking it had to be something worse than Gene drinking on the job, or losing his job; and then she finally gathered her thoughts and said, "He's dead. Gene is dead."

About another 15-20 minutes had passed as we sat and stood around the kitchen frozen, stunned, numbed. And just like any black woman who had already been through so much, my mother got up off that floor, untangled the cord she had been holding onto for dear life, put the canary yellow phone receiver back on the hook and said, "I need to go to the funeral home to identify the body. Tasha, you make y'all some bologna sandwiches for dinner, there's some red Kool Aid in the refrigerator. Y'all can watch TV until it's time to go to bed, and make sure you take a bath first. I'll be back as soon as I can."

Gene was dead? I could not believe he was dead! Every time Dr. Jekyll would grace us with his evilness, I would pray to God he would take Gene away. I even wrote in my play at school (you know the one that my teacher thought I made up but I really didn't) that Gene died in the end and we lived happily ever after. Oh my God! Did I *will* God to kill Gene? Did I have superpowers that I did not know how to use? Is it my fault my mother is in so much agony and pain because I prayed for this? I begged God to get rid of him. This was a mess! I was a mess!

Of course, I carried the burden of Gene's death on my shoulders for another 12 years, and I never spoke about it to anyone because I really thought I had the power to make God kill people. Quite frankly, when I look back on it, I know it sounds preposterous, because if I had that kind of power there would be at least several more people dead, but they are still here, so there went that theory!

But as a child, we tend to take things at face value. This is what we said, this is what we saw, and this is all we knew. There was no one to ask questions to, no one to explain things to us. My only hope was that I would get clarity on most things later in life, which is still seemingly a work in progress.

I felt badly that Gene was dead, at the young age of 33 no less. I felt sorry for my mother because she did truly love him and she mourned his death at that moment, but then never talked about it again. I felt sorry for his kids because they lost their father; Gene was dead, but then again, so was Dr. Jekyll.

Chapter 6

THE MAN IN THE PICTURE

The sixth and seventh grades were a very difficult and dark time for me. Several months after Gene's death, we moved back to Lil' Mama and Lil' Daddy's house. Shortly afterwards, Lil' Daddy died of lung cancer. We experienced so much loss in a very short time period, maybe within less than six months of one another.

Right when I felt like I was living under this dark cloud, Floyd's father, Johnny Murrell, started coming by Lil'Mama's house for visits. I'm not sure if he stepped in because we had just lost our grandfather and stepfather, or if this was just his timing. Nonetheless, we were happy he would even think of us.

Johnny was a thin, frail, older gentleman. I saw the resemblance of him with the picture I had of my father from a few years ago. Those Murrell smile lines ran deep and I had them honest. Johnny wore eye glasses, as most elderly people would, and was always dressed to impress. Typically when he came to pick us up he would have on a church suit, as he was coming over right after church on Sundays. Johnny had a very calming demeanor, and appeared to be very peaceful. He was also soft spoken in a nurturing kind of way, and seemed genuinely sincere with his intentions.

When Johnny Murrell showed up, he wanted to first apologize for not enforcing his son to acknowledge us as his children.

"I am so sorry. I know I did not stand up for what was right and I have spent many years dealing with the guilt. At the time, I was married to your grandmother, Fatima, and she was totally against having Floyd be accountable for getting your mother pregnant both times. He was definitely a spoiled Mama's Boy, being the youngest of 8 sons total, but that did not serve him in his manhood. Also, I was more interested in keeping the peace in my household, versus standing up for what was right. I was a coward and I can admit that. I should have fought harder for you kids. This was not fair to you at all. I want to make it right with you, and I am working on getting your father to do the same, to own up to his responsibilities. I hope you both will accept my apology."

When my mother first got pregnant with Lewis, at 15 years old, my grandparents of course, asked her who the father was, and she refused to tell them. So Lil' Daddy, being the man he was, kept demanding she tell them who she's been having sex with and who got her pregnant. She finally told them she was walking home from school one day from the bus stop, which is about a one mile walk, when a white man attacked her and forced her into the woods and raped her!

Lil' Daddy was furious! He called the Sheriff's Department in a frenzy! The Sheriff had come out and taken a statement from her and had someone do a sketch of the description of this 'alleged' rapist and there was a manhunt out for this white man who had raped my mother. My grandfather was even combing the woods with a gun in hand in the middle of the night. Then lo and behold, months later, when the baby was born, he came out black as tar!

Well, if you were raped by a white man, and you are a dark-skinned woman; nine times out of ten, your baby is not going to be black as tar, so they knew she was not telling the truth. They just didn't know who she was protecting and why. So then 18 months later, she's having another baby, that would be me. My grandparents, again, demanded she tell them who is the father of these children? She finally confessed to them that it was Floyd Murrell.

There are a number of reasons why my mother did not want to tell Lil' Daddy the truth. She was still in high school with two children and was not even in a dating relationship with this dude, but was just messing around with him. Floyd had already threatened her he would tell everyone she was lying. But the ultimate reason, she did not want Lil' Daddy to kill his ass!

Shortly thereafter, my grandparents met with Floyd's parents, Johnnie and Fatima. I was pretty much a newborn baby and Lewis was a toddler. Lil' Mama and Lil' Daddy set up this meeting at the Murrells' house to discuss our well-being.

"We would like to know if you all are willing to help raise these grandchildren with us since our kids are still teenagers themselves?" my grandparents asked.

"Oh, no!" Fatima, Floyd's mother, chimed in defensively. "My baby did not do this! Don't come in here blaming my son and accusing him of being your daughter's babies' daddy! I can assure you; he is not the father of these children. Matter of fact, they don't even look nothing like us!"

"Well, our daughter, Arlene, told us your son is the father of these children," my grandparents continued, "and we just want to know if you are willing to help with..."

"Like I said," Fatima was adamant about protecting her son. "My son did not do this, and your daughter best be careful about who she's going around town spreading these lies on!" We had heard later that Fatima wore the pants in the family and could be mean and controlling.

Fatima hastily jumped out of her chair, "It's time for you all to go! You are wasting my time, lying on my son....I know my son, and he would have never touched that girl!" She ranted and raved and Johnnie did not say ne'er a word! He just allowed her to control the entire conversation.

I've never known my grandparents to beg anybody for anything and this time was no exception. So they left with us two grandkids in arms, and they did what they had to do as grandparents, without the help of the other grandparents. Basically, my father got off scot-free! He never had to take care of his children. He never had to own any of it, no accountability whatsoever!

I often wondered why my mother never filed for child support later in life since she had to go on welfare. Then I found out that child support was not a law until 1975. This was not something that people thought of back then and definitely not something that went through the court system as it does now. I know men who are arrested for not paying child support these days. Like I said, Floyd got off scot-free.

There was always something in me throughout my entire childhood that yearned for a father figure. Maybe it was because of my mother being in abusive relationships all the time. Maybe I thought my father would have been a better example for us. Maybe he would not have been... Maybe...

Well Johnny was here now, showing up, wanting to be our grandfather. What were we going to do? We knew we couldn't change the past. There was no reason to hold what he allowed to happen in the past against him and he seemed to be sincere about his intentions now. Plus, Johnnie was a bit docile, so it kind of made sense he would have to go along with whatever Fatima said to do.

At 13 and 11 years old, my brother and I didn't know much about holding grudges and carrying that type of burden. We experienced plenty of burden carrying with my mother, but gratefully 'letting it go' was more of our forte. It was the only way to survive this life of turmoil and keep a healthy mental state of mind. We were accustomed to moving on, so this would be no different. We were just glad he was here now, and that we had an opportunity to know someone else who was close to our father. However, Lewis couldn't care one way or another about meeting our father.

"What do I wanna meet him for? He ain't never tried to find me or reach out to me. I could care less," is what he would always say in his nonchalant, emotionless attitude, as most older brothers would typically have in this situation.

But I was the one who pined over my father my entire life. I looked at this as being another avenue for me to get close to him, to bridge the gap, and to get to know the man they call, "your Daddy."

Our newly found Grandfather, AKA Grandaddy, would consistently come to pick us up on Sunday afternoons and take us out to eat, or else he would cook for us at his house. He even started taking us to meet some of our cousins in the Murrell family.

These family meetings continued for several months before they had their Murrell Family Reunion. Prior to the reunion, we met aunts, uncles, and cousins. The Murrells are a huge family! There were seemingly like a thousand of them! They were also well known from the small town, Hopkins Park, IL. Grandaddy and his wife, Fatima, who I never really got to know before she passed, had eleven kids and eight of those were boys! Floyd was the baby boy. All these boys were good-looking, handsome men, as I could tell Granddaddy was back in his day. Most of them were also playboys, playas, man whores; with a lot of charisma, and could probably charm the panties off any girl they wanted, and oh, they did! Consequently, most of them had many children, some out of wedlock, mostly in the double digits, thereby being fruitful and multiplying.

Of course, Granddaddy was excited to invite us to The Murrell Family Reunion at the State Park in Kankakee, Illinois. He had already assured us our father would absolutely be there and we would have an opportunity to meet him. Although Lewis wasn't all that excited about meeting Floyd, I sure was! Grandaddy would come pick us up the day of the reunion. I already had a relationship with my father, in my head that is, prior to ever meeting him. I was a dreamer and lived out my life in my head quite often.

I was in love with my father, or at least the thought of him for as long as I can remember. As a little girl, I used to sit and dream about what type of father he would be to me. Like most little girls, I made him out to be this Superhero, a man who could swoop in and save the day! Swoop in and save my life even. A man who could do no wrong. For those of us who felt like we needed to be saved, that is all we could ever hope for. I just knew that something must have happened as to why he had not yet come for me. I was always awaiting the day I could be safe in my father's arms. He was everything to me even though I did not know him.

I daydreamed about him constantly, doodling on my notepad at home or at school. I would visualize what we would do together. Playing in the park while he's pushing me on the swing and I'm screaming,

"Go higher! Go higher, Daddy!"

"I don't want to push you too high because I wouldn't want you to fall off and hurt yourself," my daddy would reply, as most fathers who cared for their daughters would.

Afterward, we would go to the Dairy Queen to get some ice cream.

"What kind of ice cream do you want, Baby? You can have whatever kind you want."

"I like the one with the chocolate covering! Can I get two of them, Daddy?"

"Oh no, I think you should stick with one because I wouldn't want your tummy to hurt if you eat too much ice cream," my father would reply as most fathers would who care about their daughter's well-being.

Then my father would teach me to ride my bike for the first time.

"Now I am going to make sure that I hold on to the bike as you balance yourself until you are comfortable and then I will let go."

"You promise you won't let go too soon, Daddy?" I imagined saying.

"I promise, Baby, I will never let you go until I know that you are comfortable enough to ride by yourself."

"Okay Daddy! I trust you."

Then my father would always read me a bedtime story and tuck me in every night. I would not have cared if he read the same story over and over again. The fact he would be there by my bedside making sure I was safe and sound every night would have been enough for me.

Of all the conversations that did not happen between my father and me, I still had these conversations in my head. The only problem is, no one witnessed these conversations but me and God. I am not sure why I loved this man so much; I just did. The love was just built inside of me for him. It was real, it was genuine, and it was unconditional. Even if he *was* just a figment of my imagination, at some point I would have given anything to be his daughter, and for him to be my Daddy.

What little girl did not have the hopes and dreams of her father walking her down the aisle on her wedding day? He would be the father who would show up at every basketball game, every play I was in, every cheer competition, every chorus event. In my mind, he was that father who cared about his kids and would give his life for us.

Ever since my sister, Tabula, gave me that picture of him, I put my father on a pedestal. Whatever he was, it had to be better than my stepfather James, right? If there was the slightest chance of my real father being a part of my life, I was willing to take that chance.

I was constantly hopeful. As a little girl with wide eyes, a big heart, and dreams that could stretch from here to Africa, I was totally and utterly in love with my father, for just being my father, although he himself had not acknowledged that... not yet. At the time, I knew nothing about using positive energy to attract what I wanted from life; seemingly, that is exactly what I was doing.

I was going to the seventh grade at this point, and I was so enthusiastic to be able to meet my father for the first time at his Family Reunion! In real life, that is. The man in the picture I had slept with under my pillow for years, is finally coming to see *me*! I felt like Cinderella meeting my Prince Charming! This was about to be the best day of my life and hopefully the start of a new relationship. One I could depend on, and one I could grow with. I was so eager and anxious all at once. I did not know what to expect, but I was so looking forward to this meeting. I was definitely praying for the best possible outcome!

I remember getting up extra early that day as my anxiety was through the roof! I could not sleep much the night before. I had my bath, brushed my teeth, and Lil' Mama cooked Lewis and me a huge breakfast. It was like a buffet spread. Bacon, sausage, eggs, grits, pancakes, and breakfast potatoes. Lil' Mama always wanted to make sure we had more than enough food to choose from. "Just in case, you get out there and they not cooking nothing y'all like to eat!"

I even had my Auntie Terri do my two French braids with some extra cute bows! I wanted to make the best first impression I possibly could.

Grandaddy came to pick us up right on time as promised. Tabula and Ron also rode with us in Granddaddy's brown station wagon. When we arrived at the State Park the boys went to play softball with the cousins, while I saw Tabula run up and hug this man. This man! This is the same man in the picture she gave me in the third grade.

"That must be him!" I thought. "That really is him!" All of my dreams were about to come true. I was about to meet my father, the man in the picture, for the first time in my life!

My grandfather pointed out, "That's your Daddy over there, Tasha. Why don't you go over there and talk to him?"

My father was cooking on the grill and I heard he considered himself a Grill Master. He stood about 5'9, the same complexion as me, and with wavy hair. Or he probably just wore a do-rag to bed at night, but nonetheless, his hair was wavy! This was a far stretch from the afro in the picture I had of him. He was extremely handsome if I may say so myself! I can see why he was such a 'Ladies Man' and consequently why he had so many kids, as condoms were not used much in my neighborhood back in the '70s. The total head count for his kids at this point were 8 children with 7 different baby mamas and counting!

Grandaddy and my Aunts and Uncle kept encouraging me to go and talk to my father.

One aunt, Auntie Sylvia, would say, "Did you see your father over there? You need to go on over there and talk to him."

Another aunt, Auntie Yvonne, would say, "Go on over there baby, don't be scared Ms. Tasha. He ain't gon' bite you."

One uncle, Uncle Alvin would say, "Did you see your daddy over there on that grill? He's right there, go on over there!"

I always wondered why they were constantly rallying me, a child, to go and talk to him, the adult. I would think it would've been the other way around. Shouldn't he want to talk to me? Didn't Grandaddy already tell him I was going to be there and wanted to meet him? I did not really understand it, but in my heart of hearts, I just wanted to meet him, and I just wanted him to like me and get to know me. If I had to be the one to make the first move, then I would have to figure out a way to do it.

I got up enough nerve to go where he was grilling and talk to him, or at least to introduce myself to him. However, my shyness began to take over. With great hesitation, I walked slowly to give myself time to rehearse in my mind what I would say when I was close enough to speak.

I could smell the scent of marinated chicken and beef ribs on that grill! Delicious! I could not wait to sink my teeth into that! I stood there in front of the grill, smoke all in my face, day dreaming of my Daddy making me a plate of food for the first time in my life! Sitting together to break bread, talk about school, and catch up on all the conversations we missed out on. Palms sweaty, heart beating out of my chest, I took a deep breath and said, "Hi," forcing a nervous smile on my face while putting my hand out so he could shake it. I did not know if a hug was appropriate or if it was even something he would even consider, so a handshake would have to do.

He looked up from the grill at me and said, "H-H-Hi," as I noticed at that point he was a huge stutterer. He came over to the other side of the grill and shook my hand. The awkwardness left a certain thick tension in the atmosphere. The pensive look on his face had me wondering, curious about what was to happen next. We stood staring at each other for some moments on end, in silence. I was expecting I would have a conversation with him, even if it was just small talk... anything. But nothing was happening. While stuttering as if he was trying to get something out, no words left his mouth until...

Taking several steps back after shaking my hand, he stuttered. "Well, I, I, I, I, I don't know why my, my, my, my family is t-t-telling you that I-I-I'm your father." He finally stammered through a complete sentence which seemed to be jibber-jabber-ish.

"Wait, what?" I thought, standing there like a possum or a deer in headlights. The very first conversation I have ever had with my father was this gut-wrenching, heart-stabbing words that would forever remain in my sea of rejection. Then he said, "After your m-m-mother got p-pregnant with your b-brother, L-L-Lewis, I n-n-never saw your m-m-other again, so I'm not sure wh-wh-why everybody is t-telling you that I'm your father, because I-I-I'm not, there's no way I could be."

Another gut punch right below the belt!

"B-but if you want to h-have a father d-d-d-aughter relationship, w-w-e can."

I saw his lips moving, but what the hell was he saying? I'm just standing there. Not breathing, yet heart-pounding, feeling faint. Breathe, Tasha, breathe, before you fall on the ground! I had to remind myself to stay in this disastrous moment even though it was killing me!

I thought this was going to be the best day of my life, but it ended up being the worst day of my life to hear those words come out of his mouth! I'm looking at this man and it's like I'm looking in the mirror at myself. Same complexion, same eyes, same cheeks, same smile lines, same hair texture! That's just how much I resembled him. His family genes are extremely strong so *why* would he be denying me to my face when I see myself in him?

I thought about his words, 'If you want to have a father-daughter relationship, we can'??? Why the fuck would I want a father-daughter relationship with a man who just denied me to my face and told me he was not my father, and I was not his daughter! And these words, "After your mother got pregnant with Lewis, I never saw her again." Well, if *he is* not my father, then who the hell is!

He doesn't want me, doesn't give a shit about me, and clearly did not respect my mother! Father-daughter relationship my ass! Get the fuck outta here!

I was pissed! I was mad! I was furious! But most of all, I was hurt...heartbroken! Broken in places I had never been broken before. I felt defeated! Subdued! All those dreams I had about him were now shattered! All those prayers must have fallen on deaf ears! Why was God allowing this to happen to me? What had I done so terrible to deserve this type of treatment? No one deserved to be treated this way! My heart was filled with the anticipation of knowing him, loving him, but at this moment, it burst and exploded into a million pieces. Why am I giving my heart to a man who doesn't love me, who doesn't even like me, and who clearly doesn't want to have anything to do with me!

I just stood there as tears welled up in my eyes, knees buckling, struggling to hold it together. I could hear the faint sounds of the children still playing in the park. I wondered if anyone saw or heard what I just experienced... I hoped not.

I reminded myself, "Don't you shed not one tear in front of this man. He is not worth it! Where is that poker face, Tasha? He does not even deserve to see how hurt you are, since he is the cause of it all. Don't give him the fuckin' satisfaction!"

I finally let go of the breath I seemed to be holding since the handshake. I didn't say anything else because there was nothing else for me to say. I was so done with this picnic! I was done with this family reunion and this entire family! I was just done!

Why would this family push me on this man, not knowing if the outcome was going to be in my favor? Why would they put me in this predicament to be devastated by the one they call "your daddy"? Why wouldn't they protect me, a child, from having to go through this? There were so many unanswered questions.

I rushed back to Grandaddy's car in hysterics. I could barely see my hand in front of my face as I finally released the bucket of tears that clouded my vision, with snot profusely running down my nose. Once I arrived, I climbed in the back seat of his station wagon, hoping nobody would find me, and I just cried. I cried my little heart out. I was so embarrassed they had pushed me off on him, that I was naive enough to fall for it, and he did not want to have anything to do with me. I was ashamed I had invested so much time and emotional energy into loving him, a man who I never even knew.

A while later, my sister Tabula came looking for me. Out of the hundreds of people who were at the family reunion, she was the *only* one who realized I was missing. Not Grandaddy, not my aunts, not Ron, not Uncle Alvin, and not even my brother Lewis. She sat in the back seat of that station wagon with me and wrapped her arms around me.

"Shhh... don't cry Tasha," Tabula attempted to console me. "I'm sorry...It's gon' be alright."

She didn't ask me what happened, but she was just there for me. She was there *with* me. She knew I had gone missing and she came to look for me and found me in the back seat of that station wagon all alone, and we just cried together until the sun went down.

By this point we were true sisters, blood sisters, bonded at the hip, because Tabula knew what probably had transpired since Floyd had been denying me to her the entire time.

Although this was a very devastating time, it brought us closer together as sisters, and that is why we have been there for each other along the way, through thick and thin, through ups and downs. I thought I needed my father in my life because of the way my life was, because of my environment. But if the adult father does not want a relationship with his own children, what can you do? There was nothing I could do, and no amount of hoping, praying, and dreaming about it was going to make it happen. The biggest heartbreak of my life was done by my own father. The man I loved on purpose was my biggest disappointment to this day, EVER!

Chapter 7

WE MEET AGAIN

I had several dealings, or shall I say, run-ins with my father after that dreadful initial meeting in the park that day. The following year, Floyd attended our eighth grade graduation. Me, Ron, and Tabula's! No, wait, he came to Tabula's eighth grade graduation while Ron and I just happened to be graduating, too.

Hopkins Park, IL was composed of about 90% African-American, lower to middle-class people. This was the land of cornfields. The place where my grandfather moved his family in the 60's to get away from the rising crime in Chicago. There definitely was not much to do so we had to learn to make friends and play outside like normal kids. This was way before the age of video games, iPhones, and the fact a child had the audacity to think it was ok to talk back to a teacher, or to any adult for that matter. However, I believe we had some of the best teachers in the entire world. Teachers who gave back everything they had, which was not much, but they genuinely loved us. They taught us how to respect ourselves, and we definitely respected them. My middle school years were between 1980 and 1985 when the teachers were able to discipline the kids, even if you didn't like it, you respected it, with hopes of trying to be a better student.

In 1985, I graduated from Lorenzo R. Smith school as Valedictorian. I was the Valedictorian of the entire school! You would think Floyd would have wanted to be associated with the *smartest* kid in the school! I was also voted May Day Queen of the eighth grade class, but even that did not seem to impress him.

This honor did not come easily, as I had actually tied with another girl because we had the same grades, perfect attendance, and did equally as well on our year-end tests. The tie breaker, however, was the teachers had to interview us and then they decided who would be Valedictorian and who would be Salutatorian.

Throughout the interviews, they asked certain questions about our family's lives and livelihood, our relationships with our parents, things of that nature. I do not know if they felt sorrier for me than they did my running mate, Franchan Lafayette, who was also a good friend of mine, because Franchan came from a two-parent household. Her parents were into the church, but they were also involved in her schooling. She was a Christian, her father had a decent paying job, and she seemed to have much more family structure and stability. Life was much easier for her than it was for me. I asked Franchan about her childhood just recently, and she replied, "Quite honestly, Tasha, I didn't even know we were poor back then!"

Awww, bless her little sweet, little precious, little innocent, little naive heart!! Oh we were well aware how *po' we were*!

My teachers never saw my mother because she never came to the school for any reason. No parent/teacher conference, no open house, no school activities, no nothing. She never even made it to any awards ceremonies when I would receive an award for being on the A honor roll. She was just uninvolved, never showing any interest. I was also on the volleyball team, ran track, was in the band, and starred in some school plays. She never made it to a game, track meet, concert, or play! Not one! She never showed up to any of my sibling's activities either, not just mine. This was before she was married to Gene, during the marriage and after Gene died, so I cannot even blame it on him. I was just happy she made it to my graduation, although she showed up late. It was a miracle she was even there, if I must say so. Nevertheless, the teachers knew I had recently lost my grandfather and stepfather, all within the last year, but I still managed to be in this tight race for Valedictorian. They also knew they had never seen nor heard me mention my biological father, and could draw their own conclusions from there.

My mother was on welfare after we divorced James. Yes, I know I said *we* divorced James because it was a family effort to get rid of that bastard! But at some point she did work in the jewelry department at Kmart. I'm not sure if we ever came off welfare since she was only married to Gene for a few months before he died. We remained in Gene's house for several months after he died, but it seemed like everything started to fall apart in that house. There were plenty of times when we had no running water. Gene had renovated this house prior to us moving in with him, and there was a well on the property for water, but after his death for some reason, the well ran dry. There was no water for drinking, bathing, or cooking. I recall we had to drag these large 5-gallon plastic containers to the neighbor's house to fill them with water. Of course, returning these containers to the house was a challenge, but we hauled them across the bumpy, non-manicured lawn to our house whenever we needed to; careful to not allow much spillage over the top. Mrs. Gillenwater, our neighbor, allowed us to use her outdoor water spigot anytime we needed. All we had to do was ask. She was very nice to us and was also the school librarian. Back then, people did not hesitate to assist when and wherever they could. We were grateful for the kindness of the neighbors 'out in the country.'

Water was scarce and it was embarrassing enough to ask Mrs. Gillenwater every time if we could get more water. We were careful not to use too much, as it would increase the number of embarrassing trips. It felt like begging to me. I mean, who doesn't have running water in the mid 1980's! We didn't.

We never took baths in the tub since it would require too much water. We only washed up at the sink. Yes, we were doing this long before the term 'Ho-bath' became popular! Of course, we still had to visit Mrs. Gillenwater's spigot several times a week, especially on the weekends. We used most of the water for washing our hands and flushing the toilet every time somebody had to poop. If it's yellow, let it mellow, if it's brown, flush it down! Do not forget, we still had to wash our hair, cook, and clean with this water. It was a hot mess, but continued for months and months until we finally moved back in with Lil' Mama. It's safe to say we did the best we could with what we had. We had no choice.

In the winter months, we would be out of propane gas and my mother would just run the kerosene heater in the living room. We would all sit there and watch television until it was time to go to bed. When we went to bed, we would wrap up in 4 or 5 blankets and quilts in order to get warm enough to fall asleep. My sister and I shared a room and my two brothers shared another room. We at least had our own twin beds. This is in the dead of winter where the temperature could get 20 degrees below zero. Winters in Illinois were ruthless!

At any rate, there was the challenge of trying to keep my grades up and to even make it to school every day. I always tried to look on the bright side of things, no matter how dim it appeared.

"At least they had heat and water at school," I thought. They also had free breakfast and lunch programs for those families who qualified. We had no problems qualifying with low or no income! "Who would want to miss school and endure our living arrangements at home?" It seemed pretty logical to me as to why I had perfect attendance. Shoot! I was never missing a day!

I remember my very first job was working in the cornfields. We were already living with my grandparents when Lil' Daddy died, but Lil' Mama was the only one working; so that summer all the kids in the house were getting jobs to help out, or at least be able to take care of themselves. I was only 12 years old at the time, but my Auntie Terri's in-laws, and my older brother Lewis, were getting jobs detasseling corn in the cornfields.

"Can I go to work, too?" I asked Lil' Mama.

"Naw, baby, you too young to work," Lil' Mama answered, rubbing my hand. She was such a nurturer.

"Who says I'm too young to work?"

"Well, I believe you have to be 13 years old to work in this state. Ain't that right Terri?" my grandmother turned to ask my Auntie Terri.

"Yeah, but I don't think they are expecting her to have an ID on her, so how would they know how old she is?" Terri explained.

Lil' Mama was still rubbing my hand, "Baby, why do you want to work?"

"So that I can have my own money and buy my own school clothes. I don't want you to have to worry about how you're going to take care of me, Lil' Mama. I don't want to have to worry about Mama not being able to buy my school clothes this year, I want to be able to take care of myself. I know I can do this! Please let me go to work with everybody else!"

Lil' Mama looked at me with that 'I know you're not going to let it go until I say yes' look on her face and a slight smile and said, "Ok, you can go, but the minute it gets to be too much for you, you let me know, ya' hear?"

"Yes ma'am, I will!" I hugged and kissed her on the cheek. This was my first sense of what independence felt like!

Auntie Terri filled out my employment application and lied, saying I was 13 years old, even though I was only 12. I got up every morning at 4:30 am with sleep in my eyes, made my lunch, caught a ride to Watseka, IL with my cousins, and worked in the cornfields detasseling corn from 6am to 6pm that summer. Some weekends they were offering overtime, where they paid time and a half, which I was always volunteering for as long as I had a ride. Most of the other family members wanted to rest on the weekends or hang out and party with their friends, but I just wanted to work and make money!

Lewis and I still lived with Lil' Mama while Punkin and Adrian lived somewhere else with my mother. One day guess who the people hired to detassel corn? Yep! My Mama! Oh Lord. She was out there in the hot sweltering heat with two of her girlfriends, yapping more than they were working. They wanted to take a water break at the end of every row, but the rule was only every 30 minutes. Every time I saw them, they were sitting on their asses, drinking water, and complaining about how hot it was, and how they were ready to quit.

"Goddamn it! Y'all just got here!" I thought. Not surprising, by the end of the day Mama and her girlfriends were fired!

I heard them mumbling as they stumbled off the field. "Well, I know one thing, they better pay us for the hours we did work!"

All I could think of was I was glad my mama and I had different last names!

I managed to save well over $1000 that summer and Lil' Mama and I opened up my very first bank account. "Don't ever spend all your money at once. You take half your money and buy your school supplies and fall and winter school clothes, then you save the other half of the money for spring."

That was good advice and I did exactly that. The only problem is, my mother knew I had worked all summer and would save my money for what I wanted, even though she could not last one day on the same job. So you can imagine what happened next. Yes, she did! She came to me and asked if she could borrow some money and laid a guilt trip on me!

"Tasha, how much money you got saved?"

"Why?" I really wasn't trying to be disrespectful, but dayummmm!

"Well, I don't get my check until next month and I don't have any money to buy Punkin and Adrian any school clothes."

My mother knew goddamn well school starts every year in August and her check comes the first of every month. So why didn't she buy Punkin's and Adrian's school clothes with the August check???

"I need the rest of my money for my spring school clothes, Mama."

"Spring is a long ways away! You have school clothes now. Do you want your little brother and sister to be without school clothes and you get to go to school with new clothes?"

That's where she got me. "No," I replied sadly just thinking about my younger siblings and feeling sorry for them.

"Then let me borrow the rest of the money and I will pay you back next month."

"Fine." I said reluctantly.

We got with Lil' Mama and went to the bank, withdrew over $500 and gave it to Mama. Of course, next month never came and I never got my $500 back! Over the course of the next few years, I would bring up this incident to my mother and the fact she still owes me money, and she would just say, "Well, you eating ain't you? You got a roof over your head?" Basically, this means she did not owe me nothing! I ultimately learned to lower my expectations of my mother to reduce the disappointments.

I guess if you are really looking at it, I was the candidate who had come the furthest and who had a much longer way to go. Not just physically and financially, but mentally and emotionally. So, I took it for what it was worth. I was ecstatic to be elected Valedictorian of the school! Either position would have been a great honor. Valedictorian was an epic accomplishment for a teenager coming out of a place and environment like the one I had to endure. But honestly, I was just glad to be surviving!

My father had no idea what it took for me to get here. The struggle was real! He was apparently too busy saving face and telling lies because he did not want to take on the responsibility of more kids. How was that my fault? Why did the children have to pay for the mistakes of their parents?

Consequently, Floyd showed up to the graduation just to see Tabula graduate and to give her gifts and take her out to a celebratory graduation dinner.

I can remember giving my Valedictorian speech with much more fervor, passion, and intensity after knowing my father was going to be there! I was determined to show him what he was missing in me, and what he missed out on not knowing me! He chose to disown me, so I had to choose to be *GREAT*, despite his choices! Yeah, this should make him feel appropriately small now, missing out on having anything to do with me receiving this Valedictorian honor. Ha! The highest honor of the school! He should be ashamed! I hoped he felt two inches tall! I even received a standing ovation from the crowd and saw him stand up. Maybe he did not want to be the only one sitting. "Sit yo' bitch-ass down!" I thought. "You have no reason to be standing as if you're proud of me, when you know you're not!" I felt like he had no right to even *appear* to be associated with *The Valedictorian*!

After we had all received our diplomas and shifted the tassel from left to right, we were excited to be going to high school!

Our eighth grade graduation field trip was to Great America the next day, which is now the Six Flag theme park on the north side of Chicago, about two hours north of Kankakee.

Tabula stepped away from our group to talk to her father. "Daddy, is it ok if Tasha and Ron go to dinner with us?"

"Uhhh, I-I don't think that's a good idea. I h-h-hadn't planned f-f-for them to g-g-go with us," he stuttered nervously. " I-I already t-t-told you, they are n-n-not m-my kids!"

"Well, but they are my friends, and I would love for them to come with us!" Tabula was adamant and was always trying to stand up for us, although Floyd was not budging.

Then Floyd's father, Johnny Murrell, AKA Grandaddy, came over as he overheard the previous conversations.

"So I guess you're taking all the kids out to eat, huh?" he said to Floyd, but not as if he was asking, more like insisting.

"No-nah, I wasn't p-p-planning to t-t-take them all o-o-out to eat," Floyd replied.

"Well if you take one of them, you gon' have to take all of them. That's just not right!" Grandaddy was not letting up. He was not accepting 'no' for an answer. After what Floyd did to me in the park a year ago, Granddaddy needed to step up and force his hand!

"A-A-l right, then I-I-I g-g-guess they c-can go," Floyd replied reluctantly as to not cause a scene with his father.

It was weird, awkward, and uncomfortable, if I'm being completely honest, to witness how all this played out. Floyd was so determined to continue to throw us away as if we were worth nothing! As if there was no value to our lives whatsoever. As if our feelings just did not count! Grandaddy was forcing Floyd to do something he clearly did not want to do, and I am not sure that pushing him to take some responsibility was making things any better.

I was pretty much done with this man after what he had already put me through, but Ron was begging me to go so that he wouldn't be the only outcast. I guess two outcasts were better than one! Ron needed me to be there with him, unwanted and all, so that is what I did.

We eventually went out to eat, mostly in silence, but Floyd did force some small conversations, so we just went along with it. Never reading too much into it and keeping our expectations low.

After that, my brother Ron would periodically call me because he would have had some bad dream about our father, and he just wanted to be able to talk to him. He wanted to be able to get to know Floyd, even though Floyd was not 'checkin' for us'. So, when Ron called me up and said, "Hey, Tasha, I want to know if you would call our father?"

"Why would I call our father? He hasn't been trying to call us." About this time I had given up hope.

"Well, I understand that," Ron said, "but I already got the phone number."

I said, "Where did you get the phone number?"

"I got it from Auntie Sylvia, who was like, "just don't tell him I gave it to you," but I got it and I don't want to be the one to call him, so that's why I'm calling you, so you can get him on a three-way and we can talk to him together."

Ron is about five months younger than I, and he has always called me his big sister ever since we met in the 5th grade. 'My big sister this, my big sister that.' So I guess as the *big sister*, I would step up and do things a *big sister* would probably do. This situation with Ron was no different. I knew he yearned for his father. We all did at some point, however his yearning for our father seemed to be a little more drastic. My heart went out to him, and still does to this day because there is a hole in his heart in the shape of his father. Yes, I got that from *Iyanla Vanzant*. So I agreed to call Floyd with no high hopes of where this conversation was going to go. Ron was happy and it pleased him in some way, which was pretty much the only reason why I did it.

Floyd answered the phone and I let him know I was on the phone with Ron, and asked if he had some time to chat with us; that was all we really wanted. He did not seem to mind just chatting. We never talked about our relationship with him. We never talked about when he would come see us, or if we could come to visit him. We never put him on the spot about anything we needed for school, or for after school, or for other activities we were involved in. We never, not once, asked anything of him. We never asked him for money. Never, not once. The only thing we asked was if we could call him from time to time and just chat and get to know him; that was all we ever asked. That was the extent of it!

He seemed to be pretty comfortable with just chatting about nothing serious, nothing of any importance. So I thought, okay, maybe this is a start. I even asked him before we got off the phone if he would not mind us calling him in maybe a month or two, just to catch up with him. He said he did not mind at all, that would be great, and that was that. When the month or two later came, Ron wanted to call him again. I was going to get him on the three-way just like I had done previously, but lo and behold, we would hear that recorded voice on the phone!

"You have reached a number that has been disconnected. If you feel like you've dialed the number in error, please hang up and try your call again."

"Ron, are you sure you gave me the right number?" I would get frustrated.

"Yeah, I'm positive, that's the same number we dialed the last time!"

Basically, our father would change his number. Every single time Ron would go and get his number from one of our aunts or uncles, we would go through that whole rigmarole again and again and again, and every time he would change his number! Nigga! He would let us know it was okay to call him, he would be willing to chat, then we would get off the phone with him and a month or two later, whenever Ron got an inkling to call his father again, we were right in the same place; having to get his number again because he had changed it. I have no idea how many times this man has changed his number on us, and all we wanted to do was *chat* and get to know him. He was treating us like a fuckin' bill collector! Damn shame!

I would never be able to explain how a man can look his children in their faces and deny them; how he looked at me that day in the park and would not have acknowledged me, even on his mother's grave. He had not yet acknowledged Ron either. So, I was not the only one. There were other siblings he had not acknowledged. Lisa was another one. Then there was Kenyatta; although he was married to her mom for several months, but had not been in contact with her since. Even though he told me to my face in the park that day, that after Lewis was born, he and my mother never got together again, yet he never had any contact with Lewis either. I would never be able to understand the guilt and shame that tortures him on a daily basis throughout his entire life. It's sad! Very, very, sad. All because he is a cocky, arrogant, maniacal, narcissist! I would hate to be him. Living his entire life with a mask on! A face so ugly, even God will have to turn away!

Chapter 8

DAMON

After graduating from the eighth grade, I had to move from my grandmother's house to my mother's house in Kankakee, Illinois. This was very disappointing to me as I had become accustomed to never worrying about food, clothes, or getting a ride somewhere when I needed it. Heat, water, love, attention, and other bare necessities that every child needed were never a concern.

Lil' Mama had custody of two of my younger cousins and had decided to move from Beaverville in order to have a fresh start. Eventually, I knew I was going to have to suck it up and move on. My mother would have to step up to the plate and be a mother to all her children. I was going to have to adjust to the instabilities of life once again.

I hated the thought of wondering how this was going to pan out. My mother was just too unstable for me! However, she had recently gotten a huge annuity settlement from Gene's death, and was planning on getting us a nice house to live in. About time! It would be nice to get ahead for a change! I just hoped she would know what to do with the money and not blow it! You know what happens when people who never had nothing get a large sum of money, don't you? So, I had a right to be concerned. Of course, my mother never shared with us how much money she had received, but I did hear from an aunt that it was around $150,000. That was a lot of money back then for people who came from nothing!

She had acquired a very nice house in the most decent neighborhood we had ever lived in! I figured this may be a move in the right direction since she appeared to be doing much better financially, at least.

The house was located on Hickory Street on the south side of town. It was a light blue house with a porch that had a wooden swing we could sit on when we were outside. Once you walked into the house, to the right was a sunroom, or at least that is what we called it. It looked like the previous owners had enclosed the porch and then added a new porch onto the front of the house. My mother had all new furniture in this home. Upstairs there were three bedrooms and two full baths. I later found out we were not buying this house; we were only leasing it and it came fully furnished.

At this time Mama was dating a guy named Damon. He was a lot younger than she, maybe by about 10 years, and he worked as a security guard. He was kind of short for a man, and was a little stout and chunky. I remember him wearing cornrows braided from the front to the back of his head. I really didn't have a problem with Damon. He did not mess with me, and I did not mess with him. However, when it came to his relationship with my mother, it was totally toxic. They were always fighting and arguing, no different from any of her other relationships.

One day we were having a sleepover with our younger cousins and a few friends. I was in the ninth grade and attending Kankakee Junior High School and I was the oldest of the children present. My friends were old friends from Hopkins Park who I didn't get to see much since I had to move to Kankakee with my mother, so we were happy to finally be able to get together.

We were all in one room together playing a game of 'who can tell the scariest story' when we heard some banging against the wall in the next room.

"Shh-shh!" I hushed everybody. All the kids listened intently, then we heard it again. There was loud bumping against the wall as if someone was being pushed or thrown, then the muffle of my mother's scream as if a hand was over her mouth!

"Did y'all hear that?" I asked. "That sounds like Mama screaming." Over the years I had become extremely familiar with this sound; my mother's screams ringing in my ears.

We all decided to gather and go down the hall to the master bedroom door to see what the commotion was all about. There was about 9 or 10 of us kids, ages ranging from 7-14. Imagine us lining up tallest to the shortest, as if we were in school getting ready to go on a bathroom break! But really, we were getting in formation to go to war! We just knew we were going to have to kick Damon's ass! We first strategized on how we would handle the situation. Then we began knocking on their bedroom door, which turned into banging when you have 20 fists knocking simultaneously, until Damon finally opened the door. I stuck my head in and saw my mother holding her arm and crying. I also witnessed a hole in the sheetrock.

"What y'all want? Stop banging on this goddamn door!" Damon was irritated, trying not to open the door too wide so I could barely see the damage that was done.

"We want to make sure Mama is okay!" Poking my head around the room as much as I could, I was the leader of the group and clearly the spokesperson.

"She alright!" Damon hollered. "Now get back to your room and mind your own damn business." He slammed the door in our faces and we could hear them arguing again.

Maybe 10 minutes later, we decided we should call the police, because as the evening went on, we could hear her screaming again. Apparently, he was throwing her against the wall because there was lots of thumping and bumping going on. My friend, Tamiko, and I tip-toed downstairs to the kitchen to use the phone and I called 911 and let them know what was going on in the house. Two of the other kids stood watch as they would be our lookout in the event Damon came out of the master bedroom. We returned to the upstairs room where we were all playing the game, and watched out the window with anticipation for the police to show up.

None of us were immune to these incidents. We each had our own set of dramatic experiences and stories to tell. We all lived in an environment of poverty and fear, which tends to go hand in hand. There was always some drama going on in our lives. Always something to tell. Always something we were trying to live through. We were inevitably the ones trying to survive our situations. Pent up energy, tight chest, anxiety, insomnia, depression. Yes, all of it! We could not go to the doctor and get a prescription for our issues back in the day. We could not afford to even see a doctor back then. Although we were on welfare, we had to break an arm or something serious before our mother would take us to see the doctor. While we were afraid, we always knew we had to push through the fear and do what needed to be done. There was no time to think about being scared when we were too busy thinking about how to survive.

As soon as the police car arrived, I hurried downstairs and went outside to meet with the officer to give him a heads up on the situation. The officer followed me upstairs to my mother's bedroom and knocked on the door.

"Police, open up!"

Damon quickly opened the door, and lo and behold, the officer and Damon were acquainted. I noticed the officer relaxed his hand from his weapon when he saw Damon. Apparently, they worked some security guard gigs together. I knew then Damon would not be taken to jail.

"Hey Damon!" the police officer called him by name as soon as he saw him. "What's going on here? We received a call about a domestic violence disturbance."

Damon appeared relieved when he realized he knew this officer. "Well, I do not know who called you or why, but there is no domestic violence going on here. Ain't that right, Arlene?" he said, giving her that 'look.'

We kids were all standing in the hall, telling the officer what we heard and what we witnessed. My experience with my mother was she would not tell the truth about what was happening and who was hurting her. When you are afraid of a person, you know telling on them would make it worse for you in the long run. She was not about to do that. So as usual, we were left pointing the finger as if it were all a lie. I was a believer that one day when I was reporting something bad happening to her, would be the day I saved her life....or maybe not. I was committed to reporting it anyway, if just to let the guy know her kids are not just going to sit back and watch this abuse happen without doing something!

The officer looked at my mother and asked, "Has this man physically harmed you in any way, ma'am?"

My mother looked over at me and the other kids with sad eyes and a soft, broken voice, "No, officer."

"Are you sure you do not want to press charges, ma'am?" At least the officer was committed to doing his job. He could see she was crying and in pain, while holding the arm Damon had twisted.

"Press charges for what?" Damon exclaimed. "I didn't touch her! Did I Arlene?"

The officer interjected, "Did this man harm you physically, ma'am?"

We all stood intensely, holding our breath, hoping she would tell the officer what happened. Knowing she would not, but hoping, nonetheless.

"Tell him the truth! Tell him that I did not put my hands on you!" Damon reiterated.

"No, officer, he did not put his hands on me," my mother replied robotically.

The officer hesitated, "Okay, then there's nothing that I can do here." The police officer looked at my mother, looked at Damon, and then looked at us kids, shaking his head, as if to say he was sorry. He then turned around and walked away. I followed him down the stairs and out to his squad car.

"So you're not going to arrest him for beating up my mama? You saw her crying. You saw her holding her arm in pain. You saw the hole in the wall. You know him, so I know you know he did something wrong!"

"I'm sorry," the police officer replied. "There's nothing I can do unless she says with her own mouth that he has been abusing her."

"So what is it that I'm supposed to do if this continues? Are we going to wait for him to hit her so hard that he kills her, and then you want me to call you back?" I had a way of being sarcastic when I was upset.

"I understand your concern," the officer replied to me, "but there's nothing I can do unless your mother says that he is harming her. She has to be the one to say it, she has to press charges. I am so sorry I was not able to help you."

I realized the police were no good to anybody who lived in fear. My mother was never going to admit that Damon was hurting her. No justice would ever be there for her in her life because she lived in fear. That really sucks! I've always felt sorry for her. So scared to speak up for herself. So scared to love herself. So scared to demand respect. Fear- *an unpleasant emotion caused by the belief that someone or something is dangerous, likely to cause pain, or a threat.*

I came back into the house solemnly, trying to think of a Plan B. I ran back upstairs and put my ear to my mother's bedroom door. I could hear Damon scolding her about me calling the police on him, and she better be lucky he did not break her arm. I went back to the room to let my siblings, cousins, and friends know what I heard, and we all decided we would sleep with knives under our pillows that night. How else could we take his fat ass down! The police would be of no use to us now. We all quietly went downstairs to the kitchen and I passed out every big butcher knife we could find in the house. After we ran out of big knives, I gave the smaller kids the smaller steak knives. We just knew Damon was going to die that night.

We all made a pact that if we heard my mother scream once again that night, we would figure out a way to knock the door down and stab the man to death with all these knives! If the police were not going to do something about it, we would have to do it ourselves. Although we were all very afraid, with adrenaline pumping, we were ready to "Set it Off!" We had no idea what we were getting ourselves into, but we had a plan, at least for that night if the circumstances would have taken a turn for the worse.

Morning came and thank God we did not have to kill anybody! I wonder where we would have been if we had? God made sure our house was quiet that night! And I'm so glad that He did. I did not really understand the magnitude of what could have happened here. I was just thinking we would have all told the judge we were just taking up for my mama when we killed the man, and everything would have been fine. Clearly, God protects the children and fools!

My mother did not stay with Damon for too long. By the end of the school year, she had already checked out, and had even stopped coming home. We had no idea where she was. Damon used to work the night shift as a security guard, and I assumed he knew what was going on, but of course, we kids were in the dark. Weeks had passed with no word from my mother, and naturally I began to worry. First, I had to make sure my little brother and sister were not going to school talking about the fact that we didn't know where our mother was.

"When you get home from school, you get off that bus, get in this house, make yourself a bologna sandwich to eat, and do your homework. There will be no staying after school, don't invite your friends over here and no, you cannot go outside to play, so don't even ask! If you say anything to anybody, you need to know the State will come in here and take us away from each other and put us in foster care. And you know what they do to kids in the Foster Care system, don't you? So make sure you keep your mouths closed!"

Even at 14 years old I was the true sheriff in town. I knew what I needed to do to protect my little brother and sister. I also knew that included scaring them half to death so they would obey me. There was no time to be a child when I was too busy being a responsible grown up.

My mother did not even bother to call me to let me know she was even alive. About the third week, we were running out of food. Clearly, Damon did not care if we had food to eat or not, and I assume his fat ass was eating fast food every day, so he did not care if the refrigerator was empty. Then out of the blue one day, Lil' Mama showed up with bags full of groceries! My grandmother was definitely a lifesaver!

"Punkin and Adrian! Come down here and get these groceries and put them up in the refrigerator," I called for my siblings. The kids ran downstairs, hugged my grandmother, and took the groceries to put them away. My grandmother and I huddled in the sunroom to have a grown-up conversation.

"Do you know where our mother is? Is she okay?" I asked anxiously.

"Yes," Lil' Mama replied calmly. "Your Mama called me and she is okay. She wanted me to come over here and check up on you kids and bring you some groceries."

"So, what is going on with her, and how come she has not called to let me know where she is? Do you know we have not seen her in over three weeks?"

"Your mother will explain it all to you when she can. You just keep watching your little brother and sister and making sure everybody is okay. She said she will call you soon, Tasha. I'm sure she will."

My grandmother was notorious for taking up for my mother, no matter how wrong she was, and no matter how much she did wrong. I believe she felt sorry for her and at the same time, she did not want to have the responsibility of filling my mother's shoes as the mother all the time, so she didn't have a choice but to take a step back.

We kids were stuck on a road that we did not choose, but one that chose us. I was so tired of this drama! So tired of this road!

My mother never came back to the house on Hickory Street. As a matter of fact, school was out for summer about a week or so later when I received a call from my Auntie De-De.

"Hey, pack up as much as you can and tell Punkin and Adrian to pack some clothes because I'm coming to get y'all."

"You coming to get us and take us where?" I questioned.

"Well, your Mama is going to let you stay at my house for the summer and Punkin and Adrian are going to go with her to the new place where she's living now," Auntie De-De replied.

"So basically my mother hasn't lived here with her children and her boyfriend for the past month. Yet, she already has a new place where she is living and has not said a word to the oldest child that she left in the house with the boyfriend that she is not even with anymore!" I was clearly perturbed with this whole situation and how my mother chose to handle it. I did not get it. Adults should be able to make better choices for their lives and for their kids! I just did not get it!

"Well, at least can I go see my mama to make sure she's okay?" Auntie De-De took us over to Ms. Mary's house, which is where my mother was staying with her new boyfriend, Rusty. Edward was his real name. Ms. Mary was a white, redneck, trailer park, chain-smoking, fat, sickly woman, who always sounded like she was about to cough up a lung! Rusty was a mixed race, redneck, trailer park, chain-smoking, broke man who lived in his mama's basement. Y'all, I cannot make this shit up!

So I asked myself, "How is this better than what we had???"

That summer, I lived with Auntie De-De. My younger brother and sister lived with my mother at Ms. Mary's house in the basement with Rusty.

One day my mother called me to ask me to do her a favor.

"What kind of favor?" I asked.

"I need you to go down to the house at 2'oclock when the mailman runs. I'm supposed to be getting a check today and I don't want Damon to get his hands on that check."

"Well, if it's your check, then how come you can't go get it? What is he going to be able to do with a check in your name?"

"I just don't want him to get the check. If he does, I'll have to wait to put a stop payment on it and have them re-issue it. I really don't have time to do that because I need to get us another place to live before y'all start school. Plus, he might try to do something to me; he's not going to touch you."

"How do you know that?"

"Has he ever put his hands on you before?"

"No."

"Then can you just do me this one little favor? He's not going to be up when the mail runs anyway. He never even checks the mail, so you should be ok. Just walk down to the house and be there by 2'oclock and get the mail from the mailman, then go back to De-De's house after that. Once you get the mail, call me back. Can you just do me this one little favor, Tasha?"

"Okay, Mama." I replied hesitantly and with an attitude.

I hate that my mother put me up to things that I had no business being involved in. It's been that way all my life. It is very hard to say no to your mother when you know she has no other options. She has built her life around not having any options, or at least believing no other options existed for her. I hate seeing her like that. Carrying the burden of her life on my shoulders once again, as I had done my entire life! But what options did *I* have at this point?

I paced the floor at my aunt's house all the next morning until it was time to walk down the street to intercept the mail from the mailman. I was on my way to the house a couple of blocks away, and I could see the mailman down the street dropping off the neighbor's mail. We arrived at our house simultaneously and I spoke to the mailman and he put the mail in my hands and drove off. As soon as he drove off, Damon came running out of the house, grabbed my arm and snatched all the mail from me and pushed me almost to the point of falling to the ground. As I stumbled to catch my fall, I knew there was nothing that I could do because after he snatched the mail he ran back into the house and locked the door. "Punk ass Bitch! Fat, sloppy, mothafucka!" These were the only choice words I could come up with!

I went back to my Auntie De-De's house crying and let her know what happened.

"Don't worry Tasha, it's not your fault," she told me.

I did not like putting myself in these predicaments with my mother. Why would she have me confronting the issue with her boyfriend anyway when I'm just a child? How come adults around here do not know how to be grown-ups? They are worse than teenagers. Worse than kids! They are terrible! They are the worst!!!

I do not know how my mother eventually got that check, or maybe she had to call and put a stop payment on it and get them to mail it to Ms. Mary's house. By the end of the summer we rented another house on River Street, right before the next school year started. It was a white duplex and we lived on the right side facing the street. I was beginning my sophomore year at Kankakee High School. At least we were out from under Damon, and I was not going to have to worry about dealing with him ever again. I was relieved, for the moment, that is.

Chapter 9

THE GRASS IS NOT ALWAYS GREENER

My sophomore year in high school I dated a guy by the name of Fredrick Clark. Fred, who was a senior, was one of our high school's track stars, and he was also in the band. I was a Cheerleader and was also in Show Choir. I met Fred on an activity bus on the way from the Lincoln Cultural Center to Kankakee High School.

"Hi, I'm Fred Clark. Frederick." Fred had walked up from the back of the activity bus and sat next to me in the front seat. He seemed a little shy, but at least he was willing to put himself out there.

"Hey, I'm Natasha Bostic." I had been staring out the window dreading the ride home.

Fred seemed to be interested in getting to know me and he also had a good sense of humor. We talked and laughed the entire ride to the High School and then the magic happened.

"So can I get your phone number and maybe call you sometimes?" he asked nervously.

I looked up at him with a slight smile on my face. "Sure, I would like that. The number is 944-9267." That was back in the day where the prefix was not required.

He quickly wrote the number down on a notepad and I could tell he was shaking in his boots.

"What? What's the matter?" I asked. I already knew he was nervous.

"I honestly didn't think you were going to say yes."

"Really? Then why did you ask?"

"Because I was *hoping* you were going to say yes," we both laughed.

I knew if my very existence made a guy nervous, then he genuinely liked me. There was something pure and innocent about this type of nervousness. Like he wanted to please me. He wanted to make me happy.

Fred was medium build, 5ft 10in, dark brown complexion, with wavy hair and was a very handsome young man. He was on the quiet side, but cool, funny, and popular. Not popular because he got around, but his family was very well known in the area. The Clarks were a larger, middle-class family in Kankakee. There were 4 girls, 3 boys, and of course, the mother and father. Mr. and Mrs. Clark were a fun couple, always joking and playing with each other. They kind of reminded me of a younger version of Lil' Mama and Lil' Daddy, with less financial worries.

I was a light skinned, skinny girl, about 5ft 5in, long shoulder length hair and cute, with a nice set of 'cheerleader's legs.' Like me, Fred had many extra teeth in his mouth and would later wear braces. Fred was smooth, like Keith Sweat, but kindhearted and generous, and would do anything for me. He was very genuine and admirable. Not too cocky and arrogant like lots of other guys. In a few short months I had fallen totally and completely in love with Fred Clark. He was everything a girl could want and more.

We were High School Sweethearts, paving the journey together. Everybody just knew Fred and I would be together forever. You couldn't see one of us without seeing the other. Fred was my first serious boyfriend, and first true love.

The Clarks were a pleasant family and possessed good morals, values, and character. Both his parents had seniority jobs at the local tobacco factory, and were considered middle-class citizens. They had a very nice house on the north side of town, also drove nice cars, one I remembered being a brand-new Cadillac.

Although Fred was two years older than me, he asked me to his Senior Prom. I was ecstatic as I was only a sophomore being asked to prom by a senior! When I asked my mother if I could go, she said she did not have any money to buy me a prom dress, so the answer was no. It is funny how they had money to buy drugs or anything Rusty wanted, but when it came time for us to need or even want to do anything...

"You know I don't have any money," would be my mother's rehearsed answer. When Rusty wanted something, they sure had a way of *finding* the money for that!

I told Fred I was not able to go to prom with him because my mother "didn't have any money." However, when his mother was taking him shopping to pick out his tux, she invited me along with them. Of course, I did not want to go since I wasn't able to buy myself a dress; but I still went for moral support. Once we got to the mall, Mrs. Clark asked me to try on a particular dress. I let her know I wasn't one for window shopping and I really did not want to try it on. She was extremely persistent, so I tried on the dress. It fit like a glove. It was a long white strapless dress just above the ankles. The very top of the dress was satin and down the middle was sheer with rhinestones. The dress was tapered at the waist, accentuating my petite figure, and from the waist down it flared out with a sheer layer over the satin portion. I felt like a Princess from a Disney movie! Mrs. Clark told me she would buy the dress for me as a gift, so I could accompany her son to Senior Prom. The Clark family was really good to me, despite my circumstances. I later found out that Fred bought the dress for me and had just given the money to his mother. He did not want me to feel uncomfortable about him buying my clothes just so I could go to prom with him. How embarrassing that would have been! Yes, I was one of those proud, poor black girls! I do not need no handouts! I don't need nobody feeling sorry for me!

I learned so much from the Clark family just by hanging out at their house, how they interacted, how they supported one another, shared, took trips together, and sometimes would invite me to ride to Chicago with them to visit Fred's older sister, Betty. Betty had such a nice apartment in the big city and I was ultimately drawn to how they lived their lives and the quality by which they had achieved not only material success, but also with their family and relationships. I cherished these moments with the Clark family, and I could see myself being a part of it. Everything about this family made me wonder what type of family I would have when I was older. It gave me insight on family dynamics in this generation.

Yes, I had experienced family life with my grandparents, and even after Lil' Daddy died, I was still able to experience that family life with Lil' Mama. Since I had been living with my mother, there was not much 'family' going on. I yearned to be around Fred and his family. I just wanted to continue to experience what that family structure felt like. The love, support, and camaraderie were what I looked forward to when I thought about having my own family. The Clarks were always doing something together and going places. I loved that! They may have game night, cookouts, or take short trips, and I was always more than welcomed. They were my new extended family and I was very appreciative.

After Fred graduated from High School in December 1987, he joined the Air Force, as his older brother, Dennis, was already in the Air Force. This is how he had money to purchase my prom dress. We had been dating for about 9-10 months. I was still a sophomore in high school dating an Air Force man! After Basic Training, Fred bought himself a brand new car. I do not recall the make or model, but I do remember it was black, sporty, and a 5-speed. Oh, and did I mention brand new? Right off the factory lot! I did not know how to drive a stick shift, but Fred was willing to teach me. He would take me out to a vacant parking lot so I could practice driving. Of course, men are not the best teachers, so he decided to let me drive myself around so I could practice without him trying to tell me what to do. I learned how to drive that 5-speed in no time in the parking lot by myself! He definitely trusted me and I trusted him. Fred and I were the best of friends, and I knew he had my back. Fred knew everything about me and the type of environment I lived in with my mother and her boyfriend. Neither he nor his family were judgmental of my situation and I loved him for that.

Fred was never allowed to come over to the house when we lived in the duplex on River Street with Rusty. Actually, Rusty was living with us. Remember, he used to live in his mama's basement! Oh, did I mention, he did not have a job? I do not know if the man ever worked a day in his life! I hated Rusty's guts, and it seems he hated mine, too. We were like oil and water; we just did not mix! Plus, I would much rather be over at Fred's family's house where there was love, friendship, and everybody got along.

I never actually invited people over to our house because I never knew when a fight might break out, or if Mama and Rusty would be doing drugs, or if the police or ambulance would need to be called at any given moment. It was best that people stayed clear, and I would just go to their house for visits and sleepovers.

One time my best friend, Rolanda, invited herself over to our house because she wanted to go trick-or-treating. We also had a basketball game to attend as we were both cheerleaders. I never wanted to invite her over to our house because I knew my mother and Rusty would probably embarrass me in some way. She insisted on coming just so we could walk to the basketball game as her parents were out of town and my house was closer to the school. Besides, I was always at her house, so now I guess I needed to suck it up and return the favor.

After we got off the bus and began walking toward the house, I could not help but pray there would be no drama going on once we arrived. When we approached the front door and entered the house, the very first thing we could smell was drugs. My mother and Rusty's drug room was a den at the front of the house. The room had two glass doors that reminded you of patio doors, but they were covered with curtains so we could not see in. But there was always smoke coming from underneath the door, so we knew what was going on in there.

"What's that smell?" Rolanda asked, innocently.

"Girl, don't worry about that! Let's go upstairs and get this homework done."

I rushed her upstairs so I would not have to explain to her that my mother and her boyfriend sat around doing drugs all day, every day.

One time I had gone to a carnival with a few friends of mine; Loreal, Terrence, and Jarvis. Once Terrence, who was driving us, got to the stop sign near the corner lot where I lived; there were police cars in the driveway.

"Tasha, looks like they must be having a drug bust at your house!" Terrence said jokingly. Little did he know he was right.

"Boy, shut up and stop playing!" I replied back jokingly. I tried my best to deflect from the truth.

I hurriedly rushed out of the car, slammed the door, and ran across the corner lot lawn to my house. As soon as I got through the door I saw my mother bleeding from the side of her head and crying. I saw Rusty handcuffed, and the police holding his arms behind his back. I saw my younger brother, Adrian, crying and Punkin was also crying while cursing out Rusty.

"What is going on here? What happened?" I hollered as I entered the house.

"He put his hands on my Mama! We saw him punch her in the face and that's why I called the police."

Punkin turned to Rusty as the police were dragging him off to jail in handcuffs. "If you think you gone be hitting our motherfuckin' Mama and getting away with it, yo' ass is trippin'. Fuck that!"

Punkin had seen me call the police on my Mama's boyfriends many times. This was her first time having to do it since I was not at home. I had no idea that girl could curse so well! Even better than me. "Well done Grasshopper, well done indeed!"

Just like all the previous times before, Rusty would be hauled off to jail and Mama would bail him right out of jail. But this time, he did not come right back as if nothing had happened. This time it was days, maybe even a couple of weeks. I would even say he sent her flowers for the first time, and a bird. Like we needed another mouth to feed! I guess it was the best gesture he could think of. Then, in the middle of the night, I started hearing Rusty sneak through the back door and up the stairs to their bedroom. Mama would sneak him back out before she woke us kids up for school. Little did she know I would already be awake and overhear the entire transaction every night. They were not fooling nobody! Then one day my mother finally asked me the million dollar question.

"So, how do you feel about Rusty coming back home?"

Ha! As if I didn't know he was already back home! "So what's going to be different this time, Mama?"

"He knows he can't be fighting me and calling me names and all that stuff. He really is trying to change."

"And you can tell he's trying to change because of what? The flowers? Because he bought you a bird? In exchange for another black eye!" I knew I was being hard on my Mama, but I was getting way too tired of their shenanigans!

"Well, I want to give him another chance."

"I don't know why you're asking me anyway, when you know your mind is already made up! So do what you wanna do, which is what you've always done, and will continue to do."

My living situation with Mama and Rusty was worse than my living situation with her and Damon. Rusty was bigger, badder, louder, scarier, and just downright ruthless! He didn't care about doing things behind closed doors. He was so ruthless, did it right in front of our faces. He was more like James; except we were not little babies anymore. He would curse out our mother, call her demeaning names, even punching her right in the face in front of my little brother and sister. This one was bold I would say! I started to think about that old saying, "The devil you know is better than the devil you don't!" On one hand, maybe Damon was a better devil than Rusty was; but on the other hand, who wants to live with the devil, having to deal with his ass every single day?

Many times my mother would get into terrible fights with Rusty, whom I had grown to hate, literally. I know they say it is wrong to hate, but try telling that to the feeling within! I have learned it is simpler to not mask my true feelings, so then *hate* it is! Anyway, I would sneak out of the house and walk over to my boyfriend Fred's house late at night. Fred had already returned to his military base in Champagne, IL, but his mother was very welcoming and understanding. She would call my mother to let her know I was at her house and that I was fine. She also asked my mother if I could stay a few nights just to have a breather, and she would bring me back home in a couple of days. Thankfully, my mother agreed to this arrangement.

Other times, I would ask a simple question like, "Can I go to church with Rolanda tomorrow?"

"No!" Rusty would scream out for sport.

"Ain't nobody even talkin' to you!"

"But I'm talkin' to you!"

Ignoring Rusty, "Mama, can I go to church with Rolanda tomorrow?"

"Rusty already said no," the parrot had spoken.

Ughhhh! She made me so sick! And I hated Rusty's controlling ass!

One Sunday, I decided I was going to go to church anyway. God probably would not be upset about it. Since I didn't want to get Rolanda's parents mixed up in my drama, I wouldn't dare ask them to come pick me up for church. So, the next day, I woke up early, got dressed, and climbed out the window of our 2-story duplex. Outside of our window was a pole; I scurried down in my church dress scuffing up my shoes and walked several miles to church. I was so tired by the time I got there, I had missed the entire service, but I was just in time for the food they had in the basement after service.

"Hey girl! How did you get here?" Rolanda asked, knowing my mother would not have dropped me off.

I was so tired and distraught I could not even respond, so I just began to cry. Tears ran down my face like a waterfall! Rolanda ran to go get her mother, Mrs. Turner.

"Are you okay Tasha? Are you hurt? What happened? How did you get here?"

"I walked."

"You walked all the way over here to the church?"

"Yes."

"Does your mother know where you are?"

"No."

"Are you afraid?"

"Yes." The best thing I could do was give her one word answers as I was still bawling my eyes out!

"Are you afraid that someone will hurt you at your house?"

"No. I'm afraid that I will hurt him."

Rusty wasn't no fool! He knew who he could push around and who he could not. He could hurt my mother physically and had been getting away with it, but if he had put a hand on me, he knew he wouldn't live to see another day!

I started to become defiant and disobedient like all the other kids who grew up in my environment. I was growing angry and hostile living in this toxic situation. I was very disappointed in my mother. For one, why didn't she love herself enough to demand respect from these men? Secondly, why was it so easy for her to love them more than she loved her own children, the people she gave birth to? Note to self: never put a fuckin' man before my own children!

I was constantly trying to figure out a way to get from under that roof with all the fighting, bickering, and name-calling going on day in and day out. It is a wonder I kept my sanity through all of these years. God's blessings were surrounding me, even when I did not know it.

Chapter 10

UNCLE JOHN

After my sophomore school year ended, Lil' Mama was planning to visit my Auntie Nita and her husband John, who lived in Jackson, Mississippi for the summer. Lil' Mama knew how bad the situation had gotten for me at home with Mama and Rusty. Their relationship had become as tumultuous as her and James' relationship had been, except now I was much older and refused to stand for that shit! Now I had started rebelling against Rusty, standing up to him, talking back, jumping into my mother's fights, and calling the police on him. I even attempted to set up a drug bust against his raggedy ass by snooping on them when they were planning to throw one of their drug parties at the house. We were all supposed to stay that weekend at Lil' Mama's house, but at the last minute the party got changed to the next weekend. That was when I realized someone on the inside was always involved in these ordeals. Someone had leaked the fact there was going to be a drug bust! Anyway, the cops came on the previous weekend where there was no party, but they still ended up taking Rusty to jail on some minor drug paraphernalia charges, but nothing much more.

I even started running away from home and sneaking out of the house at night just to get my mother's attention. I would go to my grandmother's house and my mother would *drag* me right back home. I always thought my mother was jealous of my relationship with Lil' Mama, but it was not my fault Lil' Mama was a better mother! It wasn't my fault Lil' Mama loved me when my mother couldn't!

"I just can't stand him, Lil' Mama," sobbing on my grandmother's chest referring to Rusty. "Mama always takes his word over ours! She always believes what he says over her own kids! It's just not fair!"

"I know, baby," Lil' Mama tried to console me. "It's gon' be alright. We gon' think of something, I promise."

"I'm telling you Lil' Mama, I hate Rusty's guts! He's nothing but a big ole' mean, loud bully, and I hope he gets what's coming to him one day!" I was still crying, but fiery mad!

Then there was a knock on the door. It was my Mama.

Lil' Mama went to the door and opened it.

"Is Tasha here?" My mother bum rushed Lil' Mama as if she had a search team looking for me all night when she knew this would be the first place to start.

"Yeah, she's here, but why don't you just let her stay?" Lil' Mama tried to reason with her.

"No, I told her not to leave the house and she left anyway." My mother was trying to stand her ground. Wonder where all this machismo was when she was dealing with Rusty. Oh, I am sure he had put her up to this just to prove a point to me. He liked throwing his big ass weight around!

Lil' Mama did her best to convince Mama to let me stay, but Mama was there to prove a point. I am sure she did not want to disappoint Rusty and get beat upside her head if she did not have this teenager back home with her when she got there.

She walks into the living room where I was sitting on the couch listening to her and Lil' Mama go back and forth and says, "Come on Tasha, let's go!"

"No!" I ain't going nowhere!" I screamed at her.

"I said let's go, and I'm not gonna say it again!' My mother was not one to raise her voice, but I feared the intensity that grew stronger and stronger. She grabbed my arm with one hand, and the hood of my coat with the other hand, and began to drag me off the sofa, out of the living room, through the kitchen, and out the door! The whole time I was kicking and screaming!

"No, let me go! Leave me alone! I don't wanna go! Lil' Mama! Help me! Lil Mama! Don't let her take me! Please!" I was crying and wailing through the whole house!

"Arlene, don't hurt her!" My grandmother was trying to stop my mother from dragging me, but the woman was too strong. "Please, you don't have to do this to her!"

"This is my child Mama, not yours, remember that!" My mother continued the goal that was set for her.

There you have it. My mama *was* jealous of Lil' Mama, just as I had anticipated. She eventually dragged me down the stairs, shoved me into the car, and drove me back to that prison they called home. I could not understand why she was forcing me to live in the same prison that she volunteered to live in. Why did I need to be a part of this shitty group of people they called family, when all they did was argue, fuss, and fight. Where was all that talk when it came to standing up to Rusty for herself? Where was that strong woman who dragged me out of Lil' Mama's house? I'd like to see her use that strength to go upside Rusty's head instead of her letting him go upside hers all the time.

On the ride home, I had thoughts about how I would kill Rusty. Mama was starting to take on the personalities of her suitors. She had never put her hands on me up to this point in my entire life. And yes, I know I was being rebellious, but I had to! I could not keep sitting around twiddling my thumbs and watching this big giant of a monster jump on my Mama! I refused to keep letting him call her all kinds of 'black bitches' and 'stank whores' in front of my little brother and sister. Sooner or later, there is bound to be some retaliation! Sooner or later, somebody's gon' lose some teeth, or get a jaw broken, or an eye for an eye. I mean, sooner or later something is going to have to give! If I kept sitting quietly doing nothing, they would think what they were doing was okay, that we were not being bothered or affected by this shit. But that could not be further from the truth. Sleepless nights, cries, screams, drugs, police sirens, blood, ambulances, sleepless nights, cries, screams, drugs, police sirens, blood, ambulances. Hit play, pause, repeat. Play, pause, repeat again. My life.

I am not sure if my mother ever knew herself, or ever discovered who she really was. So, if I got rid of Rusty, she would not be acting all big and bad towards me. Rusty was quite a large motherfucka' though, so I would need to wait for him to go to sleep in order to take him down. Maybe I would suffocate him with a pillow, strangle him with an extension cord, set the house on fire with him in it when everyone else is gone. I do not know. How about a pot of hot grits for a little first degree burn in the face? Rat poisoning in the food?? I am not saying I could have really done it, but I am saying there were thoughts and many of them, on how he could die. He was a mean bastard and I just could not stand him! Period!

Now, since Lil' Mama was going to visit Auntie Nita in Jackson, MS, and a little bit of time had passed since the 'dragging incident,' Lil' Mama and Auntie Nita came up with a plan to have me go to Jackson with her, but *not* return. My grandmother would do anything to put me in a better environment and give me an opportunity for a better life. As Lil' Mama shared their plot and scheme with me, I was all for it!

"How would you like to go live with your Auntie and Uncle in Jackson, Mississippi?"

"What? But I am only 16. You think Mama will let me go?"

"Well, your aunt and I already asked your mama if you could go down south with me just for the summer, but I'm going to come back and your Auntie says you can stay down there and finish high school. Then you can go to college from there."

Lil' Mama and Auntie Nita already had this plan worked out. They both had already talked to Mama before bringing it up to me. I am not sure what they told her or how they convinced her to let me go, or maybe Rusty was just tired of me 'back talking' him, and was not going to put up a fight this time.

It was a beautifully crafted master plan! I was so excited about this plan, and the favor I had with my grandmother and Aunt. They saw something in me that needed to flourish, and they were willing to assist in the blossoming process.

My grandmother truly feared I would kill Rusty one day, and so did I, and wanted to get me out of that place. She knew I was of the age where I was just not going to sit back and let Rusty beat my Mama, without there being some type of recourse. Anywhere there was recourse, there were bound to be consequences. She was not willing to allow me to risk my future and what I would be able to accomplish in life because of some low-life, good for nothin' nigga like Rusty.

"We gotta get this baby outta that house!" I overheard Lil' Mama talking to Auntie Nita on the phone about it one day.

Lil' Mama and I took the Greyhound bus all the way to Jackson, Mississippi. I remember I had to borrow a couple of suitcases from my Auntie Terri since we never traveled anywhere. On this long bus ride, there are miles of flat land throughout Illinois. Once we got to Tennessee, we headed through some beautiful mountainous terrain. Once we finally reached Mississippi, there were fields and fields of black people picking cotton. This was my first time ever seeing a cotton field, and for sure my first time ever seeing someone picking cotton! Then I thought, "Are we sure Mississippi will be a better place? Well, I am not going to be pickin' nobody's cotton. So, stay positive!"

I remember feeling excited to be getting a new start in life. A new beginning! My grandmother told me my aunt and uncle were doing very well financially and could afford to take me in. It would be strange living in a different environment, but I was always up for the challenge. Hell, if I could live in the environment I was in, I am sure it would be better than what I was used to.

I did not know Auntie Nita as well as I knew the other aunts because she graduated from high school early at age 16, and had moved on with her life. I heard she had done some traveling to California, back to Illinois, and now to Mississippi. All I know is when I saw her again, she was driving a brand new car, and always wore the latest fashions in clothes, and all name brands. Even when she moved back to Kankakee, she had a beautiful apartment. She was the one who people would call "bougie." Auntie Nita was extremely 'proper' and stood out from the rest of the family. And "yes," I wanted to be just like that! There was something about her that was poised, professional, classy, attractive, and highly intelligent, that I was drawn to. Even when I was growing up, the other aunts would tease me and say, "You talk just like a little white girl like Nita!" White girl or not, I accepted it as a compliment to be like my Auntie Nita. When Lil' Mama told me Auntie Nita agreed I could move in with her, I was overjoyed! I felt special, significant, that they would agree to accept me into their home. That they would take this chance on me.

Auntie Nita was married to Uncle John. They had been together for a very long time. As I recall they were together even when I was in elementary school. Once they moved to Mississippi and had lived together for seven years, they were automatically considered married by Common Law. We've always called him Uncle John, even as a kid. I did not know much about John except he was very pleasant and friendly. I am not sure what he did for a living, but I know at least as a side hustle he did construction type work as a handyman.

After my second stepfather, Gene died, there were many things in the house Uncle John would come over and fix. Since Gene had renovated the house from a previous fire, many of the renovations were nigga-rigged. When he died, no regular repair man would touch the nigga-rigged repairs without a proper permit. Uncle John did not mind taking care of those repairs anyway, and he was at the house all the time. Seemingly, for days and weeks in a row. But we were grateful since we would not have had lights or water without him!

I always found myself getting up in the middle of the night to check on my mother after Gene's death. Sometimes I would hear her in the room crying, but even if I did not hear anything, I was prone to check on her just out of habit. One morning, after I had gotten up, I walked past the living room and saw Uncle John's green camouflage coat hanging on the back of the chair. It was the dead of winter in Illinois, well below freezing outside. "How did Uncle John forget his coat as cold as it is?" I asked myself. I tiptoed down the hall to my mother's room and the door was ajar. I slowly pushed the door open a little more and peeped my head in and saw Uncle John and my Mama butt naked in the bed together! He laid there with one leg and butt cheek exposed to the brisk cold from under the sheet, and she laid there with half her breast uncovered!

"Oh my God!" I gasped for air as I put both hands over my mouth, pulled the door back up and quickly tip-toed back to my room.

What the fuck did I just see?? I am so ashamed! No, *she* should be ashamed of herself, sleeping with her sister's husband. No, *he* should be ashamed sleeping with his wife's sister! Wait, Auntie Nita and Uncle John are not married, so what? But they have been together forever, and everybody knows she is pregnant with his baby! Well, they should both be ashamed! I never said a word to anyone about this; I was all of 12 years old at the time. Why was I trying to explain to myself how grown folks should handle their business? It was clear to me, most of the time they did not know what they were doing anyway.

That was about four years ago. Now my Auntie Nita and Uncle John were giving me a chance for a new life. A better life. Apparently they had resolved their issues and were doing well in their marriage in Jackson MS, according to Lil' Mama. My aunt also had several miscarriages, unfortunately. Stress, I guess. But then again, it was none of my business. I had better keep my mouth closed. I was accustomed to maintaining my silence, and this would be no different. Hell, I had my own problems, and I was just trying to survive those!

Once I arrived at my Aunt and Uncle's house, I was sure this would be my paradise. I finally had my own room for the very first time in my life! I can remember sleeping 4 and 5 to a full-size bed at my grandparents' house in the past. No more sharing a room with Messy Marvin's twin sister Punkin at my Mama's house! This room was nicely furnished with a chestnut brown queen size sleigh bed, a color TV, a VCR (it was 1987), a stereo system, and a telephone! I had my own TV in my own room! They lived in a beautiful, two-story brick townhome with a two-car garage and they both drove nice vehicles. One was a sleek red Camaro convertible! They had no children, so everything in their home was impeccable. Glass coffee tables, glass dining room table, artifacts throughout the home, custom window treatments, mirrors galore, and paintings on the walls. It was beautifully decorated! I was so excited I could barely maintain my composure. They both told me they will help me to find an after-school job, buy me a car before school starts, and buy all my school clothes to make sure I will be prepared for the new school year. My aunt worked as a radio station Accounting Associate, and my uncle was a manager at the major mall in Jackson. They had comfortable salaried careers, and were willing to share some of the fruits of their labor with *me*. They were both very welcoming and hospitable, and seemed more than happy to have me there. I was feeling blessed beyond measure!

Shortly into my stay, my Aunt kept asking Uncle John if we could take a trip to New Orleans. When they go to New Orleans, they like to stay in the French Quarter. My Uncle kept replying that money was tight and he was not willing to pay for the trip. Money did not seem tight to me as it appeared they had everything they could ever want. Then again, who am I to be counting their money?

Before I left Kankakee, I had some photos taken by a photographer at Bird Park. The photographer was the cousin of my boyfriend, Fred Clark. Fred was now stationed at Tinker Air Force Base in Oklahoma City, OK. He scheduled his cousin to take the photos prior to me leaving. After the pictures were developed, the photographer sent all the pictures to Fred. Fred kept the ones he wanted, and he sent the other ones to me with some *sweet nothings* written on the back of each picture. Fred was a regular Casanova! He was so charming and loving, and he was the best thing that happened to me at this point in my life.

The day I received the photos in the mail, I sat them on top of the dresser as I went downstairs to the kitchen to have lunch with Lil' Mama. When I came back upstairs to the room, the pictures were on the pillow and some were on the bed!

"Wait, I didn't put these pictures on this bed like this, did I?" I thought to myself. "Why would I?" Lil' Mama never even comes upstairs, as her bedroom was downstairs, and Auntie Nita and Uncle John were at work. Weird!

There was another time I was coming out of the bathroom and I opened the door and Uncle John was standing right there at the door as if he was listening or something.

"Oh!" I screamed, "Oh my God, you scared me!"

"I'm sorry, I didn't mean to startle you. I just wanted to make sure you had some extra towels in your bathroom," he said as he handed me the towels.

"Ok, thank you," I tried to receive the towels from him without touching his hands, but he made it a point to touch my hand for longer than the one second rule while catching my eye.

"Just let me know if you need anything, Tasha." Suddenly, he paused the transfer of the towels between our hands.

"Ok, got it." I tried my best not to look into his eyes.

"Anything at all."

His stares started feeling creepy, so I put a little more force into pulling the towels towards me. "Yes, I-I got it, thank you, Uncle John." I was finally free to walk away, towels in hand, and to let go of the breath I had been holding since I caught him outside the bathroom door.

Uncle John seemed to be very natural around my Aunt and Lil' Mama. We went to the museum one time, went to the aquarium, and the entire family had such an amazing time. There were no strange stares, uncomfortable feelings, or tense gestures, just pure family fun. Had I miscalculated Uncle John? Had I judged him based on my own misperceptions? After all, I was only 16 years old, and did not have enough experience to decipher if a man twice my age would be trying to manipulate me. I would try to let my guard down, and more importantly, not allow my own preconceived notions interfere with my living arrangements here in Jackson. I had a good thing going here, and I did not want to mess it up. I just was not sure what would happen if I had to go back to Kankakee with Mama and Rusty. I think I was more afraid of that than anything!

Uncle John had a fetish with the video camera. When we went to the museum, when we went to the aquarium, the grocery store, everywhere we went that video camera was all up in our faces. With his very charismatic personality, he would ask my grandmother, "So Mama, how would you say your stay has been so far?"

"Oh, I'm enjoying myself! The museum is beautiful, but my feets is tired, and I'm hungry!" Lil' Mama cared very little about showing off in front of people.

He'd ask me, "So Tasha, I hear you moved to Jackson so that you can get a fresh start on life. Tell us a little bit about that."

"That's right. Thanks to my Auntie Nita and Uncle John, who I am so grateful for, I have moved to Jackson, MS to finish high school here. I will be visiting colleges in the upcoming year, and hopefully will get a scholarship to the college of my choice."

"So what will you be majoring in Tasha?"

"I'm not sure yet, but it will be a field where I can help people and also make a lot of money so that I can buy my grandmama a new house!"

I was just like those basketball and football players who came out of the projects and made it to the NBA or NFL. All they wanted to do was buy their mamas and grandmamas a new house.

"And Nita, how do you feel about having your family here visiting for the first time?"

"Well, I'm always grateful to be with my mother, but I'm equally as happy my niece is here. I'm happy to be a part of her journey as she goes off to college and then goes on with her life from there. I'm just glad we could be here to assist in the process."

Lil' Mama chimes in, "We always knew this baby was gon' be somebody. We always knew that!"

Lil' Mama was always my number one supporter! Unlike a lot of other people's stories, there was *never* a time when I did not believe in myself, because of my grandmother. I trusted and believed everything this woman said, because every word from her mouth, and every action she lived in front of me was *TRUE*. She did not have to say much, and it wasn't every day, but when she said what she said, it stuck because it added value. It meant something. It was worth something to me. It was priceless. She may not have been perfect, but Lil' Mama was the TRUTH! And she had the love of God inside of her and those are the facts!

Things had been going fairly smoothly these last few weeks. After we left the aquarium, we also went to the grocery store as Lil Mama would be cooking dinner for the family. I was assisting her in the kitchen by unloading the groceries. I finally made it upstairs to my room, and lo and behold, those damn pictures! This time they were all stuck in between the mirror posts on the dresser. I know for a fact I left them sitting in a pile on the dresser before I left the room. Uncle John! Ugh! I was extremely confused by these actions. The fact he would be roaming through my room, digging through my personals when I am not there, was growing increasingly uncomfortable.

Then Auntie Nita came and knocked on the door post. "Hey, Tasha, can we talk for a moment?"

"Hey, Auntie, sure." I hurriedly changed my facial expressions so she would not question the disturbed look I had on my face about the pictures.

"Well," she hesitated, "I'm not going to be able to buy your school clothes like I thought. It's just not in the budget."

"Oh ok." I was quite surprised because Auntie Nita seemed to be a woman of her word based on what Lil' Mama says about her, but I quickly transformed into solutions mode.

"That's fine, I can wear the clothes I have from last year."

"Well I know you only brought summer clothes down here."

"Yeah, but I can have my boyfriend send me some money for a winter coat and a few pairs of jeans. And then I'll get a job and I'll be fine." There was no way I was being sent back to Kankakee over a lack of school clothes!

"Ok well, you know you can always go back home when Mama goes back since you probably won't have enough clothes to go to school here."

"Nope, no problem." I literally cut her off. "I'll be fine, I promise! I never have a lot of clothes at home anyway." The thought of me going back home was *not* an option!

What was it with her? Suddenly she seemed to have a problem with me. I had not done anything wrong! She started treating me like I owed her money or something. She's the one who invited me down here to live with her. She and John came to me and told me they were going to do all these wonderful things for me, I never asked them for anything! That was on them. All of a sudden, she is flipping the script? Now her words do not mean anything? Now she is going back on promises made? I guess I shouldn't be surprised. This is what I was accustomed to, people never kept their word. People never meant what they said. Your word is never your bond like back in my granddaddy's day, when all was required was a handshake to bind a contract. Only my grandparents' word was good, that's about it. I would not even mention this to Lil' Mama, at least she got me down here, and I did not have to be in Kankakee. I did not want to put this on her. At least I was still better off, even though it wasn't as good as I thought it would be.

After Auntie Nita left, John must have been lurking in the hallway as their room was right next door to mine.

"So are you getting settled in ok?" he would stick his head in while leaning his shoulder against the door post. John was an attractive looking man, medium build, dark complexion, and stood about 5'9 and he had a smile that could charm any woman. But there was a certain twist in that smile that turned upward in the right corner of his mouth. John had a certain aura that exuded innocence; you wanted to believe the best about him, but his Gemini ways would eventually shine through.

"Oh yes, I just want to thank you again for letting me come and finish high school here," I tried to force a smile and not give confrontational vibes. "Uhmmm, did you see my pictures?" I knew it had to be him rearranging my pictures in my room, who else would it have been?

"Oh, I was just coming in here to drop off some clean linens and towels for you. I saw the pictures on the dresser and I pulled out some of the ones that I liked the best. I didn't mean any harm. Did I offend you?"

"Uhh, no, I was just asking." I replied abruptly, I didn't want to start any trouble. I tried to consider my own personal situation. I needed my Auntie Nita and Uncle John so I could stay here in Jackson and not have to move back to Kankakee. I am not sure what games Uncle John was trying to play here, but I was trying my best to ignore them.

"How is everything going with your Aunt?" he quickly changed the subject.

"Auntie Nita came and told me that she was not going to be able to buy my school clothes like she thought."

"Awww, don't worry about that. I'm a manager at the mall and I will be more than happy to buy your school clothes," he stated confidently. "Tell you what, I'll pick out some dresses and outfits that I think you would like and I'll bring them home for you to try them on. Whatever you don't like, I'll take it back to the store. Fair enough?"

"Ok," I replied reluctantly.

Why would he pick out my clothes for me versus letting me go to the mall and pick out my own clothes? Why was he willing to purchase my school clothes and my own aunt was no longer willing to do so? Ok, Tasha, maybe you are overthinking things. Why do I care as long as *someone* is willing to buy my school clothes? It was difficult to interpret why people acted the way they did. Adults! No harm, no foul. I would go along with it for as long as I could.

Later, Uncle John came home from work with about 10 new outfits which consisted of long flowy dresses, a couple of pairs of jeans and shirts, and a new winter coat. As I was writing a letter to my boyfriend, Fred, I told him about the dresses and how I couldn't see myself wearing them because they were more for an older woman, like my aunt. What 16 year old girl is wearing a long flowy dress, back in the 80s? As a teenager, I did not even wear dresses that much, and for sure, not to school. The quality of these dresses, however, were top of the line. Who would pay over $80 for a dress I probably would never wear? I do wish he had allowed me to pick out my own clothes, but I figure it was a nice gesture. I told my boyfriend in the letter I did not want to hurt Uncle John's feelings, and have him take all these clothes back. But those dresses were straight ugly! The only items I would have chosen to keep were the winter coat and the jeans.

It seemed like he was doing a nice thing, but it was the way he was doing it I did not quite understand. It felt like he was controlling me or something. Like I did not have a choice. I would accept the clothes as a gift, and whatever it is they were willing to give me, with a level of gratitude and thankfulness. I would keep my real comments about the clothes to myself and only share them with my boyfriend. You know what they say, "beggars can't be choosy."

When I initially arrived in Jackson, my Aunt had promised she would also get my hair done for me, just like she said she would make sure I had new clothes for school. Then something began to change. Auntie Nita would come to my room and apologize for not being able to keep her word as she was not going to be able to get my hair done after all. Getting my hair done was not a big deal for me. I had to learn to do my own hair over the years and could give myself a relaxer. Later, Uncle John came to my room to ask me if my aunt had scheduled my hair appointment for me. I would then tell him that she broke her promise and said she wasn't going to be able to do it because money was tight.

Uncle John would then say, "Oh don't worry about it, I'll take you to get your hair done. You know sometimes your Aunt is just moody. You'll just have to cut her some slack. It'll be fine, though, I'll take care of it."

"Uh, ok." I thought it was a little strange, as I felt like I was in the *Twilight Zone* or something. I mean, do they even talk to each other? Does the right hand know what the left hand is doing? What is really going on? I had no earthly idea!

Uncle John was being super nice, but I always thought he was a nice guy. He came home from work early one day to take me to the hair salon to get my hair relaxed and styled. I had that Asymmetric Salt-N-Pepa hair-do. He went and ran some errands during my appointment and then picked me up afterwards.

"Oooo-weeee! Look at you! You lookin' good, girl!" he complimented me.

"Thanks," I replied blushing. I honestly did not know how to take his level of enthusiasm. Of course, it did cross my mind as to why he was taking me to the hair salon instead of my aunt. Why was he buying my clothes, instead of my aunt? Why was my aunt making such a big deal about the money and Uncle John didn't seem to have a problem with it at all?

On the drive home he asked me, " How would you like to go to New Orleans?"

"Oh wow! That sounds like a lot of fun! Auntie Nita had been asking you if we could go to New Orleans, but she said you kept saying no because money was tight."

95

"Well," he said, "If *you* want to go then that settles it, we'll go. As a matter of fact, we'll go this weekend!"

As soon as we got home from the hair salon I jumped out of the car and ran into the house to let my aunt know the good news.

"Auntie Nita, Auntie Nita! Uncle John said we can go to New Orleans this weekend!

"Oh, he did, did he?" She turned around with a perplexed look on her face.

"He also got my hair done; how do you like it?" Turning around and modeling the new hair style for her, I was just excited he had finally changed his mind about New Orleans because I knew she wanted my grandmother and me to experience that city.

"Your hair looks beautiful, Tasha. Go upstairs and pack your bag for the weekend. It looks like we're going to New Orleans! We'll leave in the morning." My Aunt seemed to be somewhat excited about the trip, but not really.

After dinner that night, John pulled out the video camera so we could watch the footage from the previous week's outings. I did notice that at times when he was asking Lil' Mama questions, he had the camera on me. Other times when he was interviewing Auntie Nita, he'd have the camera on me. When he interviewed me, he lingered, getting a lot of closeup shots of my face and breasts. There was something very peculiar about Uncle John, but I mostly ignored it as I tried to figure out how I would wait out this two year sentence as it was still better than the one I had waiting for me back in Kankakee.

Sure enough, early the next morning, we packed up the car and headed to New Orleans for the weekend. Consequently, we stayed in the French Quarter at the Hilton Hotel in adjoining suites. I do not recall it being some special holiday, but apparently in New Orleans they party on any given day for any given reason, no questions asked! I remember a slew of vendors selling everything from food to sweets, to drinks to souvenirs, to clothing. Every kind of person from every walk of life was there in full effect. All kinds of music, all kinds of dancing, masks and costumes, beads, Black people, White people, Asians, Hispanics, Africans, French, everyone! Everyone enjoyed the massive festivities of this bizarre city. Women on balconies with their titties out! I even thought I saw a man swinging his ding-a-ling! All types of musicians in the streets playing their hearts out for coins; and not with real instruments, but drumming on the bottom of car wash buckets and tin cans! Most people were eating, drinking, and smoking, while walking down Bourbon Street, enjoying the festivities! It was without a doubt, an experience I would never forget!

I believe there was a change in the level of humidity from Mississippi to New Orleans as I had a serious headache the next day. My Auntie Nita wanted to go visit one of her girlfriends, and of course John did not want to go because he did not like any of her friends, or basically he just did not want her to have any friends. When my grandmother told me we were getting ready to leave, I told her I had a headache and wanted to stay at the hotel. She tapped me on the leg and said, "I have some Advil in my purse baby, you're coming with us."

No questions asked, I took the Advil and got in the car with Auntie Nita and Lil' Mama. Uncle John stayed back at the hotel. I noticed the tension of these two ladies in the car as they kept looking at each other as if something were the matter. As we were driving along the highway, all of a sudden, I noticed my aunt pulled the car over to the side of the road. I thought we were going to one of her friend's houses. Instead, we were close to the Superdome as I recall looking out of the window and staring at it. We all sat in silence for a while.

"Why are we pulling over? Are we meeting your friend here?"

My aunt finally took a deep breath and spoke, "Tasha, I'm so sorry to have to tell you this, but when Mama goes home, you're going to have to go back to Kankakee with her." My Aunt's voice sounded as if she was a doctor delivering bad news to her patient.

"What!" I was so shocked that she was telling me this! "What! What did I do? What did I do wrong?" I began to cry.

"You didn't do anything wrong," she said. "I'm afraid if I don't get you out of this house now, then John is going to do something bad to you. Somewhere in his mind, he's looking to go to all the baseball games with you and I will be left out in the cold."

"What could she possibly be talking about?" I thought to myself.

My Aunt begins to explain in her softest, most proper voice. "You may not understand what's going on, so let me tell you. John is trying to make me look like the bad guy and he wants to be the Superhero. Although he and I discussed what we were willing to do for you as far as buying your school clothes, getting your hair done, helping you get a job, and buying you a car, he has forced me to renege on all those promises to you. And then he comes right behind me and does those things for you so that I can look like the Wicked Bitch of the West and he can look like your favorite 'Uncle John.' I am so sorry that I invited you down here to be mixed up in this drama. But now I need to protect you, and I need to get you out of here, safely!"

"No, I'm not moving back to Kankakee!" This was the only thing I could think about.

"John is infatuated with you! He acts like he is in love with you, but in a stalkerish way! I mean, you're still a child but he looks at you as if you're a woman!"

"What the fuck!" Only I did not say the word "fuck" since my grandmother was in the car, but I for damn sure thought it. I mean, I knew Uncle John was a little *cra-cra*, but d-a-y-u-m! I was constantly taking deep breaths to deal with the woes of my life.

"He's been spying on you and invading your privacy. He opened your letters to your boyfriend before taking them to the post office."

"He what?" I was so surprised he would do that! Or was I? I was just so confused right now!

"He told me how you thought the dresses that he bought you were ugly and how you didn't want to hurt his feelings so you kept them. He told me that you wrote how your auntie is acting like a bitch and your Uncle John was treating you like a princess."

"Oh my God!" I had written many letters to my boyfriend, Fred, about everything that was going on here. I had said some hurtful things about the way my aunt was acting towards me, and how nice John was being towards me. How low of John to snoop through my letters, while volunteering to drop them off at the post office on his way to work, and then go back and tell my aunt all those horrible things to make her feel bad when he was the one setting us up the entire time! How conniving! That low down, dirty, manipulative, controlling, maniacal, Bastard!

"Tasha, this is just his scheme to try to make you fall in love with him and make you hate me! I would never let anything bad happen to you so when we get back to Jackson, I need you to pack your bags, and I'm going to get you and Mama a bus ticket to go back home."

I couldn't believe this was happening! Every time there was a slight glimpse of surviving, life had a way of sucking me right back into a hole. A sinkhole!

I just cried, and cried, and cried some more. I began to recall all the strange things John was doing and I was petrified! I was hysterical! I felt like everything I kept trying to do to make my life better, just kept ricocheting and backfiring, and slapping me right back in my face. Although I did not want to go back to Kankakee, the devil I knew was so much better than the devil I did not know. I had to settle with this reality, and I knew I would have to deal with Rusty when I got there.

The 2½ hour drive from New Orleans back to Jackson would prove to be a daunting one. Not much was said, and I pretended to be asleep most of the time. Lil' Mama and I rode in the back seat and we would sometimes give each other stares when John would try to ask us more 'interview' questions about our stay. You could cut the tension with a knife!

Once we returned to Jackson, I quickly rushed upstairs to begin packing and to plan my escape.

While I was folding my clothes and packing them in the suitcase, John peeps his head in the door.

"Knock, Knock."

"Hey," I said nervously.

He pretended not to notice I was packing. "I was just stopping by to check to see if you were ready to start school in the fall and just wanted to make sure you had everything that you needed."

"I'm actually a little homesick and decided to go back to Kankakee when my grand-mother leaves." I was hoping Auntie Nita was able to get those bus tickets so that we could get the hell up outta here!

"What!" He took his forearm that was already leaning against the doorpost and balled up his fist and hit the doorpost with all his might! I literally felt the house shake! I could tell he was one of those people who could go from 0 to 100 in one second flat. He was like a ticking time bomb, waiting to explode! "This is very disappointing! After all your aunt and I have done for you, you're just going to leave! How ungrateful! We went out of our way for you, getting your hair done, buying you all those school clothes, spent thousands of dollars! Your aunt was working on getting you an after-school job. I was even out looking for you a new car! And now you're telling me you're leaving to go back to a place that you hate? You're choosing them over me!" John was officially irate and had lost his *motherfuckin'* mind!

I stood there, frozen, possum style, poker faced. I had been practicing that face all my life! "Don't move, don't make any facial expressions, and don't speak." I'd remind myself. Because I used to have to fight a lot growing up, I learned to allow people who had episodes of bad energy to use it all up. I would have to save my energy for the real fight. Also growing up with James, Gene, Damon, Rusty, and now John, unfortunately I have had to cross different kinds of crazies a lot by the time I was 16. I almost felt numb to the situation. I never really knew how I was going to get out of a situation, but I was always confident I was going to get out.

I remember that same night we were eating fried catfish for dinner on that nice glass dining room table. John brought up to Auntie Nita that I said I was leaving to go back to Kankakee with Lil' Mama, and if she was aware of it?

"Yes, she told me," my aunt replied hesitantly.

He was not happy at all to hear this. He literally slammed his beer can down on the glass table and everyone at the table was shaken. Every time he picked up his beer to take a drink, he'd slam it down on the table. He drank beer, after beer, after beer. I believe he drank an entire six pack in one sitting!

We just sat there, as still as possible, and all witnessed him losing his temper, throwing an 'adult tantrum', if you will. None of us said a word as to not add fuel to the fire. I had no idea how crazy John was. I also had no idea if Auntie Nita knew she was married to a crazy man! I didn't know what he was capable of. What I did know was I am not about to stick around and deal with 'crazy.'

I slowly got up from the table, so as to not make any sudden moves, but I knew I needed to remove myself from this hostile situation. I went upstairs to finish packing my clothes, so I could make sure we were ready when it was time to go.

Hours later, I heard my aunt crying in the next room, and I went to her room to see what was the matter. She told me John told her she could buy my grandmother's bus ticket, but she could not buy mine. He actually told her that I wasn't going anywhere! He went roaming through her purse and saw the receipt for both tickets, got upset, and slapped her in the face.

I was horrified at this point and was trying to think of every scenario I could to get myself out of this house. The master and guest bedrooms were on the second floor, and my bedroom window faced the backyard. I was thinking I could throw my suitcases out first, then jump out the window and hopefully the suitcases would break my fall. If I had to go that route, I was definitely willing to do so. I went ahead and finished packing the rest of my clothes and hesitated to go down the stairs. While I was at the top of the stairs, I could hear Auntie Nita and John arguing about the fact that I ain't going nowhere. My grandmother was trying to mediate the argument. When John saw me at the top of the stairs with my bags he hollered,

"You may as well put those bags down, and put those new clothes that I bought you back, because you ain't going nowhere!"

"I don't care nothing about these clothes, but I guarantee you I will be leaving this house with my grandmother!" I hollered back. I've never been one to not have something to say back!

I had no earthly idea how I was going to make it out of this house, but I knew there was one option with three steps that I had been thinking about in order to escape this tragedy. Jump, drop and roll! I was terrified out of my mind, but was willing to do whatever it took to get out of there!

Moments later the police showed up. Thank God my aunt had enough forethought to call them ahead of time, to let them know I was in danger, and that we would need an escort to the bus station. John's crazy ass really thought he was going to hold me captive in this house so he could do ungodly things to me, and that was going to be alright with me, with my aunt, my grandmother, and even the law? I am not one to try to understand the mind of a crazy, deranged, person like this. The sickly, unwholesome, contaminated, diseased minds of some people in this world.

Clearly, a great number of people have gone undiagnosed for mental illness. I cannot explain how a grown man thought he could get away with having his way with a minor, and there not be any consequences. Ughhh! R. Kelly! I rest my case! Well, whatever thoughts he had conjured up in his mind were to be buried on this day, because they were never going to come true. The police officer stayed at the house with John while my aunt drove us to the Greyhound bus station. John was still ranting and raving about how I was supposed to live at the house with him, and how Auntie Nita fucked up everything! This crazy bastard should have been strapped up like a mummy and taken to the mental institution because that was clearly what we were dealing with here!

Lil' Mama just held me all the way to the bus station as I trembled and cried. We arrived just in time to get on the bus since John was trying to hold me hostage. We found a couple of vacant seats toward the center and took those. I sat by the window as Auntie Nita waved goodbye to us. She looked so sad, so confused, so disappointed, but also as if she knew what she finally needed to do.

"What happens if he tries to follow us?" I asked Lil' Mama while still staring out the window at my aunt.

"He's not going to try to follow us. The police will hold him until we get far enough away. Nita will press charges against him if he tries anything else." Lil' Mama replied.

"Is Auntie Nita going to be safe going back there?"

"She's only going back there to get some clothes, and then she will go to a friend's house. After that she plans to move. The police will stay there until she gets her things packed. She will let me know when she's out of the house."

"Why would Uncle John act so crazy, Lil' Mama?"

"I don't know, baby. Some people are just crazy. I can't explain why."

It was the longest bus ride home and I am sure I slept most of the way. Exhausted. I had left one hell hole for another hell hole that was better looking on the outside, yet just as filthy and contaminated on the inside. Now I was going back to the first hell hole. They say the more things change, the more they stay the same.

To my disappointment I arrived back in Kankakee with my mother and Rusty. It was like I never left... The saga continued.

Chapter 11

SHE'S OUTTA HERE!

I never talked to my mother about what happened at Nita and John's house. I never talked to her period, and she never talked to me either. If I did ask her a question, she would never answer it. She would normally say something like, "Stop asking me questions." She did not know I was planning to stay in Jackson beyond the summer anyway. No point in bringing more drama to her world, and it is not like she would be able to do anything about it.

I was gone for all of two months and of course, nothing had changed. Rusty was up to his same old mean, maniacal, controlling ways, and Mama was still putting up with it. What was it with her? She was so afraid to speak up for herself, as if she did not have a voice. She would let Rusty talk to her in a very demeaning fashion, call her ugly names, and physically and emotionally abuse her. I was so sick of him, and could not stand to be in his presence. After my experience in Jackson, MS, I was definitely not up for his bullshit this time around.

Thankfully, Fred was home on military leave from Oklahoma City. I missed him so much. He was the only constant in my life! After knowing about all the turmoil that was going on with Mama and Rusty, and then Uncle John, Fred was definitely a sight for sore eyes. My safe place. My knight in shining armor. Not the kind I used to dream about, where he was untouchable or so far away that he could not be reached, as in my father. No, Fred was right here with me every step of the way, and he was always willing and ready to prove that.

"Hey, let's go over here to this store. As you know, this is one of my favorite stores." We had been walking along the strip mall and he wanted to stop by Kays Jewelers where he'd get his silver chains and bracelets cleaned. Fred was always sharp and clean as a whip, but not gaudy! There is a difference.

"Ok, no problem." It is not like I had anything else to do, or any place else I'd rather be but with him.

As we roamed the jewelry store for earrings and necklaces, he finally asked me what I thought about this one particular ring.

"What do you mean, what do I think about it?"

"I mean, do you like it?"

"Of course I like it! It's beautiful!" It was a one carat marquis cut shining diamond bling bling! What was there not to like! The sales lady sized my finger and the ring fit perfectly. She handed the ring to Fred, who in turn got down on one knee right in the jewelry store in front of all its customers.

"Will you, Natasha Anne Bostic, marry me?"

"Oh my God! Wait! What? How am I going to do that? I'm only 17 years old! I can't marry you. That is not even legal in the state of Illinois is it?" I was guilty of spoiling a moment based on logic. If it does not make sense, how can I be happy about it?

"I want you to wear my ring, until we can legally get married. You'll be graduating next year which is right around the corner. I want to know that you'll be mine, and I want you to know that I will always be yours. You are my Best Friend Forever. The love of my life. My Baby Girl!"

I told y'all he was smooth like Keith Sweat! "Well in that case, Yes!" I mean, who could say 'No' to all of that?

My engagement to Fred Clark was kept secret and I had not even shared it with my best friend, Rolanda, in High School. I was not going to tell my mother. Plus, I knew I loved Fred, but I also knew I had not lived long enough to know what I did not know. Fred was from my small town, he was a good guy, but we tend to have a small mindset. I dreamed in color and I have always wanted something larger than the typical mind could fathom. My life was at stake here; my future was on the line. I did not know if I was willing to sacrifice the world of the unknown, for this safe place with Fred. How could I be sure?

I appreciated him though. Wholeheartedly. I knew he wanted to marry me to remove me from the hell hole I was in. He wanted to save me from my environment, and offer me the love and support I both needed and deserved. I just did not want to get trapped into depending on him, on any man for that matter. I needed to know I could make it in this world on my own. I needed to prove that to myself, not to him. If I should welcome Fred, or any other man into my life in the future, it would be because I wanted to, not because I needed to. That way, if he chose to act like an ass, I would be more than happy to kick his script-flipping ass to the curb! As a woman, I must be able to take care of myself, so if I find out my man has a whole other family down the street unbeknownst to me, Imma be alright!

However, the best-case scenario is having a man who can take care of you, who loves and respects you as his Queen. Oh honey, it does not get any better than that!

Consequently, at 17 years old, I only knew what I knew, which wasn't much. I mean granted, I had been through a lot for my age, but I also knew I had a long way to go!

Not long after the fall semester started, beginning my senior year in High School, I was walking home from the bus stop thinking to myself; if they are arguing and fighting today, I am going to do something about it. You know how you just feel like today is that day? I cannot continue to go in my room, slam the door, and drown them out. That is pretty much how I survived my childhood when I lived with my mother; I drowned it out. But today, a new movement will be awakened. There is a new Tasha in town and she is not having it! If they were fighting today, I would have to do something about it. I was hoping and praying to God this was not the case, but if it was, I was mentally and physically preparing myself for the worst-case scenario.

As I walked slowly up to the duplex where we lived on River Street, I already noticed the door slightly ajar. I also could hear noises coming from upstairs. Ok, here we go! It is time for me to put on my Big Girl Panties, take off my earrings, and slap some Vaseline on my face and I was already wearing my tennis shoes! These were the necessities when planning an altercation with someone.

Rusty was a fairly large man. He stood 6ft 4in tall and weighed over 275 lbs., and not one of those pounds were muscle. Rusty was a light complected man as his mother was white and his father was black. He wore a short, curly afro and a thick Hitler mustache. He was tall and slouched, clothes never fitting quite right. He carried a full, deep, and scary voice which could be very intimidating when he spoke. Rusty did not work, but was a small-time drug dealer. Small time because he was not making any real money, smoking the products and all.

My mother always treated Rusty like a king. She would buy him name brand foods, and make us kids eat generics from Aldi's. For instance, he had Kellogg's Frosted Flakes and we had to eat Corn Flakes. He had Oreo Cookies, and we had to eat the generic chocolate sandwich cookies. We drank powdered milk in our cereal; you know, the kind you had to mix with water? While he had whole milk. He had Coca Cola, and we had the generic Cola. His 'special' name brand foods would have its own section in the kitchen cabinets and the refrigerator, and we were not allowed to touch his food. "And you better not ask for any of it either!" We would be scolded by both of them for asking. When my mother cooked, she made sure she made Rusty a plate of food first, and would hold out the leftovers just in case he wanted some later. Whatever food was left, is what we had to share among ourselves. If we were still hungry after that, oh well, that's Rusty's food and you had better not touch it! Adding insult to injury, my mother was getting food stamps to feed her children, not to feed her man!

Rusty brought nothing to the table in the way of paying rent or bills. My mother never worked when she was with him, but lived off Gene's social security and annuity benefits. All they did all day, every day, was stay in the small den downstairs watching TV and doing drugs. Our house always reeked of drugs. As soon as you stepped in the front door, you could smell it! My mother was never emotionally or mentally present for her children. Trust me, I tried everything in my power to connect with her to no avail.

That year I decided to compete in this pageant and I asked Rusty to be my escort. Not because I *wanted* him to be my escort, but because I wanted my mother to partake in something I was participating in. Sure enough, Rusty was ecstatic I would ask him to escort me in the pageant. Idiot! I just wanted to make sure they figured out a way to buy my evening gown, which they got from Donna's Dresses. They also bought Rusty a tuxedo. He was casket sharp, too! This was the first time they ever did anything for me, and I literally had to con them to get it done! Although I did not win the pageant, I did win Miss Photogenic and placed third in the evening gown competition. I won a 4-year scholarship to some college for Hotel Management in Rhode Island. Rhode Island? Do black people really live there? For my talent, I got a standing ovation for a monologue I performed called 'Ms. Cocaine.' Wonder if Mama and Rusty ever figured out that monologue was my gift to them?

I never understood why a woman would have children and not be there for them; not support them, not protect them, not fight for them, not fight for a better environment, a chance for a better life. I guess if you are not able/willing to fight for yourself, then how can you fight for your children? I often wondered why she even had all of us in the first place, if she was not willing to be present?

I entered the front door of our duplex and sure enough, the noise I heard coming from upstairs was Rusty cursing at my mother. Apparently, she had purchased some bad drugs from somebody and he was having a hissy fit about it.

"How stupid can you be! Who told you to go buy drugs from some new dude that I do not even know! You so stupid! That's why don't nobody want your dumb, black, ugly, ass anyway!" He was infuriated, and was letting it all out.

"I said I was sorry, Rusty. I didn't know it was bad," my mother said apologetically.

"You're supposed to know these things, Arlene! You're about as dumb as a doorknob! I can't teach you nothing! Cause you too stupid to learn!" he was revving up.

I was walking quickly up the stairs by this time, and I was listening to what the fuss was all about.

"You're the one who's stupid!" I finally chimed in.

"Who you talking to?" He was surprised as we were never allowed to partake in their arguments. But this time, I had decided not to play by their rules. Enough was enough!

"I'm talking to you!" I did not hesitate to commit. Once I am in, I'm committed!

"Little girl, you need to sit your ass down somewhere!" Rusty was huffing and puffing by now.

"You might want to sit your big ass down somewhere, before you have a heart attack, because I ain't going nowhere!" I was known to have a quick come back.

"Arlene, you better get your child! She thinks she's grown. I'm gonna knock her ass out," he was trying hard to come back strong.

"Oh, you gon' knock me out! You think you gon' put hands on me and get away with it! I'm not my Mama, I will fight your ass back." I was all up in his face by this time, daring him to put hands on me because I was aching to get his ass put in jail. "I wish you would touch me!" I was in full blown fight effect!

"Oh what you gon' do?" Rusty was now acting like he was about to fight a man in the streets.

"Try me! You will see what I'm gon' do!" I was not about to back down and he was not either.

My grandfather always taught us to never back down, never show fear. The minute you show fear, the enemy knows he has the advantage. I was very fearful of Rusty because I had witnessed how badly he treated my mother, and I feared for her life. Yet at this moment, Rusty nor my mother could tell I was afraid of him. Hell, I did not even recognize it myself! Once I set out to stand up to you, no fear can be present. And no fear was present.

Rusty and I were arguing like two high schoolers on the playground, except I was the only one in high school. My mother seemed to be in a state of shock as she had never heard me curse before, since we were not allowed to curse. Oh, but I learned from my peers and learned from listening to the 'so-called' adults arguing.

"Tasha, please go downstairs, this does not have anything to do with you!" The entire time she was standing in between Rusty and me as we threw insults back and forth.

"No, I'm not going nowhere! This does have something to do with me. I have to live here and listen to you let this no-good, no-working, lowlife trailer park, fraction-of-a-man call you all kinds of names in front of your own children! And you say this doesn't have anything to do with me! I'm the one who can't sleep at night while you're arguing and fighting all night, then I need to get up and be ready to take exams at school the next day. How do you let this punk-ass bully treat you like this and walk all over you as if, like he says, 'you're a worthless piece of shit?' You should want better for yourself and for your kids!" I was steaming, full blast ahead!

"Tasha, go downstairs! I'm not going to say it again. I'm going to handle this. I just need you to go downstairs, NOW!" My mother was starting to get fed up with me, but never appeared to be fed up with Rusty.

I caught my breath and turned around and walked away slowly towards the stairs, mean-mugging Rusty the whole time. I heard him say something under his breath.

"Lil Heifer," he tried to say it almost as an afterthought.

"Asshole!" I retaliated.

"You better watch your mouth!" Rusty tried to control the room with his loud, monstrous voice, but was definitely not succeeding.

"I ain't better do nothing, Bitch!" Yes, I was just a teenager and had to make sure I had gotten the last word, because that's just what we do. I was committed to this fight and was not about to back down.

"Tasha, go downstairs like I said!" I could tell my mother was getting perturbed with me. I had pretty much taken over this fight and my mother had become the referee.

We were always taught to respect our elders, no matter what. In my day, that is the way we were raised. It didn't matter how wrong they were, we always had to give them a certain level of respect. Well, that was then, this is now. My respect ran out the door today. I was up to my wits end, and the only thing I was willing to give today was a piece of my mind! I do not even understand why adults thought they deserved respect when they clearly had not earned respect. If you don't respect me as a person, how can I respect you as an adult? I was not going to continue to live up to some cockamamie standards they demanded with no recourse. If you want to get a little, you must be willing to give a little. In other words, show my mother some respect and I'll be more than happy to show you some respect. Otherwise, kick rocks with an open-toe shoe!

I finally made it downstairs and was fiery mad at my mother for making me leave the fight scene. I was in the living room pacing the floor, tears running down my face as my temper was boiling. I could still hear them going back and forth about whatever. I did not plan for the after effect of my confrontation with Rusty. My thoughts never went that far.

Finally, Rusty came downstairs stomping his feet. He ended up walking right past me and trying to bump my shoulders, similar to the high school bully trying to pick a fight in the school hallway. Instead of allowing him to bump my shoulder, I dropped my left shoulder back so his shoulder could not touch mine. He was definitely showing his level of immaturity as a grown ass man.

"You think you grown, don't you?" Rusty said once again as if that was his final statement.

My mother came behind him shortly, "Tasha, you should have never spoken to him that way."

"You should have never let him speak to you in the way that he does. I was just trying to take up for you since you don't care to take up for yourself." I had become very defensive towards my mother for coming at me like this.

"Arlene, I'll tell you this much, since she thinks she grown, it's not enough room in this house for the two of us. Either she gots to go, or I'm leaving. Your choice," Rusty seemed very sure of himself.

My mother looked at me and said, "Tasha," with slight hesitation, " I'm afraid you're going to have to pack your bags." She then turned around, walked away, and headed back up the stairs to watch her soap operas.

It was clear to me they already had a conversation while they were still upstairs. That is the reason why Rusty was so confident and cocky when he came downstairs, because he already knew what was about to happen, that my mother would choose him over her own child.

I, on the other hand, was quite stunned and taken aback! I had no idea this would be the turnout of events. That I will be the one getting kicked out of the house and not him. I thought if I showed her she is not in this alone, and I would stand up for her, she would be more apt to stand up for herself. I was merely taking up for my mother trying to protect her rights as a woman, as a human being; trying to protect myself and my well-being. I tried to instill in her the values my grandparents taught us. The value of self-worth, the fact we all stand together and take up for one another. The value of having someone to fight with you, to fight *for* you. "If they mess with one of us, they mess with all of us," was our mantra growing up. My mother insisted we give Rusty respect, but she did not require respect herself. She did not have a voice, did not want a voice, or was not capable of finding her voice. She's never stood up for herself in her life; she's never been able to protect herself nor her children, and now this woman has turned her back on me like I was just another nigga off the streets. My own mother...

"I will gladly pack my bags!"

I was so mad, hurt, and disgusted with her. I was known to have a poker face when someone hurt me. I showed her no emotions whatsoever. The disappointments in my own mother ran so deeply; I cannot express how she made me feel. What I did know is I wasn't about to let her know how hurt I was and furthermore, I wasn't about to let Rusty see how hurt I was. He had won this round for sure with his conniving ways. Once again, my mother had allowed it.

I went upstairs and thought about where I was going since I was being kicked out of the house on the spur of a moment. I didn't have time to be in my feelings about what just happened. "Just stay numb, Tasha!" I'd have to remember to give myself permission to break down later. But for now, I had to think about my next plan of action. I could not go to Fred's parents' house because I did not want that burden on them since they were not my real family, plus what happens if we broke up? The same thing with Rolanda's parents. I finally decided to call my Auntie DeDe and ask her to come pick me up. My aunt never asked me any questions, she just replied, "I'm on my way." As I began to pack my clothes in large, oversized garbage bags, I started to realize this was a positive move. I had always wanted to be from under Rusty's thumb. From now on, let my mother figure out how she was going to take up for herself since it was 'none of my business.' I needed a break from carrying the weight of her life and well-being on my shoulders anyway. Shit, she just did me a favor! I was merely a teenager, trying to focus on what I was going to do with my life, and this lifestyle was extremely burdensome. Perhaps I could find peace and freedom somewhere else. At least I was willing to try. I really did not have a choice. I am outta' here...

Chapter 12

IT'S A MATTER OF LIFE
OR DEATH

They say the grass is not always greener on the other side, and it's so true. Just because it looks greener doesn't necessarily mean greener is better. The experience with 'Uncle' John taught me that.

After my mother kicked me out of the house, I moved in with my Auntie De-De. De-De was a lot more flexible, but lo and behold, she still had the same issues as my mother, with her abusive boyfriend, Obie. Her son, my cousin Demetrius, was about four years old at the time, and so long as I was willing to babysit him whenever she needed, I could have a roof over my head. De-De was also about six months pregnant when I moved in with her. The entire first few months at her house in the Mary Crest subdivision was nothing short of what it was like at my mother's house; fighting, arguing, and him being extremely abusive to her. What is it with these women?? They just did not love themselves and it showed, based on how they allowed men to mistreat them. To love yourself means to respect yourself, and demand respect from others! If you allow a man to put his hands on you, you do not respect yourself, nor will he ever respect you. I just don't get it!

How can a young poor girl, who grew up on welfare, escape such mental turmoil when every environment in her path is a toxic one? Every time I tried to run away, I ran right into the same environment. That's what was available to me. How could I rise above my circumstances and pull myself up by my bootstraps if there was no one in my family circle to steer me in the right direction? There was no manuscript with any instructions available. I knew what I wanted in my head, my dreams, my vision for my life, yet I had no idea how I was going to go about getting it. I was determined to write this manuscript myself as I went along life's journey. Tripping, stammering, and bumping into walls all along the way... by any means necessary.

My Auntie De-De was a full figured, hippy, voluptuous woman with a huge, beautiful smile. She was about 5'6 with a big personality and one of those laughs that shook the room and made everyone around join in, even if you did not know what she was laughing about. Obie, on the other hand, was a very short, curly afro-haired guy with one of his front teeth missing. I heard he lost that tooth in a fight. I guess he lost the fight as well! Obie was not a mean dude, from what I remember, but for some reason that *Napoleon Complex* came with a temper and hostility to go with it! Obie was always over at the house, usually for days or weeks at a time. I recall a time when Obie was looking for a job, and my aunt had to help him fill out the application for the Car Wash. Obie could not even read, struggling with the simplest of words on the application.

I always wondered why my aunt put up with Obie. This little bitty man with no job, no high school education, no money, an extremely small stature, and clearly a small brain to match. Auntie De-De told me they had dated since high school, and apparently, he is all she knew and was comfortable with him. I think all women older than 30 should have experienced more than one man by this time in their lives, unless of course, they marry the first guy they ever dated. Otherwise, how would they know the differences in what they like and what they do not like? We don't know unless we have something else to compare it to. Experience really is the best teacher.

One positive thing about living at my Auntie De-De's is that I could have my boyfriend, Fred Clark over whenever I wanted. I mean, he never stayed the night or anything like that, but he was pretty much welcome to the house at any time. One night when my aunt was out and my little cousin was asleep, Fred was in town for the weekend on leave from the Air Force and he asked to come over. Of course, I was always so excited to see him as I was completely in love with him.

"Hey, Baby! It's so good to see you." He came into the house and gave me the biggest hug and passionate kiss.

"Hey Fred! I missed you so much!"

"How's my Baby Girl doing?" he asked.

"Well, I wrote you a letter and told you how my mother kicked me out of the house because of Rusty, so I'm here now, at least until I go to college."

"Just look on the bright side, at least you don't have to deal with Rusty anymore."

"That's true, but sometimes it's no better over here. I'll take it though. At least I had a place to go."

"Now I've told you, we can just get married and you can live on base with me for free."

"I'm 17 years old and you're 19. We don't have no business getting married this young."

He grabbed me and held me close, "We love each other, don't we? That's the only thing that matters. You know I want to take you away from all this chaos. You deserve so much better. Let me take care of you. Let me love you like you deserve to be loved. I'm ready."

"But I'm not ready. I need to finish out my Senior year, and then I plan to go to college."

"That's fine, you can finish senior year and then you can go to Oklahoma State University. That's not too far from the Air Force Base."

"I don't know about that, Fred. It seems too premature for us to be talking about this right now."

"You know I love you, don't you?"

"Of course, I do."

"You know that I would do anything for you, right?"

"Yes."

"Well at least tell me you'll think about it. You don't have to answer right now."

"Ok, I will give it some thought."

"You promise?"

"I promise."

It's true, I was crazy about Fred Clark and everyone knew it. Not only was he smooth, he was kind hearted, generous, and just a good person in general. I loved being around him. I trusted Fred and felt so safe with him.

Did I think he could take care of me? Of course, I did. Did I feel safe and secure with him? Absolutely. Did I think he would love me and give me the best life he was able to? Without a doubt. Then why did I not want to marry Fred Clark? One thing I was sure of at this point in my life is that I did not know what I did not know.

He grabbed my face and started kissing me passionately. Next thing I know, he had unbuttoned my jeans, rubbing gently between my thighs. He really knew how to turn me on. As I began panting heavily, he pulled down my jeans, unbuckled his belt, and unzipped his pants.

"I love you," he whispered softly in my ear. "I love you."

We both ripped off the other's shirt and he unsnapped my bra. His soft, smooth lips on my breasts made me loosie goosy downstairs as he entered my person... and we made love, right there on the floor as I straddled him in front of the oversized chair in the living room.

I loved making love to Fred. He just had a way of making me feel wanted and valued. The quality of life I had with him was one I could see myself having in my future. But what was I willing to give up for it? College? The ability to choose where I would attend college? I did not know anyone in Oklahoma! I did not feel I was ready for what he wanted at the time. I spent my entire life trying to position myself to have the right to choose for myself. Was I prepared to give that up at such an early age?

I heard a car pull up. "Oh shit, it's my Auntie De-De!"

We hurried up off the floor pulling up our pants and straightening our clothes, pretending like Fred was on his way out the front door.

"Hey Fred!" my Aunt was coming in as he was walking out.

"Hey, De-De," Fred replied.

"You drive home safely, you hear?" she looked like she knew we were up to something, but did not say anything.

"Ok, I will. Thanks."

I walked Fred to his car and we stood out under the stars hugging.

"Tasha, I love you so much, I don't want to live without you," he gazed into my eyes.

"I love you, too," I said, squeezing him tighter.

"Please think about what I said. I want you in my life."

"Ok, I will think about it. I promise. Goodnight."

We kissed once again and I watched him drive off. He would be driving back to the base first thing in the morning. My heart broke every time I had to see him leave. Oh, that man was so irresistible! I think I could have a happy life with him. Maybe I should give it some serious thought.

Several weeks later the unthinkable happened. I had missed my period! Every month I was with Fred I was constantly praying to God to let my period come on because we had stopped using condoms. We were using what he called the '*withdrawal method.*'

That is when the guy feels himself coming and pulls his penis out of the vagina prior to ejaculation. Of course, the *withdrawal method* is just a myth because it is not a method at all. Maybe I was just a fool to think it was working when it never was. Maybe it was just God's grace giving me another chance to get it right. Well now, seemingly, that grace had run out!

Since I was 17 years old, I was able to go to Planned Parenthood without parental knowledge. I already knew something was growing in my belly, even at six weeks I could tell I must be pregnant. Breast tenderness. Fatigue. Hungry all the time. Sleeping all the time. It all added up. I had no idea what I would do at this point because I thought I had a future ahead of me. I would need to make some very tough decisions about my life and my future. But let me start here.

After I got home from Planned Parenthood with the confirmation I was pregnant, I began to panic. I went back to my Aunt De-De's house to call Fred to let him know.

"Hey."

"Hey Baby Girl, how's it going?"

"Not too well."

"What do you mean, what's going on?"

"I missed my period, Fred."

"What! Awww man! Are you serious? You're going to have my baby!" he was ecstatic about the news.

I was pretty taken aback by his response. I was 17 years old and he was only 19 years old. What did either of us know about having a baby or raising a child? We weren't ready for this! At least I wasn't.

"You sound way too happy about this," I responded.

"Well, I see this as the perfect storm. A perfect opportunity for us to make our relationship permanent. We have a baby on the way! I have already given you a ring, and you know I want you to be my wife!"

"Fred, please listen to me, I'm 17 years old! I'm not sure that we have a baby on the way, because I'm not even sure if I'm going to keep this baby."

"What do you mean you're not sure? That's my baby you're carrying, too! Don't I have a say so in this? Don't I have rights?"

Rights? Clearly, I had not had any dealings with men who gave a shit about their kids, yet along with having 'rights' and a 'say so' about what the girl decided to do regarding her pregnancy.

"This is my body! Not yours! I must think about my future. And a baby right now is not something I can do, still go to college, and get an education. I don't think I can be a mother right now. I'm 17 years old! This is not what I signed up for!"

"You're not doing this by yourself. I'm here with you. I'm here to support you!"

"Yeah, you're here with me right now, but I'm the one who is going to be *solely* responsible for this baby, and *I'm* not ready for that!"

"Do you know how many girls have babies, then go on to finish college and do whatever it is that they need to do?"

"That's them, that's not me! This baby was not in the plan for me. I don't think I can keep this baby, Fred."

"So what are you saying? You going to kill my baby? Even if I'm totally against you having an abortion, you're going to do it anyway?"

"I'm not saying what I'm going to do, or what I'm not going to do. But I am saying I have to think about it and I have to make a decision because it's my life!"

"It's *my life* too! And I don't see how you're going to make this decision without me."

"Listen, I'm not saying I'm going to make a decision right away. And I'm not making a decision without you, which is the reason why I called you. I am going to take time to think about it. However, the nurse practitioner told me that I cannot wait too long to make a decision because it could be too late. I will call you by the end of the week so that we can discuss this again."

"Well, I need you to remember that I love you, and I want you to be my wife. You having a baby to me is a blessing and a miracle. I would love to have you and my baby to take care of. You know I'm here for you as I always have been. Please take our relationship into consideration because I don't think it will survive an abortion."

Well, there you go. He was basically giving me an ultimatum. He wanted this baby so badly and he wanted me to be his wife so badly that he would not consider any other options. I, on the other hand, had no choice but to consider the options.

Although Fred Clark was my high school sweetheart, and I did love him, I knew I did not have enough experience to make this decision to be married to someone from my small hometown of Kankakee, IL. I've never dated anybody outside of this little square box. What would I be giving up? What would I be missing out on? How would I even know until the experience came? But if I never had the experience, how would I ever know what I do not know? I had so many questions in my head, and I was just scared. I was so terrified! I was petrified of having a baby, I was afraid of being just another statistic. I really am a product of my environment. What they say about poor little welfare black girls, especially ones that grew up with no daddy and a mama on drugs. Especially those who grew up seeing a lot of abuse. Especially those who were molested as a child and just looking to love and to be loved. I was that girl. I am that girl.

I may have been smart, always on the A honor roll, productive, on the cheerleading squad, on the show choir team, the person who people come to for advice, a mentor amongst my peers; but I would be looked upon as being the same little fast-ass girl from the neighborhood. I could hear the people already; their words ringing through my ears:

"Girl, she's so fast, went and got herself pregnant!"

"What a shame, she could have been somebody!"

"Oh, I guess she won't be going to college. Not with a baby strapped to her back!"

"She's no better than these other little fast girls around here. Can't keep her legs closed."

I was not too much different from any of the other girls I grew up around. Same background, same environment, same lack of structure, same lack of opportunity, and seemingly the same future. A teenage mom.

I thought about where this life would lead me. Did I really want to move to Oklahoma City and marry Fred Clark and live on some Air Force Base? Is that what my future held for me? What if I get there and I do not like it, then what? What if I married him and didn't like it? Then what? It's hard to be mobile with a baby on your hip. I knew I did not want my mistake to dictate the rest of my life. I wanted more. I wanted to *be* more. I wanted to *do* more. I wanted to go to different places and have different experiences I have never had the opportunity to do before. What was I willing to give up? How was I going to handle this? I had no idea what I was going to do. There was no one I was able to talk to about this either.

Facing this harsh reality put me in a state of emotional distress. It wasn't just what other people would say about me or think about me, because what other people thought was never a major concern for me. It was what I thought about myself. All the dreams, visions, and thoughts I had invested into my life would be placed on hold being a wife to someone and a mother. How would I ever get to experience college campus life with a baby strapped to my back? How would I ever get to date outside of my hometown if I was already married at 17? I know people used to make these types of situations work back in the day, but I, on the other hand, did not think I was cut out to do it and quite honestly, did not want to do it.

I continued to go to cheerleading practice as if nothing was wrong. Even though I was having morning sickness and was tired all the time, I would still put on my little cheerleading outfit, jump around and cheer, because at this moment I was still trying to figure out my next move. Then one day my cheerleading coach, Karen Williams, came to get me out of the gym where we were practicing, and asked me to come to her office. I followed her to her office, and she asked me to have a seat.

"So, how are you feeling?"

"Just fine. Why do you ask?"

"Tasha, I'm not stupid. I can see you are getting a little chubby around the middle section. Are you pregnant?" she just came right out and asked.

Damn! She was so observant. I thought I was hiding it so well. If she had figured it out, I wonder how many others had figured it out too, but just had not said anything.

All I could do was break down in tears. I was glad Ms. Williams had called me out on it because honestly, I was crumbling under the pressure of knowing I was pregnant and not knowing what to do about it.

"Yes ma'am," I cried, hanging my head low with embarrassment.

"So how far along are you?"

"About eight weeks."

"What do you plan to do?"

"I honestly don't know Ms. Williams."

"Whose baby is it, Fred Clark's?"

"Yes ma'am."

"What is he saying about all this?"

"He wants to keep the baby, get married, and be a family."

This definitely didn't seem to be her first rodeo. Ms. Williams was shooting off these questions like a pro!

"Well, that's very noble of him, but what do you want to do, Tasha?"

Reaching for the Kleenex from her desk to wipe the tears from my face, I finally responded. "I want to have a better future. I'm not ready to have a baby, to be a mother and a wife. I just can't see myself doing that right now!" I was literally bursting out in tears.

Ms. Williams grabbed me and hugged me and just let me cry. "It's going to be alright. You need to take some time and make a final decision on what you're going to do. It's your body. You have the right to do whatever you choose."

"I don't want to keep this baby, Ms. Williams. But I feel so bad because that means I'm taking a life. I'm killing a potential person who's growing inside of me. What does that say about me as a person? I don't even know if I would be able to live with that. I feel guilty that I created this little life inside me and then I'm going to take the life away. This baby doesn't have a chance."

Yes, I used to be Pro-Life until I *became* Pro-Choice when my own body and right to choose were at stake. Everyone can have an opinion, but until you are in this situation, I honestly don't know where the strong opinion is coming from. It seems to be all political and not personal. Mine is *all* personal.

"Listen, each one of us must live and learn. Life will give you your own experiences and you must learn from them. Whatever you decide to do, I will support you 100%. Whether you decide to keep the baby, or whether you decide to go through with the abortion, but you do not have a lot of time to think about it. You literally only have about a week to take action. You call me by the end of this week and let me know what you intend to do, and then we will go from there."

Ms. Williams was a lot more than a cheerleading coach to all of us. She was the mother, the aunt, the caretaker, the ride home from cheerleading squad practice, the food in our mouths when we didn't have any. She would give me clothes she could no longer fit into, and let me borrow her car and babysit her kids for extra money. She saved many of us, just by being there for us. She was the sound mind as far as the adults were concerned in my life. She was the voice of reason. In addition, she never judged me or made me feel guilty about any decisions I made.

Once I realized I had someone to help me through this process who would talk me through it, and walk with me through it, I decided I was not going to keep this baby. I called Ms. Williams to let her know.

"So, did you let Fred Clark know what your decision is already?"

"Yes, but he is not in agreement with me. I called him last night and he ended up hanging up on me because he did not want to hear what I had to say. I just don't want to be stuck! I feel like I'm suffocating in this process!"

"Ok, just calm down, Tasha, he's just upset right now because he can't get his way, but he'll come around. Did you ask him if he would pay for the abortion?"

"He's being an asshole right now, and told me that he was not going to pay for an abortion, and so where would I get the money for it?"

It is amazing how I thought we were so close, so in love, without realizing as long as I was going along with everything Fred said, that love would still exist. But if I was deciding to do something different, that love could back-fire!

Karen was comforting. "That's okay, and his reaction is very normal coming from a man. He seems to really care about you and wants you to be a part of his future, but you must decide if you want to have a future with him. No one can decide that for you. What you need to do is get on the phone and call his mother and get the money for the abortion from her. What kind of relationship do you have with his mother?"

"I love his mother and I believe she loves me."

"Okay then, let's start there."

"Okay, I'll call her now." I hung up the phone with Ms. Williams and took several deep breaths before dialing Mrs. Clark's home phone number.

"Hello," she answered the phone.

"Hi, Mrs. Clark, it's Tasha."

"Hey baby, how's it going?"

"Uhmmmm..... I just wanted to know if you have a moment to talk?"

"Well of course I do. Is everything okay?"

I couldn't say anything at first.

"Tasha...are you still there? Tasha?" Mrs. Clark sensed that something was wrong.

"No," I cried. "No... everything is not okay."

"Well, what's wrong?"

I almost started hyperventilating as I tried to control my breathing, "I'm pregnant."

"Awwwww!" She sighed in grave disappointment. "So what are you going to do?"

"I want to have an abortion."

"Have you spoken to my son about this?"

"Yeah, he knows everything, but he wants me to keep the baby and I just can't see that happening, Mrs. Clark. I have different plans for my future and bringing a child into the world at this early age is just not in the plan for me. I told Fred I wanted to get an abortion, but since he is not in agreement, he refuses to pay for it."

"Well, I'm sorry you kids have gotten yourselves into this mess," she waited a few minutes and then said, "How much does it cost?"

"$300," I sniffled.

After another moment of silence, she finally said, "Well, come over to the house and pick it up tomorrow. And don't worry, when I talk to that son of mine, I will get my money back!"

I was so relieved I could count on Fred's mother! I was under so much stress just thinking about where I was going to get the money, and if I was going to get it in time to be able to have the abortion before I was too far along. I would have never been able to get $300 from my mother to save my life! Ms. Williams took me over to the Clark's house the very next day to pick up the money. I called to schedule my abortion appointment for that Saturday and Ms. Williams had volunteered to drive me there, stay there with me, and bring me back to her house for the weekend.

At this point in my life I had already been through so much! I had survived the molestation from James, had seen my grandfather hold a gun up to James' head when he was trying to strangle my mama. I had escaped Uncle John's attempt to hold me hostage and make me his 'love slave,' or so he thought. I got out alive without having to kill Damon or Rusty, and had seen my mother through multiple abuse and near-death situations. However, this was by far the scariest of them all! I am just glad I had someone in my life who could be a sounding board and could steer me in whatever direction I chose to go. Ms. Williams kept me sane throughout this process; she helped me to maintain my peace of mind. As a young girl trying to hold on to her dreams and still keep her sanity intact, I don't know where I would have been without her help.

I ended up staying the night at Ms. Williams house on that Friday. Early Saturday morning we were on our way to the abortion clinic for my 10am appointment. We stopped by the high school to pick up the Assistant Cheerleading Coach, Mrs. Fry. I guess Ms. Williams needed emotional support as well as I did. The abortion clinic was maybe 35 to 45 minutes north. I sat in the backseat quietly the whole time. Thinking, praying, crying. I honestly did not know if I was doing the right thing or not. How could I have known? All I knew is this fear had to be taken away from me, and it needed to happen quickly. Anxiety had taken over my mind and my body, and this was the only way out!

When we arrived at the abortion clinic, hundreds of people were outside with picket signs and megaphones. With fists in the air, they urged us to stop killing our babies. Scared girls, covering their faces, while being covered by their mother's arms, walking quickly into the clinic, to their safe place. These people were shouting very mean things to us. Didn't they know this was difficult enough? That we did not just haphazardly make the decision to show up at the abortion clinic this morning? Did they not realize there was a lot of sweat and tears, turmoil and pain, sleepless nights, prayers, and endless thinking that brought us here today?

They were shouting obscenities like, "murderers, baby killers, you need to come to Jesus."

"Is anyone forcing you to kill your baby?"

"Have you considered adoption?"

"The Bible says, 'Thou shall not kill!'"

"You are murderers on your way to hell and damnation!"

"You will burn in the lake of fire forever!"

"God will never forgive a murderer, because He hates murderers!"

I was so petrified, embarrassed, and I had a terribly guilty conscience. I realized I may have been a disappointment to God, but I would hope He would forgive a naive, teenage girl who had sex and got pregnant when I knew this was not something I would be able to handle. I knew I was going to have to live with this decision for the rest of my life, but either it was that, or bringing this baby into a life I could not afford. I never wanted my child to have to experience the poverty that I grew up in. I wanted to be prepared to give my child a better life, and at 17, that was impossible. I also did not want to go through a full pregnancy and then give my child up for adoption. I still could not be sure of what type of life s/he would have, and could not bank on that option either. So, I sucked it up and I brushed it off. I am here now. I would need to put on my big girl panties and do what I came here to do!

As we walked into the clinic, we checked in and had a seat. When they were ready for us girls, mostly all teenagers, we went to this back room. It was actually a hallway where we sat in chairs lined up alongside the wall. Everybody signed papers, disclosures, and we were each given a small cup with maybe 10 different pills. Some of these pills were to kill the pain we were about to endure, others were to sedate us, others for emotional depression.

I noticed most were teenage white girls, and a few adult white women. I saw one other black girl and another who appeared to be a mixed-race girl. I guess where I am from, not many black girls could afford an abortion, having no choice but to keep their babies. Thank God for Fred's mother, is all I could think of.

When it was my turn to go to the back room to meet the doctor and the nurse, I just became numb. There was nothing else I could do, feel, or say.

"When asked, "Did you have any questions?" by the doctor...

"No," I replied.

There was nothing else I wanted to say, but I knew I needed to have this embryo out of my body. I knew I was not going to raise a child in the same environment I had grown up in. I knew that for a fact, and while I will have to deal with the guilt and the pain of this process, I was willing to do that, versus putting another human being through some of the same shit I had to endure as a child.

I remember laying back on the table. The lights in the ceiling were flickering as my eyelids grew heavy. I only had my bottoms off, and my legs were in stirrups as when a woman gets a Pap test at the OBGYN. There was a silver bucket on the floor at the bottom of the table where I lay. This bucket was used to catch the remains, which were to be vacuumed out of my body. I heard clanking of utensils and tools, the vacuum, lights flickering, eyes heavy. More clanking of utensils and tools, the vacuum, then it was over. The medication given to me had me knocked out! I have no idea how long the procedure was, but they had us in and out like it was an assembly line or something. I do recall there being a lot of pain involved once I became conscious. After the procedure was completed, I was released to my cheerleading coaches and I rode home to Ms. William's house in silence. I was cramping so badly, and I probably cried off and on for the entire weekend.

The physical pain that came with having an abortion was probably ten times worse than a woman's monthly cycle. The cramps were astronomical! The nausea was unbelievably sickening! The very next day I had to perform in a play I was in, which was the Wiz. I was one of the good witches, Addaperle. I know, I know. You are probably thinking, why would she schedule an abortion on the same weekend where she has to perform in a play? This was the only available weekend within the first 12 weeks of my pregnancy, after I had gotten the money to pay for the abortion, so I had no choice. There was nothing I could do as we had already performed the play the prior weekend, and I could not renege on my commitment with the play I had already started. So, just like most black women would do, with blood dripping down my legs every 20 minutes and all, I performed that play! I can remember wearing these extra thick maxi pads because there was still a lot of bleeding involved after the surgery. I did the show as best I could, and when it was time for me to go on stage, I put on that poker face and ran with it.

"It's showtime girl! Pull it together! Never let them see you sweat! You don't have to look like what you've been through!" I'd pump myself up!

Anytime my character was not on stage, I was in the dressing room, curled up in a ball on the floor, cramping, and in a lot of pain. When the other cast members came to check on me, I just told them my menstrual cycle had just started and I was PMS-ing. They were none the wiser. When dealing with the loss of someone growing inside of your body, when a conscious decision was made to get rid of this someone, there was no way to be mentally prepared for that. It was by far the most difficult thing I had to do in my entire life, and coming from a 17-year-old girl with ambitions and dreams, and a vision for her life; it was a necessary trade off.

A couple of weeks after my abortion, I got a call from Fred. I had not heard from him since I told him I was going to have the abortion. I figured he would reach out to me after he got over his feelings about it. He called me to let me know his mother told him what happened, because she also told him she gave me the money for the abortion. He was devastatingly distraught to say the least. He really did not think I would go through with it.

"I have a confession to make."

"What is it, Fred?"

"I know I was supposed to pull out since we were practicing the withdrawal method, and I could have when I felt myself coming, but I didn't because I didn't want to."

"Wait! What? What are you saying?"

"I purposely did not pull out. I came inside of you because I wanted to get you pregnant so that you would not have a choice but to marry me."

"So you're saying you got me pregnant on purpose!"

Unbelievable! I could not believe this man was trying to trap me into marrying him. Fred knew I had already gotten accepted into the summer engineering program at Tuskegee University, a Historically Black College and University. The thing that excited me most about learning and studying among all black people is what scared Fred the most. I assumed he realized he would not be able to compete.

"I was just trying to show you I could be a good father to our baby and a good husband."

"A man that would be deceptive and manipulative and controlling, cannot be a good father nor a good husband! I am done talking to you!"

"Wait, just give me a chance to explain."

"Goodbye Fred!" Back then you could slam the phone down and it was the true meaning of '*hanging up in someone's face*!' which is what I did!

You always hear the stories of women trying to trap the man, trying to get pregnant by the man. That's not what I'm about, but he tried to trap me! He wanted to get me pregnant on purpose, so I would decide to move in with him, marry him, and have his baby. In other words, he wanted to be my *baby daddy*!

This was such a selfish act on his part. He knew I was young, scared, without many options, and he used my predicament to his advantage. Shame on him! I was totally done at this point, because that type of love is controlling, and I was not about to be controlled by this man, or any other man. As Miss Celie stated from the Color Purple, "I may be black, I may even be ugly, (well, I'm not ugly) but I's FREE!" As long as I had something to say about it, it would never happen. I will continue to be FREE!

I was very disappointed in Fred. I mean, I really admired him. We were truly good friends, too; but sometimes love makes people do crazy things. I was never supposed to be in a marriage with him, particularly since it never happened. It's funny how when I was in the relationship, I did not feel like he was controlling at all. He opened me up to so many new things and different experiences. I guess since I was benefiting from him, it did not really bother me. What I had with Fred was as real as it could get, for a teenager. He was my high school sweetheart, my first real love, and that is all I knew, and that is how I knew I was not able to decide about the rest of my life as far as marrying him. Fred was very good to me, for what it's worth. I learned a lot from him and his family, but it was past time for me to move on to the next chapter of my life, and that was what I planned to do. I was beginning to see what I wanted in a relationship, and what I would and would not tolerate. I was growing up, growing into the woman I would become.

Most girls my age from my neighborhood, who grew up in an environment like mine probably would not have had an abortion. Most could not afford it, others too afraid to go through with it. Some did not have a vision for their future, so this baby was not necessarily a deterrent, as it was for me. They probably have had their children and worked it out the best way they could. So, even though girls from my neighborhood, a lot of us, not all of us, end up in this predicament, I had to still choose a different route. I do not regret choosing that route because I had to choose it for myself, and for the unborn child. Although when I was going through it, I struggled with the guilt, life has taught me to release myself, forgive myself. There are no regrets. I had to give myself a chance at life. The life I wanted, not the life someone else wanted for me.

"The grass is not always greener on the other side. Until you till your own field, grow your own grass, water it, and give it the nourishment that it needs, you are always subjected to someone else's weeds."

Natasha Bostic Baymon 2022

Chapter 13

TUSKEGEE-BOUND

After all was said and done, at least I made it! Getting accepted into Tuskegee University's Fast Track Engineering Program for the summer was a move in the right direction for my future. I did not know the first thing about Engineering, but when my high school principal, Mr. Jordan, told me I had the math and science aptitude to be a good engineer, I truly believed him!

I did not get a chance to visit any college campus before deciding where I would go to college because I could not afford it. Besides the brochures I had, I knew nothing about the college campus. The only deciding factor was I had a full ride for the first year, and would have to figure out the other years when the time came. Tuskegee's summer program was to begin the Monday after Friday's graduation from high school. All I know is, I was out of this place and would never turn back!

When I left Kankakee on a Saturday morning, I lived with my Auntie Terri and Uncle Warren my senior year after Auntie DeDe went in the hospital to have her baby. The living arrangements there were much better, and it was easier to stay focused on my future. My Mama had just received another settlement from Gene's death, and purchased me a one-way bus ticket to Tuskegee. She also purchased a trunk full of items I would need for college like laundry detergent, towels, soap, and so on. I also had a small 13" black and white TV, and a small refrigerator for my room. Hey, something is better than nothing, I thought! The distance was only about 12 hours, but it took us an entire 24 hours to get there as we seemed to have to stop in every little town.

When I first arrived at Tuskegee, I was definitely in shock.

"What the hell!" This southern town was more country than I could have imagined.

Dirt roads, janky dorm rooms smaller than a New York apartment, and the cafeteria served refried beans that appeared to have been refried for a whole week!

Oh my God! I had no idea what I had gotten myself into. Most of my math and engineering teachers were foreigners, and it was very difficult for me to understand their dialect. This was very frustrating as it took me a while to catch on, and I felt like it was easy to fall behind. I had to work much harder than I was accustomed to working when I was in high school, just to keep up with the fast pace of college life.

Most students who had these same difficulties would just make a phone call to their parents and let them know they wanted to come home because they did not like it, or it was too hard, or they were just homesick. Oh, but not me! I did not have any parents whom I could call, crying and complaining to. I did not have any options. Sometimes I believe having no other options is what saved me. I had to do what I came here to do. I was not leaving Tuskegee University without that Engineering degree! There would be no Summa Cum Laude, or Magna Cum Laude, I graduated with the honor of *Thank you,* Laude!

Tuskegee University taught me so much about myself, about my people, and about my culture. Different black people from all over the world attended the Engineering program. This is one of the top HBCUs for Engineering. But more importantly, it taught me the value of self. Although I already had some of that in me from my journey growing up, my lessons at Tuskegee began to show me how to connect the many dots of my life. Instead of asking why did this happen, and why did that happen, I began to discover what I wanted to do about it, how I wanted to piece my life together to make it whole, for it to make sense. I was determined to be a healthy, whole person. A person who would eventually make a major contribution to the world. What was my true purpose in life? Why had God called me forth into the world? What was I going to leave behind? Tuskegee instilled in me the tools I needed to become whole, to take all the broken pieces of my life and put them back together, make lemonade from lemons, make a loaf of bread from bread crumbs.

The teachers here were great! Once I figured out the dialect, I noticed they gave me the extra time I needed to understand the material and lessons. Providing a student was willing to put in the extra time, the Professors would make sure you understood it. The students were awesome, more like brothers and sisters! We often stayed up all night to study with each other to get the project done. We would all be falling asleep on the living room floor at a friend's house until a certain project was complete. Oh, and let us not forget the parties! I would say the Kappas threw the best parties on our yard because they were a little bougie like me! The first and last time I ever got drunk was at a Kappa Party! I was drinking something called *Pink Panty Pu-Tang*! It was hunch punch with Seagram's Gin. I remember coming back to the dorm room after the party and had to stop by the bathroom. Somehow, I slipped and fell on the bathroom floor in the stall and hit my head on the porcelain toilet! I had the worse hangover ever. I do not drink Gin now because of that! I had it all, the family, the fun; including all the stupid things that college kids get into, the love, the camaraderie, and the support.

Therefore, I knew I could not marry Fred Clark after high school! I did not know what I might be missing in the world if I had!

Then one day, my roommate, Angela, asked, "So where are you going after the summer?"

"What do you mean? I am staying here."

"Oh no, you can't stay here. They need to close the dorms down between summer school and the fall semester."

"Really? I didn't know that. Shit!"

"Oh, I thought everybody knew that." Angela lived with her aunt since her parents died in an auto accident when she was younger. "Yeah, my aunt told me that."

"Well, I had no idea." Once again, there was no one in my family to let me know what I should expect. "I have no idea where I'm going."

Ughhh! I knew I could not go back to Mama's house, although she had just purchased a new house with the money from Gene's death settlement, but she was still with Rusty, and I honestly did not want to deal with his ass. Furthermore, once they put me out, I did not want them to think they were doing me any favors by letting me stay with them. I knew it was only 3-4 weeks before the fall semester began, but in that household, anything could happen in a short period of time and I just could not risk it!

I decided to call my former cheerleading coach, Karen Williams.

"Hey Ms. Williams."

"Hey Tasha, how are you enjoying the summer engineering program down at Tuskegee?"

"Oh it's going great! After I made some adjustments, it got a little easier."

"Well, that's very good to hear. I knew you could do it!"

"So, I just found out we can't stay on the campus after summer school, and I don't really have a place to stay if I go back home."

"Oh, that's no problem. I still have an extra room for you at my house."

"Really!"

"Of course, anytime you're in town and need a place to stay, you are always welcome to stay here."

"Thank you so much Ms. Williams! I really appreciate it!"

"No problem, just let me know what day and time I need to pick you up from the bus station."

"Ok, I will!"

"Love you!"

"Love you, too!"

God always had a ram in the bush waiting for me. As long as I was trying to navigate my life, there would always be someone there to help with the steering. Especially in this phase of my life when I was still trying to figure out this 'adulting.' Now that I had a place to stay, I would need to figure out how I was going to get home to Kankakee.

I decided to call my Mama since I would need a round trip ticket to Kankakee and back to Tuskegee for the fall semester.

'Uhmmm ok, I'll see what I can do," was my Mama's response when I called her and told her my situation at college. She eventually sent me the round-trip ticket so I was able to get home. Next year I would be more prepared so I would not have to depend on her to get me to and from school.

When I arrived in Kankakee, Ms. Williams let me borrow her car so I could go visit my mother. I figured I had better remind her of the promise she made me before it is too late.

"So, Mama." I was standing outside in the front yard and she was standing on the porch. "Are you still going to be able to buy me a car for school so I can get around and won't have to worry about taking the Greyhound Bus?"

"Car! I don't have no car money. I was just about to ask you if I could borrow $20!"

Really! There goes my wishful thinking!

"$20! Why would you be asking me for $20 when I know you just received another annuity settlement from Gene's death of at least $150,000!"

"How do you know how much I received?"

My Auntie Terri told me. My mother bought the house for 69k, loaned Terri 10k, bought Rusty a car, a van, a pool table, and some other shit he did not need or deserve; and I guess they spent the rest on drugs! All in one summer! This is the reason she could not keep her promise to buy her daughter a used car for college after the summer program, because once again drugs and a nigga were always more important than her own children! And now after only two short months, my mother is once again flat broke, asking me, a broke college student, for $20! Damn shame!

I knew I could never depend on my mother. I'd better consider myself lucky she bought the round-trip Greyhound ticket to Tuskegee and leave it at that. The following school year I made sure I worked enough jobs to be able to buy my own car. I always kept a work study job as that was a part of the financial aid program and would work around my class schedule. Any student who was on work study could also qualify for food stamps. At first, I was so embarrassed by these food stamps since we grew up on welfare and did not have a choice but to be on food stamps since that was the only way my mother could feed us. But since all the students with work study were using food stamps, it was not so bad. It was like 'the thing!" Plus, I had no idea you could buy shrimp, lobster tails, and crab legs with food stamps. Shoot! We never ate that good on welfare. It was always spam, Vienna sausages, and bologna sandwiches! I honestly thought there were limitations on the food you could buy with food stamps as if the government did not want poor people to experience a better quality of food.

The second job I had was waiting tables at the dog track on weekends. I would catch a ride with my homeboy, DeRon, from Chicago, and make those tips. The pay was minimum wage but the tips were great, especially when the customers were winning!

My third job was tutoring this little girl in math. Her grandmother attended the church I started going to, and I normally saw her on Saturday mornings.

Among work, a full class schedule, and Engineering Society volunteering activities, my plate was extremely full at Tuskegee. I also kept at least one boyfriend per year, and pledged Alpha Kappa Alpha Sorority my Junior Year.

My sophomore year I moved off campus, and had saved all my money to put a down payment on my car, purchase title and tags, and any incidentals that were needed. I caught a ride to Kankakee with my homeboy DeRon, who was on his way to Chicago, and would plan to drive back to school by myself in my newly purchased car.

"Rusty can go with us to help you find a car. Anytime you are buying a used car, you need a man to go with you so people won't be trying to swindle you out of your money," my mother warned me.

I had actually heard that somewhere, and since I knew nothing about purchasing a used car, I would take her advice. Although I did not like Rusty, could not stand him really, his presence could be a little intimidating which may work in my favor with negotiating a lower price.

I ended up picking out a gold 1984 Mazda GLC 4 speed. I knew how to drive a stick shift because Fred's car was a 5 speed which I taught myself to drive in high school. When I rode home with DeRon, his car was also a 4-speed, so I had plenty of practice helping him drive. It felt good to have my own car and to be able to purchase it myself with my own money that I worked for. I did not need anybody coming down to Tuskegee trying to repossess my shit because my Mama got a title loan out against the car or something! I would rather have it this way so I can control what happens to the car!

The car did, however, need new tires.

"Oh, I know a guy who can get you some new tires at a decent price, since you have spent most of your money on the down payment," Rusty stated. Although I did not trust him, he had done a good job helping me talk down the final price of the car.

"Uhmm, ok, how much are we talking for 4 tires?"

"$200."

"Ok, that sounds reasonable."

After we returned to their house, I gave Rusty the $200 and left the car and keys with him. I walked down to my Auntie Terri's house to visit for a few hours. Terri brought me back to Mama's house and I saw my car parked on the street in front of the house. I jumped out of the car to look at my new tires.

"Wait, these are white wall tires, but they don't look new to me!"

"Let me see," my Aunt started looking closer. No, the tread on these tires are somewhat worn!"

"So, I gave Rusty $200 to buy me some new tires and he bought me some used tires!"

"Oh, hell naw!" My Auntie Terri was livid! "Come on, we about to go get yo' money back!"

We stormed up to the front door and rang the doorbell and Mama came to the door.

"Where is Rusty!" My aunt pushed the door open and began walking in the house without a formal invite. I was right behind her.

"He's in the basement. What's going on?" My mother asked as if she was clueless.

My aunt walked right past her and down to the basement hollering, "Rusty! Rusty!" Where you at?"

My Auntie Terri was a 5'2" short, but shapely, woman who could really fight. One time when she was in high school, she was fighting this girl who went and got a hammer. Auntie Terri took the hammer from the girl and beat her ass with it! Yeah, people did not mess with her! Not a man, woman, or child! And this time would be no different!

"Why are you doing all this hollering in my house?" Rusty was forever trying to deflect.

"First of all, this is my sister's house! Now did you receive money from my niece to buy some new tires for her car?"

"Yeah, she gave me $200 and I got the new tires put on for her like I said I would."

"You know good and damn well those are not no new tires on that car!"

"How you know those are not new tires?"

"Do you think I'm a damn fool or something, Rusty? I'm not my sister. I will fuck yo' ass up!"

"Arlene, you better get your sister."

"He did get new tires put on the car." I guess Mama felt like she had to say something.

"Did you see the tires he got put on the car, Mama? I didn't think so." I just needed to shut her down real quick. My auntie was handling her family duties and it was best my Mama stays out of it!

My Mama had not even seen the tires, didn't even go with Rusty when he got those tires, and of course, did not ask him any questions about the tires, but here again, she was always taking up for him, no matter what!

"All I'm saying is," my Auntie was already up in Rusty's face, "either you produce a receipt showing you paid $200 for those tires or you gon' give my niece her $200 back or Imma kick yo' mothafuckin' ass right here in my goddamn sista's house! Your choice!"

Dayuuuummmm! My Auntie was a BEAST! She was small in stature, but she didn't take no mess! We got that ride or die nature from Lil' Daddy! We did not have to let it come out much, but when it did, pleeeease, Rusty had just gotten a taste of Tornado Terri! She was about to fuck his big, sloppy, 6'4"- ass up too. The bigger they are, the harder they will fall! And I was going to make sure I got some licks in, because I had been wanting a piece of him for years anyway!

"Fuck this!" Rusty finally came to his senses. "I ain't got time for this bullshit!" He took the $200 cash I gave him out of his pockets, balled it up, threw it on the floor and walked out the back door from the basement, mumbling something under his breath.

I just stood there shaking my head. I then picked up the money and counted it.

"Make sure it's all there Tasha," my Auntie insisted.

"It's all here." I was relieved I had dodged another fight or death, as these types of situations are known to get out of control at times.

My Auntie Terri and I were headed back upstairs to exit from the front door and had to walk past my Mama, while mean mugging her.

"I didn't know he still had your money," she stated nervously.

Really lady! Now, I was never going to fight my mama, but she did not want none of my Auntie Terri! The best thing for her to do right now was to remain silent!

After we got outside I said, "Can you believe this shit Auntie!"

"Yes, I can believe it! Arlene was going to sit there and let Rusty's ass try to run a game on you. She knew goddamn well that he didn't buy those tires. He probably went to the junk yard and had somebody who owed him a favor put them on for free, and he thought he was going to just pocket your money!

"Unbelievable!"

"The good part is, although these are not brand-new tires, you can still get another 10k-15k miles on them *and* you got your money back. So, thank you, asshole!" She hollered toward the back of the house.

"Oh wow! That's good to know." My Auntie was very resourceful. She knew things about things other women just did not even have a reason to want to know.

"Come to the house and stay the night, but I need you back on the road to Tuskegee first thing in the morning. You don't need to be here in Kankakee with all this drama!"

"Thank you, Auntie for having my back!"

"Always! We do not let people take advantage of us. Not even your mother!"

"Got it! Love you, Auntie."

"Love you too, Tasha."

The following summer I attended summer school at Tuskegee and I received a call from my high school friend, Loreal, to see when I was coming home for summer break.

"Hey girl."

"Hey."

"I was visiting my dad's house and I saw the newspaper sitting on the kitchen table. Did you hear the news?"

"What news?"

"You didn't hear the news?"

"No, I have no idea what you're talking about."

"Girl, Rusty's dead."

Silence...this silence was much longer than a pregnant pause. Loreal knew I could not stand Rusty and she also knew about the tumultuous relationship my mother had with him. She was even hesitant when she told me the man was dead. The newspaper she was reading from was already two weeks old, and nobody from my family including my mother, had bothered to tell me the man was dead.

More than a pregnant pause, maybe a few minutes had gone by because I was honestly trying to get my thoughts together, or at least some words or emotions, but I could not find either! And then I started laughing, then laughing harder and louder, then Loreal started laughing, then it just became this infectious domino effect of laughter! Not that I was laughing because the man was dead, but I was laughing at myself because I just did not *feel* anything about him being dead.

"Loreal, why are we laughing?" trying to wipe the laughing tears from my face while I was on the phone with her.

"Girl, I don't know. It was just so funny that you started laughing, it made me start laughing. Then I just couldn't stop laughing!"

Ding Dong the wicked witch is dead! They say every dog has his day. I guess Rusty had his. The newspaper article read he was trying to break into a man's house to get his wife back. The man was Jerry, Mama's new boyfriend, and his wife was my mother, even though they were not married. I guess she finally decided to leave Rusty's sorry ass and he went over to the guy's house to get his 'woman' back, and Jerry shot him for breaking and entering. Shot his ass dead! Oh, Rusty was going to die, it was just a matter of time; a matter of who was going to kill him and when. I am just glad it did not have to be me! Now I could focus on getting my Chemical Engineering degree in peace!

Chapter 14

ITS ABOUT DAMN TIME!

I never had any dealings with Floyd again after all those attempts that Ron and I made trying to 'chat' with him, just for him to keep changing his phone number on us. I had decided to let it go and continue to move forward with my own life. I had plans of my own to be successful and that was going to happen with or without him. Although I was enrolled as a Chemical Engineer student at Tuskegee University in my Junior year, I was doing an internship in Terre Haute, Indiana, at Pfizer Pharmaceutical Company. The Gulf War had just started and even though I was never a very religious person, since we did not grow up in the church, (I always believed when I hear people speak of the Bible and talk about there will be wars and rumors of wars, speaking of the last days.) This was the first war I was living through, and it was awful scary not knowing how this war was going to end, or when it was going to end, and how many people were going to have to die. "Is this the end of the world?" I was asking God. "Is this the way you will end it? Am I ever going to get to know my father?" I decided to try one more time. Not with Ron on the phone, maybe that was too much pressure, just give it one last shot. I called my Uncle Alvin, who was my father's older brother. My relationship with Uncle Alvin remained quite solid over the years, and I was happy about that.

"Listen Uncle, I'm 20 years old, I'm a junior in college. I'm doing an internship and I've made it this far without my father. Clearly, I don't need him. I just wanted to get to know him. Is that too much to ask? The war has started, I don't know if the world is about to end, and I'm just asking this one last time if you can have him call me."

I've had this conversation with Uncle Alvin plenty of times in the past, but this time it was different. This time he said, "Don't you worry about it. I am going to call your father and he *will* be calling you today." He sounded pretty convincing to me. Much more so than the last few times we'd had this conversation. So, I waited by the phone, not too long, maybe 30 to 45 minutes, then my phone rang and guess who it was; Floyd Murrell, my 'alleged' father!

When I answered the phone, he started doing of course, his specialty, which is small talk. He's very good at that because it doesn't require any in depth conversation about anything of any purpose. I couldn't go too long with the small talk because I needed to get to the bottom of it... Let's just face the elephant in the room. Let's just get it out on the table, get down to it, and figure out what we're going to do, if anything. So, I stopped him in the middle of the small talk and I said, "Listen, I need to address what happened almost 10 years ago at the state park at the family reunion. We need to address that."

"O-o-okay," he said, stuttering.

Although my heart was pounding out of my chest, I had a goal in mind, and I did not care how nervous I was, or how nerve wracking it would be. I was focused on what I needed this conversation to do, and where I needed it to go.

"You looked at me and you said that I was not your child. Everybody else says that I am your child. I looked at you and it was like looking into a mirror, but you said I was not your daughter."

"Well, I-I-I didn't know h-h-how to e-explain to an 11-year-old little girl wha-wha-what had really happened."

"Okay, well, I'm not a little girl anymore, so be free to speak your truth."

"Ww-well, my friends t-t-told me that they had run a t-t-t-train on your mama, so I didn't think that yy-you were mine. I ss-s-swear, I just d-i-d-didn't know. I did not know w-w-what to believe because they were all s-s-saying that they all got t-t-t-together that same night and had s-s-sex with your mama and they t-t-took turns, so how could I tell that to a l-l-little girl? How could I t-t-tell that to y-y-ou at that t-t-time? I-I-I'm s-s-sorry. I just didn't know w-w-w-hat I should say."

Of course, I'm shocked! My jaw is hanging down to the ground at this moment. Does he really believe I would believe this bullshit he is feeding me? Did I believe it? I mean, my mother was no saint by any stretch of the imagination, but this is clearly far-fetched, even for him to say about her.

I had to decide if the story he told was even important. Yes, I wanted answers, but did the answers really matter? Was it the explanation I was seeking, or was it a relationship with my father, before the end of the world, that I was seeking?

Okay Tasha, is this a time to get mad, to be upset, to be in your feelings right now, or is this the time to figure out if you are going to have any type of working relationship with this man as your father? Remember, it really is all you have ever wanted.

I took a couple of deep breaths and decided to just let it go. "Okay, I can't change what happened in the past. I was not there, I cannot vouch for it, but what I am asking of you today is, do you want to have some type of friendship, relationship with me now? The world is in turmoil, we're at war. I have no idea how this is going to end, and I just did not want it to end without me giving it at least one last try."

"T-t-that's all I've ever wanted. I-I- j-j-just didn't know h-h-how to a-a-approach it."

He was all for it, of course. I guess the story about his friends running a train on my mama gave him some ease this whole thing is not his fault and he is not to be blamed, so I gave him what he wanted. He didn't want to be blamed, so I didn't blame him. What difference would it have made anyway, it wasn't going to change anything; it's still 20 years after the fact. We cannot make up for lost time, and we will never be able to get that time back. The only thing we could do, in any situation, is keep moving forward.

My father and I sat on the phone that evening and literally talked for hours. It was like finding a new love, having a new boyfriend, the man in my life! The man of my dreams! This is what I have always desired, to have my father in my life. Someone I could count on, depend on, get advice from, and simply call when I needed to talk.

Life didn't get any better than this! Dreams really did come true. God really does answer prayers! I do not believe I have ever felt as special as the moment my father acknowledged me. Just to have that sense of belonging, like he really did want me in his life, and he really wanted to be part of my life. No, this surprise didn't come in a pretty gift box with a bow, maybe this was all he was able to give. That's ok. I will take it. Just to have the opportunity to get to know my father and that part of myself, was amazing! I had the opportunity to have a father, someone I could call Daddy! I'll take it! My first true love had finally arrived! The man I loved from the very beginning. The man I loved on purpose. Yes, I'll take it!

But now, what a relief to be acknowledged by a man you have always loved! What an experience! Unforgettable, significant, undeniably one of the most exciting times of my life! Such a profound turning point! I could not have asked God for more than what he was giving me at this moment. I understand some kids would never have this moment; some would never get to experience what that closure brought to my well-being. We spend the most of our childhood wondering what we could have done wrong, why he did not choose us, questioning who we are and whose we are. I was trying to find where I fit in this world. Even with confidence, still not too sure of who I was, or who I wanted to be. But at the age of 20, God decided to give me closure, and for that, I am forever grateful.

My father and I continued to talk on the phone at least a couple of times a week after he acknowledged me. I was falling deeper and deeper in love with the man I had loved all of my life. I would listen to his stories about growing up, and I would tell him about my experiences growing up. He consistently apologized for not being a part of my life and did not know how rough I had it living with my mother. He's always seemed very sincere and genuine when talking to me. I was finally feeling like my life was complete, like the void in my heart had been filled by my father. I was finally his 'Baby Girl' and he was finally my 'Daddy.'

When I was still doing my internship at Pfizer Pharmaceuticals in 1991, my father invited me to his home in Nashville, TN for a visit. At the time I was dating a guy named Dayo. He was from Nigeria, but had virtually lived in the United States since the age of two. I asked my father if he minded if I brought my boyfriend with me, since it would be my first visit to see him. He did not mind at all, so Dayo and I jumped in the car one weekend and drove down to Nashville. When we arrived, my father was extremely friendly towards Dayo and myself, but he did not hesitate to lay down the house rules.

"W-w-ell, since you all are n-n-not married, you cannot s-s-sleep in the same b-b-bedroom under m-my roof," he explained.

Of course we both understood, so Dayo was escorted to my little brother's bedroom, who only visited every other weekend, and I was escorted to the guest bedroom.

"Not a problem," I replied.

That weekend was a bit weird, but interesting. My father was extremely hospitable to Dayo and me, and life could not get any better! I recall we were watching a movie with him as his wife was out of town that weekend, so I did not meet her until later.

"T-t-asha, you all w-w-want some s-s-strawberry ice c-cream? It's f-fat-free."

"Fat-free? We don't want no fat-free ice cream! You don't have any with sugar in it?" I was still in college and could virtually eat anything I wanted without gaining an ounce.

"Oh n-n-no! We d-do not eat l-like that in t-t-this house. It's a-a-all-natural. It's p-p-pretty good. You s-should t-try it. C-come here."

I went to the kitchen to try this fat-free ice cream. He fed it to me.

"Mmmmm, it is pretty good." I do not really know if the ice cream itself was good, or the fact that my father was feeding it to me made it taste even better! "I think I'll have some after all. Dayo, you want to try it too?"

"Yeah, let me come in the kitchen with you all and get it," Dayo responded.

"Oh, n-no, you d-don't h-have to come in t-the kitchen. Tasha w-w-will bring it to you."

My father stopped Dayo in his tracks.

"Oh, it's no big deal, I can get my own," Dayo replied to my father.

"I s-s-s-said, n-n-no! Do n-not come in the kitchen, T-tasha will b-bring it to you!" My father stated, a little firmer in tone than the first time.

I did not see what the problem was. If Dayo wanted to come into the kitchen to get his own ice cream, then why not let him? What was the big deal about me having to bring the bowl of ice cream to him? This was the 21st century and I was all about being liberated. Besides, Dayo was more prone to fix my plate than I was to fix his!

"Is there a problem?" I asked my father as Dayo hurriedly went back to the living room and took his position on the floor in front of the sofa and continued watching the movie.

"No, n-no problem at all. You sh-sh-should treat your guest like a g-g-guest, that is all," my father replied.

Well technically I was a guest too since this was my first time in his home, but I left that alone.

In the middle of the movie, we had eaten enough ice cream til our hearts were content. I got up, put both my and Dayo's ice cream bowls in the sink, and came back to the living room to finish watching the movie. A few minutes later, my father gets up and heads to the kitchen.

"Uh, uh, T-t-tasha!"

"Yeah?"

"C-come here for a s-second."

I got up and went to the kitchen to see what he wanted.

"Y-y-you left y-y-your d-dishes in the s-s-sink."

"I know I left the dishes in the sink, because we're still watching the movie."

"W-w-well, we don't l-l-leave the dishes in the s-sink in th-th-this house."

"Not even while the movie is still on?"

"N-n-no, once y-you're finished e-e-eating, all d-dishes should be w-washed immedi-ately." He was very matter-of-fact about it.

"Ok, no problem." I was starting to feel like a seven year old.

I tried to stay calm about the situation because I was in *his* house and these are *his* rules, albeit as juvenile as his requests seemed to be. I wanted to respect his wishes. I did not want to ruin my newly found relationship with my father over a few simple misunderstandings or differences of opinion. If he wanted the bowls and spoons washed immediately after eating some ice cream, then so be it. If he wanted the glass cleaned as soon as you were finished drinking a glass of water then that is what it had to be. I was willing to give the relationship time to develop and grow so we could at least get to know one another and have a mutual understanding of each other. It was worth it to me, especially all I went through to make it this far with him.

Later that night when everyone decided to turn in for the evening, my father knocked on the guest bedroom door.

"Come in."

"Hey T-tasha, I just w-w-wanted to ch-check up on you and m-make sure that you d-d-didn't n-need anything before I w-w-ent to b-bed."

"No, I'm fine."

"W-well, I just f-feel like I m-missed out on s-s-s-o many years with you, I-I just kind of wanted to come and s-say goodnight."

"Oh okay, that's sweet. Can I talk to you about something though? I always wanted to be able to have this conversation with you and I always dreamed of the day of being able to talk to you about some things."

"S-sure B-baby Girl. You can t-talk to me about a-a-nything...What i-is it?"

"There was a time when I was so very young, between the ages of 3 and 7 that I needed you in my life more than I needed air to breathe. When my mother was married to James Garner, he molested me during this time of their marriage. I always wished that you would come and save me and take me out of that house, out of that environment. I *needed* to be rescued. I *needed* you to rescue me. But for whatever reason, you were not there to save me."

My father looked rather perplexed and embarrassed.

"I'm so s-sorry that m-man did t-this to you. I'm s-s-so sorry I was not there to p-protect you like I s-should have been. I would n-never forgive myself for not s-s-showing up in your life until n-now. I hope that you w-will forgive me and give me a ch-chance to make it up to you. I know I-I-I cannot go back and change what h-happened in the p-past, but I am s-s-so sorry B-baby Girl. I r-really am.

His eyes began to tear up.

"D-did he actually p-penetrate you? D-did he f-force you to have s-sexual i-intercourse w-with him?"

"No, but he forcibly had oral sex with me and he threatened to kill my mother if I should breathe a word of it."

"Oh o-ok g-good. A-at least he d-d-didn't have s-sexual i-intercourse w-with you."

"It doesn't matter, it's still considered molestation!"

"Oh, I-I didn't k-k-know, I t-thought he would have h-h-had to have i-i-ntercourse w-with you."

"The fact of the matter is, I was violated by my stepfather as a young child and had no father to protect me!"

Silence. I felt his energy shift. The room stood still for several minutes before he spoke again.

"W-well, once again I'm sorry that I was not there for you and I just hope that you can f-f-orgive me for not being there."

"Well, the good part is, I made it through. I got through it. And now we are both here together in each other's lives, and that's all that really matters to me at this point. I forgive you, Daddy."

We hugged, he kissed me on the cheek and we said our goodnights. I felt like I had been waiting to have that conversation with my father my whole life!

After I completed my internship at Pfizer Pharmaceuticals at the end of May, I returned to Tuskegee University for summer school. Within a month, my father volunteered to come visit me for the weekend! Of course, I was happy to oblige! He flew into the Montgomery Airport and I picked him up and we drove to Tuskegee to tour the campus. We had a fabulous time touring the George Washington Carver Museum, and the Booker

T. Washington House. At that time my roommate was my chemical engineering 'play' Big Brother, Anthony Deanes. I did not have a place to live that summer and Anthony already was renting a house, so he offered me the second bedroom and I paid half the rent. My father seemed very concerned I would be living with a man at 20 years old.

"Anthony and I are just friends! He's like a real big brother to me!"

"W-w-well well, I'm just ch-checking up on m-my Baby Girl just to make sure that n-n-nothing is going on."

"Oh, Daddy don't be ridiculous! Anthony is very trustworthy and plus, he has not tried anything with me since I've been here."

"I'm j-j-just saying, Baby Girl. You- you- you y-y-ou just have to w-watch out for these t-t-types of things. E-especially when d-d-dealing with men. Trust me, I-I know first-hand how these m-m-men are out here b-because when I was y-younger, I used to b-b-be just like them."

Ahhh, isn't that cute! Look at my father, trying to be a Dad and all. It was the cutest thing ever! Being a little overprotective was a father's job, in my opinion, so I dare not buck what he was trying to implement as a father. He had even given Anthony the side-eye a couple of times. Just to let him know, 'I got my eye on you, buddy! Don't you even think about crossing the line with my daughter!'

"I s-sure wish I had b-been involved in y-your l-life, Baby Girl. I have m-m-missed out on s-so much! But I am just so h-happy that you g-g-gave me a ch-chance to be a p-part of your life now. L-look at you! A j-junior in college getting your c-c-chemical engineering degree! And you did it v-virtually all by yourself. You are s-s-strong, you are r-resilient, and I am so v-very proud of you!"

He held his arms out towards me and enveloped me in his arms as I cried on his chest with an exhale.

"I-i-is something the matter?"

"Nothing at all. I have literally been waiting for you to say those words to me all my life!"

"W-w-well, I am proud. And m-m-moreso, I am just glad that we found our way to each other. I-I-I pr-promise you; I am not going anywhere. I-I-will be here f-f-for you, w-w-when-e-ever you n-need me."

I was finally in the arms of the man I loved with all my heart, and all my soul. He was finally embracing the love I have always had for him. I was finally in a safe place. My protector is here now, and that's all that mattered to me. We would spend the rest of our days making up for lost time and getting to know one another.

I was in such a happy place at this time. Everything I had hoped for and dreamed of was coming to pass. Now I have my father in my life! Physically, mentally, and emotionally. I have finally been made whole! He finally said those lingering words that I have been holding onto for dear life; "I am so very proud of you, Baby Girl," and "I'm here for you."

My father and I literally resembled a Kodak picture. Everywhere we went together people thought we were brother and sister. First, because we looked just alike. Secondly, my father looked very good for his age and furthermore, he was only 18 years older than me. He was in the best shape I've ever seen a man, and looked like a combination of a strong stallion and Prince Charming.

My father was very much into physical fitness and healthy living. Going to the gym five to six times a week was definitely his forte. Even when he had visited me at Tuskegee, he made sure he got a hotel in Montgomery that had a fitness center as this was a requirement in order for him to stay there. I was growing more and more in love with the father I was experiencing and not just the figment of my imagination. However, the pedestal was already built and it was a high one if I may say so myself. My father sat on that pedestal as if he belonged there; he knew exactly how to operate from that throne. This was his domain, where he was most comfortable, and where he was accustomed to being.

Although my father was just becoming a part of my life, I always felt like he could do no wrong. He seemed so innocent and docile on one hand, and impetuous and presumptive on the other hand. As time went on, the latter traits began to grow more and more. I did not care, and was not going to let these minor mishaps intrude on my newly found relationship with him.

About a month later my father invited me to come to Nashville to visit him and his wife, Lois. They had only been married about three years at this point. I was very excited to become a part of his overall family. I drove my car from Tuskegee to Nashville, and when I got there my father was waiting at the door for me. He opened the door and gave me the biggest hug, as if he was so happy to see me. He introduced me to his wife, Lois. "Th-thi-this is Tasha, my m-my daughter."

After her initial hesitation, she said, "Hi Tasha! Welcome to our home!" She gave me a warm hug. "Come on in! I will walk you upstairs to your room!" Somehow it didn't seem like Lois knew that I had been there before.

My father grabbed my suitcase and we followed Lois upstairs to the guest bedroom. Lois was extremely friendly and wore a huge smile. She always seemed to be happy, and was always laughing and giggling about something.

They lived in a very nice 2-story brick house, and both drove nice cars. My father was now the Assistant District Chief of the Nashville Fire Department, and Lois was a top salesperson at Mary Kay. As a matter of fact, Lois had sold enough Mary Kay to earn the Pink Cadillac!

Lois wore her hair really curly and her makeup was always flawless. She was a full-figured, yet shapely woman with a very friendly demeanor. They made a good couple aesthetically, and as I began to watch them together; they were always joking with one another. Looks like they had a good life! And I was just happy to be a small part of it.

That weekend my father cooked every meal, he did all the laundry, he took the cars to be detailed and oil changed, he mowed the lawn and cut the roses from the rose bushes, hung pictures on the wall, and made the beds! It looks like my father was doing everything, and Lois was not doing much of nothing!

I had not seen anything like the dynamics of their relationship before. Although I found it strange, I dare not say a word as I did not have enough experience to know what a man would or should do in a household, and what would be the woman's responsibilities. I naturally would sit and observe people to study the relationship's dynamics. The only example I had before this one was my Grandparents, and my Aunt and Uncle. My mother's relationships were off-limits as they were all toxic anyway. My grandparents shared all the responsibilities of the household and outside of the household. I've literally never in my entire life seen a man who did everything. He worked, he cooked, he cleaned... everything! I almost felt like she was using him in the beginning, but hey, who was I to judge?

My father would always tell me how he paid for everything for Lois. He paid for her to get her hair done, paid for her to get her nails done, paid all the bills, and bought her diamonds and furs. I thought Lois had it better than any woman on the face of the Earth being married to my father. So basically, she could do whatever she wanted to do with her money. That must have been 'The Life!'

I was just happy to finally be a part of this life! Everything I had ever dreamed of about my father had come to pass. There was no stone left unturned. He was attentive, considerate, consistent, genuine, and very humbled based on what he had experienced. He could be a tad bit overbearing at times, but hey, nobody is perfect.

After I returned to Tuskegee from my weekend visit in Nashville, my father sent me some money in the mail. I was pleasantly surprised to receive a letter from him in the mail along with three $100 bills. Cool! That can help me pay for my books this semester. I did not think twice about why he would be sending cash through the mail, since most people wrote checks back then as anybody could steal the cash. Nevertheless, I did not complain, at least he was sending me something that could help out with the semester expenses. I was just so grateful for that!

Things were going super well for my father and me. Our relationship was growing into a friendship, and finally, the father-daughter relationship I always dreamed of. I did, however, notice some things starting to take a turn. Perhaps I had begun to see these signs from the start. Perhaps I was just so enthusiastic about the possibility of this 'perfect man,' I did not want to give attention to anything that could possibly taint the idea of this person in my head. Like any new relationship, it takes a while for a person to show his true self. No one can consistently be someone they are not. If given time, you will see the red flags of a person who may have, let's say, split personalities. The next turn of events would prove this theory to be correct. After the honeymoon phase was over, reality began to set in!

Chapter 15

THE HONEYMOON IS OVER

My father wanted me to come to Nashville for a visit on another weekend. I informed him I did not have any money for gas, and I was not sure that my car could make it there since it needed to be serviced. He told me if I could possibly make it, he would check the engine and do an oil change for me, put gas in my car, plus give me money to get back to school. I figured out a way to get there and was depending on him to take care of the rest.

After arriving in Nashville, everything was as it had been on my previous visits. My father worked as a Paramedic at the Fire Department, so he typically worked 24 hours on, and 48 hours off. The day I arrived in Nashville he was working the 24 hours on. Although he was at the house when I arrived, he would be leaving soon.

As a college student, the first thing on my mind was, "I'm hungry, what do you have to eat?"

When I went to look in their refrigerator there was nothing but lettuce, frozen yogurt, and some other stuff a college student was not interested in. I was like, "Do ya'll ever have any regular food in your refrigerator?"

My father replied, "W-w-we don't eat u-unhealthy foods in o-o-ur house, so if you want s-s-something else to eat y-y-ou would have to b-b-uy it yourself."

Now what was with the hint of an attitude? I wasn't going to say anything at first since I noticed he was clearly not in a good mood. I should have just kept my comments to myself. Then afterwards I said, "Can't we order a pizza or something?"

My father replied, as in a spirit of disdain, "Huh, i-i-if you want to e-e-eat pizza, you will need to buy it w-w-with your own m-m-money."

"Now you know I don't have any money, because I told you that before I got here."

"W-w-ell, Lois d-d-on't have no b-b-b-usiness eating no p-pizza. Huh, a-a-as long as it took me t-t-to help her get all that fat o-off off her thighs!"

Clearly, I was not helping the situation, so I had better leave it alone.

After my father left to go to work, Lois and I were sitting in the kitchen talking about college, about boys, and she also told me stories from when she was in college. I really did like Lois and considered her a friend. She never shared anything about her and my dad's relationship, so we were maybe on a level 1 friendship. She also never made a comment about my father's snide remark about her weight loss. I was not about to stir the pot on that subject matter.

"So, do you really want to order a pizza?" Lois asked me after my father left the house to go back to the fire hall. Lois was a little sneaky, I see...I like!

"Yeah, but Daddy said you couldn't have pizza and told me I had to buy it with my own money if I wanted it."

"Oh, girl, don't worry about him, he's gone to work anyway!"

"Ok, I'm down!"

"Alright, but first I need to go to the ATM to get some cash and then we will pick up the pizza on the way back home. Your Daddy didn't give me my allowance this week."

Wait, allowance? Ok how does a full grown-ass woman with a job that pays more than my father's job, have to wait on an allowance from her husband? Well, I guess whatever works for them.

"How much does he give you for your allowance?" Now I was just being messy, but I was also curious about the dynamics of their relationship.

"$20/week," she replied.

Well, I for damn sure was not going to college just so my husband could pinch me off $20 a week for an allowance. That is insane!

"Ok, let's get out of here before he decides to come back," Lois was rushing.

Lois and I rode into town and stopped at her bank to withdraw funds from the ATM. I do not know if she had a separate account that he knew about, but all I know is I was becoming more and more famished by the minute. We returned to the house and were having a good ole fashioned girlfriend's talk while gobbling down that delicious pizza, and then my father walked into the house.

"Uh oh!" Lois exclaimed, "Busted!"

"Hey, Daddy, did you forget something?" I said looking straight at him while taking another bite of that delicious pizza. I thought it was so funny that he walked in right in the middle of our bites! I cracked up laughing!

My father just stood there, angry, sour-faced, and dismissive. I did not see what the big deal was. We were busted! But oh well. Nobody died! I didn't see the big deal at all. My father turned around and walked out in silence. Lois and I continued sharing our funny college stories until it was time for bed. Although I did not sleep too well, as I kept hearing these noises and bumps against the walls, perhaps I was just dreaming.

The next morning, I got up around 7am, which is very early for a college student, unless we have an 8am class. I walked downstairs and found my father in the kitchen hanging window treatments.

"Morning, Daddy," I said. He did not turn to look at me, so I figured he did not hear me. "Morning, Daddy," I reiterated a little louder this time. It seemed like he was deliberately ignoring me the first time.

He then turned around and said, "Y-your breakfast i-i-is on the t-t-table." Then he went back to hanging the curtains.

Ok, so I guess he's not going to say good morning. After I finished the salmon omelet and sugar-free orange juice, I went to the living room where Lois was sitting watching TV and drinking a cup of coffee. She still had on her robe, but with a face full of makeup.

"Hey Lois, good morning."

"Good morning," she responded.

"What's wrong with your husband? Is he not speaking?"

"Oh, he always does that, you'll get used to it."

"Oh no I won't, because I don't have to live here."

"Well, I don't pay him no mind. He does that all the time."

"But why?"

"Because we went against his will and ate that pizza last night."

"Girl, shut up! Are you serious?" Lois was more like a girlfriend than a stepmom, as her age was right in the middle of mine and my father's.

"Serious as a heart attack!"

"Oh my God! How do you deal with all that bad attitude?"

"Well, he's not as bad as my first husband. He was just mean and abusive for no reason and never did anything for me. Never bought me anything and never helped out around the house. At least Floyd will buy me things and do things around the house. This marriage is way better than the last one."

Lois' thoughts and feelings regarding her marriage stayed with me for many years to come. Although Lois said her situation with my father was not as bad as her previous marriage, how bad was it? Was my father abusive to her as well, but would buy her gifts and do things around the house to make up for his 'misbehavior?' Was the bumping against the wall and noises heard in the middle of the night not just a dream I thought I was having? Was this the same bumping I would hear in the middle of the night when growing up with my mother and her exes? Why did Lois wake up with a full face of makeup? I know she did not sleep in that makeup as she was always telling me about the importance of cleansing my face at night to keep the skin smooth and clear.

None of this was adding up to me, but we were always taught to stay out of 'grown folks' business. So be it!

On Sunday morning, I was ready to leave to head back to Tuskegee University. My father had not spoken two words to me since the Friday night 'pizza' debacle and the few words mentioned Saturday morning.

I had to bring my suitcase downstairs, which normally he would have done for me. When I got outside I saw him under the hood of my 1984 Mazda GLC. Great! At least he is taking care of the car. Maybe he is in a better mood today.

"Hey Daddy, did you get a chance to change the oil and get the engine checked?"

"I-I-I added a-a-a quart of oil."

"Oh ok, but I thought you said you would *change* the oil?" I was known for holding people to their word, even when they didn't like it. Silence. Not a word from him. "Well did you at least put gas in the car like you said you would?"

He reached in his pocket and pulled out a $10 bill. "Th-th-this is all I h-h-have."

I looked at him and started to boil! He knew I did not have money to get here and get back to school! He knew I was having issues with the car engine and oil. He did not get the engine checked, he did not change the oil like he said he would, but just added a quart of oil. I was very clear in stating this, and he assured me that he would take care of the car before I put it back on the road. He was to fill up the gas tank, plus give me money for gas so I could get back to school. But no! He hands me a fuckin' $10 bill and says this is all he has!

I stared at the bill for the longest time going over everything in my mind as to how we got here and more importantly, how I was going to get back to school on $10! I figured I had better go ahead and accept this $10 and pray that Jesus would multiply it like he did the five loaves of bread and two fish!

As I reached for the $10 bill, my father let it fall to the ground instead of handing it to me. Initially I thought, ok, maybe it slipped out of his hand by mistake, because why would he intentionally let it fall to the ground? As I waited a few seconds to see if he was going to pick it up and he did not budge, I knew for sure this was not an accident. This mothafucka was deliberately putting me in a position to beg for his help, to ask him for forgiveness for going against his will and eating pizza with Lois. He wanted to see me grovel, down on my knees, crying, in need of his help. But me, being the black woman I am, I began to talk to myself, the same as in the park that day, "Don't you dare shed a tear! Where is that poker face, Tasha? Do not give him the satisfaction of seeing you hurt by him. He is NOT worth it!"

I finally bent down to pick up the fallen $10 bill, looked at him with a smirk on my face, shook my head, turned, then walked to my car without ne'er a word! I backed out of the driveway, turned the first corner, got to the next stop light, and pulled over to the side of the road. By this time, I was bawling my eyes out for about 20 minutes, having not a clue as to how I was going to make it back to school to Tuskegee on $10.

How could my own father do this to me? He didn't care if I made it back to school or not. If I was stranded on the highway or not. He did not give a shit about me! He was merely doing what he did best. Pretending. He was a pretender. A phony. A fake. Always wearing a mask. Showing himself to be one person, when he is really someone totally different! Hadn't he already done enough damage? Hadn't he already caused enough heartache and pain? And all this over some pizza??? Unbelievable!

After I got control of myself, took the knife out of my back; I then began to pray. "God, what am I going to do? Who do I know that can help me get back to Tuskegee? My roommate was in Atlanta for the weekend and for sure wouldn't be back until late. This was 1992, so there were no cell phones where I could call or text for assistance. If I were to run out of gas, I would have to walk to the nearest gas station and use a pay phone to call 911, but then again, I would not have any money to get the car towed!

I began to think about my grandfather, Lil Daddy. Lil' Daddy had passed away when I was in the sixth grade, but he was the father, the teacher, and the protector. He would have never treated me as such! There will never be another like him. Lil' Daddy also taught me a lot of things for safety purposes; he taught me to be prepared for life. We would do things he told us to do, but then would forget all about it if there was never an emergency or problem such as this.

"Always keep cash in different places in the car in the event something happens when you are on the road," I remember him telling me. I did not even have a license back then and was not even old enough to drive!

I quickly checked the glove compartment and found a $10 bill there! I checked the middle console and found a $5 bill there; then checked under the mat and found another $5 bill. In my sun visor was a $20 bill hiding behind a couple of credit card bills! Thank God, I had enough money to get back to school! Hallelujah!

The funny thing is, I don't remember when I put this money in these different compartments in my car, or even IF I did this. All I know is, the money was there when I needed it and I was able to get back to my safe place, which was Tuskegee University. It will be a cold day in hell before I come to visit Floyd's ass again! What a mess!

On the ride home to Tuskegee, I was simply exhausted at the turn of events. I had never seen this side of my father before, although I had only known him for a measly year. They say you never know someone until you *know* someone. Everyone is the ideal person until they are not. No one can consistently be someone they are not.

In my mind, my father was the epitome of fatherhood. I had him up on a pedestal, a throne, if you will. Not because he qualified in any way, or had proven himself in any way, but simply because he was my father. I did not have to know anything about him. I did not have to make sure he lived the life he preached about. It was just pure unconditional, unadulterated, love, and admiration.

Once I began to experience the man he truly was by his actions, not just actions towards me, but towards other people, I had to make some decisions for my life. My first decision would be to never depend on him again. Fool me once, shame on you. Fool me twice, shame on me. My Grandmama did not raise no fools!

Secondly, I will never put another person, man, or woman, higher than God! My father never belonged on the pedestal I put him on. He never deserved that! Being a child, I did not know this until my personal experience with it. God is my source, my beginning, my end, and everything in between. When man does not come through, God shows up. Trusting in God was a necessity, while trusting in man could be a casualty. I constantly reminded myself, when a person shows you who they really are, believe them. While giving people the benefit of the doubt, do not give them too much credit as they are prone to disappoint you. If you are disappointed by people, that means your expectations are too high. You are the only person you can control. Remember that!

That's it, my expectations of my father were far too high! Especially for a father whom I did not grow up with. How would I know who he really was and what his core values were? I would not. I had no clue. How would I know if he had integrity or good character? I did not. This experience was such an eye opener for me. If I were to make-believe I had a father who was perfect in my eyes, and who could do no wrong; I was still living in my head, as when I was a child. I am not a child anymore. There is no more pretending who I think he is since I now know him and have had my own experiences with him. I had to grow up very quickly and get this fairy tale love out of my head, because the honeymoon was over, and reality was the real factor!

Chapter 16

THE WEDDING

It was the spring of 1993 at Tuskegee University, Probability Statistics class. I walked in with my roommate, Wendy, and noticed a guy I had not seen on campus before. He was tall, dark, and handsome, and sat towards the front of the class.

"Who is that?" I asked my roommate.

"I don't know, you like him?" she replied.

"I think he's fine," snickering as a shy college girl would.

"I guess, if you say so...but he looks a little corny to me." Wendy was always putting in her two cents, that's for sure. Wendy was from Plant City, FL, a small town outside of Tampa. She was not afraid to wear her cut-up booty shorts, halter tops with her flat stomach out, and was so not afraid to speak her mind.

There was something that stood out about this guy, in my opinion. Corny was right up my alley, in a sense. I was only interested in a guy who was smart and intelligent. This would at least give me someone I could grow with in life. Rarely would I be attracted to the guy who had 'game.' That guy was only good for playing around with, not for being serious with, hence the term, 'game.' I knew I needed someone I could work with, and who had something to offer. I was only willing to put forth my energy into dating guys who could actually provide a stable future. Yes, I was bougie like that!

"You want me to get his number for you?" Wendy asked.

"Girl, no! You better not ask him for his number!"

"You know I'll do it." By this time, Wendy was already halfway out of her seat. "Hey! Hey you! What's your name?" She was adamant about getting his attention.

The guy turned around and looked our way, "Charles, the name is Charles," he said with a slight smile on his face. His voice was full, deep, and calm. Sexxy, I thought.

"My roommate wants to know your number. Can you give it to her please?"

Here we go!

Charles writes his number on a sheet of paper and Wendy goes to his desk to get it while I'm sitting there as embarrassed as I could possibly be. Wendy was not scared of anything or anybody, and whatever she wanted to do she did. I, on the other hand, lived by much more strict laws for myself. I called them standards, oh, but maybe they were just laws. Nonetheless, now I had the guy's number and had to decide if I was going to use it or not.

I waited a couple of days to use the number simply because of how I had obtained it. Will he ask me why my roommate did such a thing? Did she embarrass him enough to where he did not want to talk to me? I do not know, but I took a couple of days to try to come up with some answers in the event he asked, before I decided to call him, since I was going to have to see him in class every Tuesday and Thursday anyway.

I called Charles just to see what his conversation would be like, and was greatly disappointed! He was talking about the weather, and other things that did not matter to me, or most people in the world. I figured this may have been a waste of time because I really did not see this going anywhere. Wendy called it from the start, he *was* corny!

A few days later, Charles called me and we had our second conversation that went much better than the first, to my surprise. We shared information about our families, our journey to Tuskegee, and other facts of life. I could still sense a glimpse of corniness, but the personality of this person started to shine through a little brighter. You should never judge a book by its cover, until you've had a chance to read through at least some of the pages.

I found out Charles was considerably older than me, and of course had much more experience. I would not say it was a negative at the time for me. There was something about an older gentleman that meant he was more mentally stable, in my opinion. I was 22 years old and Charles was 30 years old. He left college to pursue a career with a band that traveled all over Africa, then decided to come back and finish his electrical engineering degree. He also told me he had a three-year-old son who lived in Tuskegee with the 'Baby Mama.' I found out I knew who the mom was, as we both attended Shady Grove Missionary Baptist Church. That could have been a deal-breaker, but there was something about him I was attracted to, and I was willing to see where it would go from here. Although I have always said I would never date a guy who had children, clearly, I learned through life's experiences you never know what you will do until you find yourself in that situation.

After about six months of dating, we both ended up interviewing for the same company and getting jobs at Westinghouse in Richland, Washington, after graduation. Truthfully, Charles had gotten a job offer at Westinghouse first. He then spoke to the hiring Human Resources Manager about interviewing me. I interviewed with them and was also offered a job. We would move to the State of Washington come December 1993. I was so excited to begin this next chapter of my life; entering into true adulthood where it included an actual paycheck!

Charles found his apartment first, and by the time I came to Washington, I found an apartment I would share with a roommate named Samantha. We only had this set up for a couple of months before Charles asked me to move in with him. At this time, I did not know what other things I should have considered, so I went along with it. Of course, I was not the type of woman to be 'shackin' up' with somebody, but here I am! Charles and I lived together for about three months prior to getting engaged.

We had gone to look at engagement rings together one day, then he went back to get the ring to propose. We had dinner one night at Red Lobster, which at one time was a hot dinner spot! He got down on one knee and asked me to marry him. I am not sure I was excited to be married, but I was excited because I guess it was the next thing to do in life. All the professional black women I knew who were married, suggested this is the next step in my journey. Was I ever ready to get married? Did I even know what that should look like? There are so many questions that I never answered for myself, or never had inquired about prior to this moment. One thing I knew about myself was if I were to commit to it, then I would stick to it and see it through. Marriage would be no different for me than anything else. Even if it were not the right decision for my life, I was in it to win it. I could make it work just like I had made everything else in my life work. Perfection does not show up on its own, it's molded into a masterpiece.

Charles and I knew this couple who had gotten married in Las Vegas. They were showing us their wedding pictures and talking to us about the price of the wedding which sounded good to us. Because of this, we decided we would get married in Las Vegas, too. However, Charles' mother refused to come to the wedding if it was going to be in Vegas.

She was adamant about the fact she did not want her son getting married in such a sinful place.

"Oh no! I am sorry, Chuck, if you are getting married in a sinful place like Las Vegas, I will not be there!" Charles' mother told him.

Okay, that meant getting married in Vegas was out of the question. We then decided to get married in Kankakee, Illinois, my hometown. This is where we were having our Murrell Family Reunion anyway, so everyone will already be there and most of my family lived there. That way Charles' mom and sister could fly to Illinois from Baltimore, MD for the wedding. His mom was okay with this arrangement. Regardless, all the same stuff happening in Vegas, would be happening at this family reunion/wedding!

I had recently become acquainted with my father two years or so prior to this, and was excited about the possibility of him walking me down the aisle. Although our relationship had its challenges, he would still call me from time to time, but we never talked about the $10 bill he gave me that day to get back to college...How he never even checked on me to see if I made it back to school is beyond me.

Months later, he just started calling pretending like nothing ever happened and picked up where we left off. I realized our relationship had stipulations on it and I just left it at that. He did come to my college graduation though, flaunting and popping his collar as if he had anything to do with me achieving my Chemical Engineering degree. Hmmmph! I digress.

A girl's biggest dream in life is to have her father walk her down the aisle. It's what every girl dreams, right? When I asked my father to do the honors on July 2, 1994, his first response was he didn't know if he could get off work. Work!?!? Who can't get off work for their daughter's wedding? Especially the daughter he had absolutely nothing to do with until she was 20 years old! I thought he and I were gaining some traction on bonding at this point. He worked as a Paramedic. As a matter of fact, at this time he was the Assistant District Chief Paramedic. Why wouldn't the Assistant District Chief Paramedic be able to take off work for his daughter's wedding? My disappointment in him ran so deep, but as usual life had groomed me to bounce back in the face of adversities. So, I chalked it up as, 'it is what it is,' 'let me keep it moving'. I requested my Uncle Alvin, who was one of my father's older brothers and my older brother Lewis, to both walk me down the aisle. I have always believed in a back-up plan. Plan A, B, and at least C. I rented their tuxedos. They made it to the wedding rehearsal as they were supposed to, and we knew exactly how this was going to go on the day of the wedding. To my surprise, on my wedding day, my father shows up, tux and all, ready to walk me down the aisle!

When the wedding planner, Mrs. Turner, came to tell me my father was here, I was about to get upset. How does he come to my wedding and not even say that he's coming? Did he just find out he did not have to work and decided to come? Was it some kind of ploy to control me like he had done to me in the past, like he does to everyone else in his life?

"Take a deep breath, Tasha," said the wedding planner. "I've already worked everything out with your father, your uncle, and your brother. Everybody is okay with letting your father walk you down the aisle, which is what you wanted from the start, right? No worries, everything has been taken care of." Mrs. Turner was my best friend's mom and always the voice of reason.

"Deep breaths indeed," I would tell myself to stay calm. "This is my wedding! Nobody is going to mess it up! Not even my father!"

I was trying my best not to let Bridezilla show up, but she was well on her way! Again, put on that poker face and let's get this show on the roll!

This was just like my father, to show up at the last minute after all the adjustments and improvisions had been made to deal with his absence, then not say anything about it ahead of time. He knew he was able to get off work, it did not just happen that morning. He had to get a plane ticket, rental car, etc., yet no one even knew he was in town for the wedding, then he just shows his ass up! That nigga!

I met my father down the aisle as he walked me to meet my groom. I had my two best friends from high school, Rolanda and Loreal, as my maid of honor and bridesmaid, my college roommate, Wendy, and my favorite Sorority Sister, Kim were bridesmaids, also. My maid of honor sang with the best man, Chris, who was Charles' best friend. Charles also serenaded me with a song he wrote. He was very adamant about singing this song on our wedding day. I honestly do not know why because he could not sing at all! But since he could play the piano, it was not so bad. It would be like Kirk Franklin, he really cannot sing, but he sure can play! Sometimes you compromise just to keep the peace, and that's pretty much what I did.

I knew I loved Charles for what I knew love to be at that time in my life. At 23 years old, how much do you really know about yourself? Love is a notion we dream up, however, the experience of love changes over time. Love means different things to different people. The only standards I knew to have at that time was that he was not abusive, I was physically attracted to him, he was educated, and talented. Those were my standards in dating, and ultimately in marriage. There is no way that I would have known anything more at this age. I knew what I knew, and what I didn't know would be learned through life's experiences.

I wanted Pastor Vince Clark to do our nuptials because I knew him. I dated his younger brother, Fred Clark, in high school. Since I did not grow up in the church, I had to choose where we would get married. My Auntie Yvonne, who was a member of Morning Star Missionary Baptist Church, suggested this as the location. Since Vince Clark was an associate Pastor there, I was excited to know someone who would be involved with my wedding. Vince Clark was more than happy to preside over the nuptials, however, the senior pastor, Pastor William Copeland, decided he was going to do the nuptials at the last minute. I have no idea for the life of me, why he would want to do the nuptials because he did not know me at all. Nevertheless, during the wedding ceremony William Copeland continued to call me by the wrong name, Natalie, instead of Natasha. Every time he would call me Natalie, Charles would correct him.

"It's Natasha!"

I understand Natalie is the root name for Natasha, but if you are reading from your notes, why do you continue to call me by the incorrect name on my fuckin' wedding day? It must have been three or four times he said the wrong name! Talk about embarrassing! This must be a sign! Was God trying to tell me something? The entire time I was standing up there getting ready to repeat my vowels, I kept thinking, "I hope to God Fred Clark walks through those doors and stops this wedding!"

Unfortunately, Fred Clark did not bust up the wedding as I had imagined he would. As Pastor Copeland continued to mispronounce my name and Charles continued to correct him, I was daydreaming of the episode of A Different World when Whitley was supposed to marry Byron, who had just become the State Senator, and Dwayne Wayne stood up and crashed the wedding when the pastor stated, "if anyone objects, let him speak now or forever hold his peace." And of course, Dwayne and Whitley were married instead! Yes, I really was hoping that would happen on my wedding day, but it did not. Damn! I do, I did, I'm done! Damn! Too late to turn back now.

There was some part of me that knew I was not ready to be married to this man, or any man for that matter. How could I have been? Ready to embark on a journey with a man when I did not even fully know myself yet? Your twenties are a time of discovery, a time to experience different things and different people, so one day you will know what it is you like and what it is you do not like. I did not have the luxury at that moment, on my wedding day, to do things differently. It was too late; I had already committed to it and I did not go back on my commitments. Fred Clark did not stop the wedding that day, the minister continued to call me by the wrong name. And now I'm married? I guess I'm happy? Except at 23, I wasn't even sure what happiness was for me.

We spent our honeymoon at the Sybaris Resort in Frankfort, Il, which is north of Kankakee. It was gorgeous! It is in a residential area, but the inside of the suite has full-blown indoor pools, jacuzzi tubs, and all the perks that can come in a room. It was posh with rose petals, champagne, big screen TVs, and delicatessens. We decided to go to the pool after the wedding reception and Charles was planning to teach me to swim. I had a bad experience at the YMCA when I was in junior high school, where two guys tried to dunk me and I thought I was going to drown. I came up fighting mad! Needless to say, I am fearful of the water! Knowing this, Charles suggested he could be the one to teach me to swim. He did not get anywhere with that because I did not trust he was not going to let me drown. This is another indication I was not ready to be married, that I had bitten off quite more than I could chew. Like I said, I am in it now, I chose it. I'll stick it out. I'll find my happiness. Somehow.

Things are always much clearer looking back, than projecting forward, hence the saying, "hindsight is 20/20." There were plenty of red flags about Charles I should have paid closer attention to had I known any better. For instance, his lackadaisical attitude, his lack of communication, his nonchalant behavior regarding important things such as finances. He did love God and that was a plus because I was just coming 'into the fold' when we met. He was educated, had a promising career as an IT/Computer Engineer, so I think I chose reasonably well under the circumstances.

We only lived in the State of Washington for two years as there were just not enough black people for us. We both interviewed for jobs to take us back to the East Coast. I say 'back to the East Coast' because Charles was from Baltimore, MD. Although I was from the Midwest, I definitely wasn't too keen on moving back there. One thing is for sure; I will travel! Charles ended up getting a job interview with Lowe's Hardware as an IT Consultant. That was great! We would take the Voluntary Reduction of Force from Westinghouse and get paid to move back to civilization. I had an opportunity to fly back with him for the interview, then a second time after he received the job offer so we could look for housing.

The first year we were in Winston-Salem, I found out after we filed taxes, married filing jointly, that Charles was behind on his child support. How I found out was they took our tax refund and said it was due to back child support. At this point we had been married for two years and we both worked very stable engineering jobs. Now why are you owing back child support?? This was the first sign of him being fiscally irresponsible. You know you have a child; you know you must pay child support, you are working a stable job, not just a college student. So why are you behind on your child support again? It did not matter how many times I asked him this question, he would never give a real answer. I guess even if he had given a real answer, the answer would have never been good enough. Your child is in need of things every day, every month, every year. You're making money as an engineer, and refuse to pay what's due? I just don't get it!

As the wife, I had to come in and try to make things right. That was my job. At least that is what I believed my job to be. To fix what's broken. To mend the rips in this type of idiotic thinking, in order to make things right. I suggested to Charles that we set up the $485 child support payment to come directly from our checking account every month. This way it will never be late and there are no surprises. Although $485/month was a lot of money in the mid 1990's, it had to be done! He never gave me a hard time about it; he never gave me a hard time about most things. As long as he didn't have to be the one to actually do the work, he was okay with it. This is pretty much how we lived out most of our marriage. If he didn't have to be involved, he was okay with it. For now, I was ok with it too.

Chapter 17

CHURCH-BOUND

S hortly after moving to Winston Salem, we joined Cleveland Avenue Christian Church. Since Charles was a musician, i.e., piano player, organ player, keyboardist, we were always close to the Pastor and First Lady of any church we attended. No church is anything unless they have a good musician. Historically speaking, he who brings the music, brings the singers out, brings out the Praise and Worship, brings in the tithes. At least that is the way it is presumed to be in the African American churches. Music is next to holiness. Every church wanted a good musician!

I enjoyed attending Cleveland Avenue Christian Church. They were a young Pastor and First Lady, maybe Charles' age, Pastor Sheldon and Joyce McCarter. We would have Sunday dinners at their house often, and sometimes visit out-of-town churches with them. We deemed them to be friends of ours. The church was growing by leaps and bounds when we joined, and we believed God had sent us there to be a blessing and it also blessed us! It was exciting to see what God was doing. I sang in the choir and Charles played for the choir. I also volunteered by teaching the Teen's Praise dance.

There was a lady by the name of Lisa who I befriended at the church. She was quiet, pretty much to herself, and a nurse at Baptist Hospital. Lisa and I did not live too far apart, maybe a few miles, and we would go for walks around the track for exercise after she got off work. At this time, I was not working after we relocated for Charles's job. The job was paying much more than Westinghouse, so we did not necessarily need the money. Lisa and I became very good friends over the course of about three to four months.

One day I called Lisa at work even though I felt God was telling me she was not at work on this particular day. I thought it was strange I would know that information because

I know Lisa never misses days from work. So, I called her job anyway, just to get the confirmation she was not at work that day. Back then, in the 90's, we didn't call people on their cell phones to use up their cell phone minutes. We would call their work or home phones first to see if they were there prior to calling their cell. I then called Lisa on her cell phone and she answered. As I began to tell her the funny story about how I knew she was not at work, there was silence on the other line. And then crying.

"Lisa? Lisa, are you there? Is everything okay?" I said, feeling a little nervous at this point. Lisa managed to muster up a response.

"I'm okay. I'm okay. I'm at the top of Pilot Mountain and I was contemplating driving my car over the cliff. I wanted to kill myself, Tasha!" now bursting into tears.

"Wait, What! Driving your car over the cliff? What is going on with you?" I questioned.

"Yes," she was now gaining some composure, "but then I heard the Holy Spirit say if you drive your car off this cliff, you will not die, but you will be paralyzed and you will not be able to take care of your son."

Lisa's son was about three years old at the time.

"Lisa, I'm coming to get you. Stay there! Don't move!"

I had become nervous and anxious. I had no idea where Pilot Mountain was since we had only lived in the area for several months. Even though I had heard about it, I had never been there. But that was not going to stop me from going up on that mountain to drag this girl back down to reality!

"No, Tasha I'm fine, I'm going to come to your house now," I could tell she was calming down.

"Are you sure? I can make my way up there with no problem."

"Yes, I'm sure. I'll be there in about 20 minutes."

This was the longest 20 minutes of my life! I began to pace up and down the living room floor praying to God that He would give me the words I needed to encourage my friend when she arrived. Of course, I understood there was a possibility that she would never make it to my house, that she would follow through with her plan of driving her car over the cliff as she initially intended. I understand that people say, "prayer changes things". However, sometimes I believe prayer does not necessarily change the outcome of things, as much as it does the person's perception of the outcome.

Luckily for me, Lisa arrived at my house in one piece. At least her physical body was in one piece; her mental state would remain to be seen.

Upon her arrival, we sat down in the living room and talked. I had no idea something was going on with her that could cause her to want to attempt to take her own life!

Lisa began to tell me how she thought her husband was cheating on her because she found some panties from a lingerie set under the backseat of her husband's car. They would switch cars sometimes as most couples do and this is how the panties were found. Of course, she had confronted her husband about these panties and he never came clean.

"I'm just going to be frank with you and come out and tell you," Lisa began. "I cheated on my husband."

"You what? With whom? Was this some type of retaliation because of what your husband did to you?" I was so shocked! Lisa was this very reserved, conservative, and uncompromising type of woman. I'm not saying she never did anything wrong, but I am saying she was always so careful to cross her T's and dot her I's. I had only known her for several months, but I felt like I had a good grasp on who she was. Always giving, volunteering, assisting, and most importantly, consistent in every duty at hand. Lisa was a beautiful woman, fair skinned with long hair, nice smile, and mild tempered. She was extremely supportive as a friend and a dedicated servant at the church. I know she told me she battled with being overweight. At the time I met her she was a size 4, so I figured she had to be strong enough to commit to getting the weight off. There was definitely a physical transformation, but what about the mental and emotional transformation?

Lisa began to share with me what happened. "I met a guy at this apartment as he was reading the Bible at the kitchen table. We started talking at first, then he started telling me what a fool my husband was to be messing around on such a beautiful woman. Marriages aren't always what they're cracked up to be. It takes a lot of hard work and sometimes you still don't get the proper treatment you deserve. I told him about my apprehensions with having sex with my husband because I knew he had been unfaithful. Then I started doubting myself, like is my husband no longer attracted to me since I had our son? There were just so many things going through my head. I began to cry and he would gently touch my hand and let me know everything was going to be alright."

I sat on the sofa next to Lisa, nodding, and listening intently, careful to not interrupt her story.

"He began to tell me how beautiful I was, and all the great and wonderful things he sees in me. My strength, my passion, my sensitivity. I was feeling all sorts of emotions at the time. He stood up from the kitchen table where he was studying the Bible, leaned down and kissed me on the forehead. It was the most intimate and passionate kiss I've ever experienced. He started hugging me, consoling me, and then… kissing me. As his hands slid up my dress, he began to caress my inner thighs. Next thing I know, we were on the floor, with my legs up in the air, and we were having sex. Tasha, the whole time, all I could do was cry!"

Lisa began to cry more and more intensely. I knew she regretted what had happened, I knew she was sorry, I knew this guilt was eating her up inside. However, there was a burning question I had been wanting to ask her since she began to tell me this story.

"Did you have sex with Pastor McCarter?"

"What? Why would you think that? Why would you think it was the Pastor!" She started to get defensive.

"I know you, Lisa. You would never find yourself in such a predicament unless it was involving someone who you really respected, and someone who had some type of authority over you. You gave that man too much credit! Who else would meet you at some apartment with the Bible out on the table, but the Pastor! He knew good and damn well what his intentions were with you! Dirty bastard!"

I would go all in for people that I cared about. That's what they call "Ride or Die!" I am that way as a mother, a sister, and a friend!

Lisa continued with the story, now that I figured out who the story was about, it began to make more sense.

"I had multiple counseling sessions with Pastor McCarter at his office at the church. He then suggested that we meet somewhere more private. He said the people in the church are nosey and are always in and out of the church building knocking on his door when he is in a counseling session. Thinking nothing of this, I agreed to the off-site meeting. Several days later, we met at this apartment. When I walked in, he was reading the Bible at the kitchen table. He even gave me some scriptures that would help me to get through this ordeal with my husband. I was really confused. On one hand, this meeting did not feel right at all, on the other hand, it was all very innocent. One thing led to another and basically I had sex with the Pastor! The entire time, tears were running down my face, but that didn't seem to bother him at all. He just kept going until he was done. I have never felt so badly in my life! I don't think God can forgive me for this!"

In my mind, all I could think of was Mista on top of Celie 'doing his business' in the Color Purple! I tried to find the words to console my friend, but I was still trying to wrap my head around what she was telling me.

"God can forgive you and He will. If you've asked for forgiveness, you are already forgiven. It's not God who has a hard time forgiving. You will have to learn to forgive yourself." I was a natural born encourager. Shoot! I'd been encouraging myself in my own head all my life!

I leaned in to give her a hug and she wept in my arms.

"Why were you contemplating suicide, Lisa?" I asked.

"Tasha, I just cannot live with this guilt. The guilt is killing me. I can't sleep, I can't eat, I'm missing days from work. This thing has really gotten the best of me. I talked to Pastor McCarter about telling our spouses the truth and he was totally against it. He said that God has forgiven us and that's all that matters. We don't ever have to bring it up again. Nobody needs to know, so let's just keep this to ourselves! But I am not able to live like this, Tasha! I just wanted to leave this life! I wanted to end it all!"

Lisa was clearly hurting and struggling with the guilt of this sin she committed with the Pastor. I could see her heart and how sorry she really was for allowing this to happen. She was very vulnerable, damaged, and confused!

"Ok, Natasha, choose wisely what you should advise next," I thought to myself.

"Well, if this secret is causing you to want to kill yourself and take your own life, I suggest you talk to your husband. Save yourself, save your family, and talk to your husband! You must be able to release what you've done and ask your husband for forgiveness so you can move on with your life."

I believed this was the right thing to do, even though it would not be pretty.

Lisa went home that evening and told her husband, Ron, what happened. Ron was literally livid because he and Pastor McCarter were best buddies and had been running a game on the women in the church, but had vowed to never touch each other's wives.

"The Pastor has crossed the line! That Motherfucker had the nerve to put his hands on *my* wife!"

Ron was furious. He was not even too upset with Lisa for allowing it to happen as he was with the Pastor for making it happen. He went to confront the Pastor about breaking their pact; they had words, and even some physical altercation. Ron was prepared to go before the church with this drama and expose not only himself, but the Pastor, too. Cleveland Avenue Christian Church was under the umbrella of the Disciples of Christ denomination. Their church holds congregational meetings once a month. At the congregational meeting, members get to voice their opinion about any church issues. The congregational meeting was coming up this Wednesday. Lord, this is going to be a hot mess that I did not want to miss!

When Charles came home from work, I could not wait to inform him about our beloved pastor and what had been going on in our church. I told him all about my meeting with Lisa. Later, I overheard him having a telephone conversation with an old friend. He called Frank, one of his Pastor friends from college, to ask for his advice on what to do. Frank told him that the Bible says if your brother has done something to offend you, you need to go to him and confront the issue and bring another person with you in the event he doesn't want to listen. If that doesn't work, you will have to take him in front of the church.

"Well, Ron is already going to take the Pastor before the church for sleeping with his wife. So what are we going to do?" I asked Charles.

He shrugged his shoulders. "Looks like we're going to have to find another church to go to. We definitely can't stay at this church with all this mess going on! But first, we need to confront the Pastor ourselves, in private."

That was good to hear as I was not planning on going back to Cleveland Avenue Christian Church. EVER! I told Charles that Ron and Lisa were going to go to the congregational meeting, and Ron was going to have his peace. I told him I wanted to go to support Lisa and he was fine with it, but was not willing to go with me. Charles was known for 'staying out of it,' but as a woman, I was committed to be there when my friend needed me to be there. Word had already gotten around the church that Ron was going to expose himself and the Pastor regarding sleeping with other women in the congregation, not just Lisa, as bad news travels very quickly.

On the date of the Congressional Meeting, one of the Deacons stood up and walked to the podium announcing if any member had something he needed to discuss with the congregation, to please come forward. Ron then went up to the podium and started singing like a canary! Most of the members of the congregation booed him to sit down and be quiet. Others shouted he was being disrespectful to our Pastor. Some called him Satan and stated he has no place in this church. Even some members suggested he was just jealous of the Pastor. Ron stood his ground. From the beginning all the way to the end. He stated when new female members came to the church, if they were beautiful, in particular, he and the Pastor would make a bet to see who could get that woman in bed first. It was all a competition, a battle of the egos, if you will. Who had the most swag, the most game, the most play? But there was one thing they had to promise to abide by, and that was to never touch the other's wife as the wives were off limits!

Ron was determined to get his truth out, yelling over the shouts from the Congregation. "Pastor McCarthy crossed the line when he touched my wife and had sex with her by luring her over to an apartment that he, myself, and other men of this congregation pay for every month!"

Dang! It was like that? My heart was starting to race. Thinking about other women in this church that may have been victims. Could I have been a potential next victim? What about her, or her, or her, as I looked around the church. Wow! This shit is crazy!

The head Deacon was trying to take back control of the meeting.

"You are out of order, Deacon!" came the shouts from the membership.

Oh yeah, did I mention Ron was a Deacon in the church also?

"Somebody remove him from the stage!" More shouts. "Turn off the mic!" Other shouts. "Get him out of here!" Someone yelled. "We cast you out, Satan!"

They were binding devils all up and through, but clearly were not binding the devil that needed to be bound!

Several of the deacons rushed to the podium physically binding Ron by his arm, hands, shoulder, and literally dragged him out of the church! He never stopped speaking his truth the entire time while being dragged! I swear it was like something straight out of the movies! The only thing I could think of was I needed to grab my purse and run out of here as fast as I could before God strikes lightning down and burns up this place with all these people in it. And that's exactly what I did!

I could not wait to get home to tell Charles about the shenanigans I had just witnessed at the church house! And they called themselves Christians! Jeesh! Charles was not really concerned about that as much as he was about setting up a meeting to talk to Pastor McCarter and his wife, at the direction of his pastor friend, Frank. We ended up meeting them at the church a couple days later in the pastor's office to have this couple to couple, friend to friend, face to face conversation.

The Pastor started off by stating what most people do when they know they are living foul.

"I am not perfect, and I make mistakes just like everybody else, and it takes two to tango." He tried to appear humble but I was not buying it!

Of course, I let the Pastor know how disappointed I was in his actions and how offended I was at his comment, "it takes two to tango."

"Clearly, I understand that it takes two, however, being a person of authority and using or abusing that authority and power that you have over people to take advantage of them is much more than a "mistake." Spearheading what was going on in the church with other Deacons in regard to being in competition to see who can get the next woman is downright atrocious!" I was disgusted at his arrogance and inability to even fake humility.

And you call yourself a Pastor! Hmmmmph!

Of course, the Pastor denied most of the accusations Ron spewed out. He did however confess that he had sex with Lisa, but it was only that one time and she was the only other woman.

His wife Joyce chimed in saying, "Well Natasha, David committed adultery and God didn't throw him away. How can you just throw your Pastor away?"

"Throw him away?" I thought. I was thinking more like throwing him into a lions' den and then watching the lions pick his flesh out of their teeth!

Clearly they had pre-planned to show up having a united front, but this was my time to express how I really felt about it.

"It is my choice to decide not to be a part of a church where I know the Pastor is a master manipulator. At some point he will be trying to manipulate me too, if he hasn't already. This is not the type of church environment where I wish to sit and grow spiritually, with so much distrust, sinful ways, and hypocrisy. So I'm just letting you know so that you get it straight from the horse's mouth that I won't be coming back to this church!"

People who know me know I say what I mean and mean what I say!

Thinking back, I recalled the time when Charles' son, Corey, came to visit us for a couple months in the summertime. He was about 8 or 9 years old at that time and I was doing everything for Corey. I made his lunch, I cooked his dinner, I took him to the YMCA for summer camp, I picked him up, I made sure he bathed, I made sure he talked to his mom every night. I spent all my time with him when I was not at work! This is Charles's son, not mine, yet I was doing all the work, and it was wearing on me. Charles had not even taken time off from work or choir rehearsals to spend time with his own son. I went to meet with Pastor McCarter to let him know what I was going through. Pastor McCarter was an extremely affectionate man. Always kissing, hugging, and calling everybody "Baby," just seemed to be a run-of-the-mill type of thing for him. I do remember feeling a sense of uneasiness with these gestures. Thank God I was strong enough not to fall into his trap! I could solve my own problems eventually. I was used to this shit!

The whole time Charles is sitting there not saying a word. This meeting was basically for me and the Pastor to speak to each other face to face, so I can let him know exactly how I felt. Charles may have said two words at most. I was assuming at this point he just felt sorry for the man.

We drove back home in silence because I did not feel the support of my husband in that meeting. Although he told me we were going to have to find another church, that is not what he expressed to the Pastor. As a matter of fact, what he expressed was next to nothing since I was doing most of the talking.

When Sunday came around, I woke up and asked Charles if he wanted to visit a different church today. He then stated he was going to go to Cleveland Avenue Christian Church.

"What! I thought we already talked about finding another church?"

"Well, if everybody who is of the *Light* leaves the church then there will be nothing but *Darkness* left. Darkness needs light in order to survive. If you remove all the good seeds, then how will the other seeds grow?" He tried to reason with me.

"This is some bull shit!" I thought. After four years of marriage, I still could not explain or even predict the actions of my husband. He will say one thing, and mean another thing. He will say one thing, then do another thing. There was no rhyme or reason to his decisions. There was no understanding why he chose to go one route over another one. I never knew what he was thinking because he never would communicate it. Until the eleventh hour is when I would know he made a different decision than what was previously discussed. I had to wonder what type of man I married who could not, or will not stand up for what is right. It is disheartening to know I am no more protected than when I was single, by being married to this man.

The challenge for me, as a woman, is I have always had to defend myself. After my grandfather died, there was no other man who had protected me. No father, no stepfather, no brother. No one. Now that I am married, I thought things would be different. I thought a marriage was meant to be different. I've always heard the preacher say when presenting an analogy about the purpose of the wedding band, "The husband is a band or a wrapping of protection around his wife." Clearly, they didn't know what the hell they were talking about! Somehow the real world never operates the way they say it should. I wish there was more faith in it, more hope for it, and more actions that lined up with it. But there simply is not. Actions can only be determined by one's character, not necessarily whether they are in the church or not, love God or not, decent people or not.

I have got to stop looking for other people to take a stand and do the right thing. Once I realize that people are going to be who they are no matter what God they say they serve, I could better accept the fact this is just the way people are, and there was nothing I could do about it.

The goal in this life is not to correct other people's wrongdoings or judge what they consider to be commonplace, but instead to live a life worth living. A life that teaches the art of raising the standard above mediocrity. Where taking a stand for what's right is not an isolated incident.

The next six months were a challenge in my marriage with Charles. We coexisted as he went to Cleveland Avenue Christian Church every Sunday, Bible Study on every Wednesday, and choir practice every Thursday. I in turn, continued to visit different churches with Lisa and another friend of ours, Kelly. Kelly had also left the church when we left. Kelly had her own experience with Pastor McCarter because Kelly's Aunt visited the church a few times, and told her that she was sleeping with the Pastor on the side. This did not come as a surprise to Kelly as years ago this behavior was already in the works. Yet, she was still going to that church and singing in the choir! But not me! I refused to pay my tithes to some church where the Pastor was using money to fund apartments to meet and have sex with his concubines! Oh, hell naw!

Chapter 18

OOPS! THERE IT IS!

Meanwhile, Charles' sister Kim had been calling the house and left several messages on our answering machine. I would tell Charles this when he came home from work, but he never seemed to be in a rush to call his sister back. Why was his sister calling so many times and leaving messages, as this was not the norm? It seemed like it was an emergency and Charles really needed to call her, but he did not express any urgency in the matter.

Several months passed when Charles finally told me he decided he was not going back to Cleveland Avenue Christian Church because he felt it was a strain on our marriage.

Hallelujah! Finally, he had come to his senses! Pastor McCarter and the Cleveland Avenue Christian Church debacle was finally behind us! Well, not really. Shit was still going on and it was heartbreaking. The people were divided, the congregation was split. Many people left and found a new church, but most people stayed. I was told, "Natasha, this is not the first time the church has gone through this same type of scandal. Our last Pastor was caught having an affair with the church secretary who was also the First Lady's best friend. The church consisted of mostly families, and it did not only split up the church, but it also split up the families. We really cannot afford to let these scandals tear us down again. If we leave every time a new Pastor comes in and messes up, we will never have a church home."

I finally began to understand why people had church in their living rooms. I think I would rather go back to the basics!

Although several other women had come forth that Sheldon McCarter had relations with, or attempted to have relations with, nothing was ever done about it. He continued to preach every Sunday, and the naive saints of the church continued to invite their naive friends and family members to join, so the church continued to grow over the years. They eventually built a new building, but in the last five years had to file bankruptcy and it was foreclosed on. Pastor McCarter was quoted in one of his sermons as saying, "To hell with all the fake folk! I'm only looking for the real folk in this season! I ain't playing no games no mo'! You can kiss my a**! I'm sick of fake and phony negroes!"

And these people were going up to the pulpit high fiving him and shit! Ridiculous!

Now I think we can all agree this mothafucka has a serious problem! Doesn't he know the time will come when he will have to eat these words? Doesn't he know he will be held accountable for the souls who have gone astray because of him? Is he not afraid of what God is going to do to him? The Devil in sheep's clothing! I just do not know what these so-called 'anointed ones' are thinking they are getting away with. I just do not understand it!

When we first met Pastor and Sis. McCarter, we took to them right away. Pastor McCarter was very charming, charismatic, and fun. He could hold a conversation with you about pretty much anything, whether intellectually, spiritually, financially, or emotionally. If he did not know something, he knew someone who knew someone who did. He was the go-to person in church, and consequently in the town of Winston Salem. He was just a likable person, and most people got along with him for the most part. So, I think when the rumors began to spiral out of control, people wanted to believe the truth, but they truly liked this person. Pastor McCarter had a personal relationship with most people in his congregation. He had invested his time and energy for a time like this. When it was time for a person to decide whether they would leave the church or not, most people were like, "Leave this church and go where? We had the same problem at my last church, which is why I came here in the first place! At least we're growing over here and the choir is good!"

I know it is a shame, this is why so many people, including those of us who are Christians, do not like organized religion. Too much power belongs to one person, and most people are not equipped to handle that type of power responsibly. Most people are selfish and do not care about the people or their congregation; they only care about themselves. They will use the church's money to buy themselves airplanes and helicopters, take lavish trips when their members are living out on the streets, or sitting at home with their lights off because they put their last paycheck in the offering! I am still waiting for it to make sense, and it just does not!

The two ministries I have been affiliated with, and know for a fact my tithes and offerings were doing some good in the world, are Bible Witness Camp in Pembroke IL, and Lakewood Church in Houston TX. I am sure there are many others, but these are the ones I have personal experience with.

And First Ladies, let us talk about you for a moment. I know you feel like you need to 'cover' your husbands, but this is just ludicrous! You are doing too much!! You cannot continue to cover your husbands' sins that clearly hurt other people! It would be like covering up a crime he committed. Are you ready to go to jail for your man, too?? Why do you keep putting yourselves on the backburner trying to be his 'help mate,' when clearly the help he needs is a psychological evaluation? Please, First Ladies, it is past time for you to start speaking out against this nonsense. So what if other women in the church are going to try to steal your man, but you know he is probably already sleeping with them anyway, so what do you have to lose? You have a voice, use it! Don't you know you will have to pay for the part you played while sitting back watching him destroy people's lives? Trust me, in the end, he is not worth your sanity!

Years ago, when Charles and I lived in Richland, Washington, we attended Greater Hope Missionary Baptist Church. I believe it was Pastor Mitchell. His wife Kathy was my sorority sister, and we had grown close. One day, a few of the sorority sisters met Kathy at the church for a Sunday afternoon program, and the First Lady smelled like liquor! What the hell! I understand the pressures of life, but it was clear she just had a drink before pulling up to the church parking lot, and it showed! I was really worried about her, but did not know how far I should insert myself into her personal business. But hey, that is what sistahs are for!

"Come with us!" Another sorority sister Toni, and I grabbed Kathy and escorted her out the front door of the church after the program was over. "What is your problem?"

"What are you talking about?" Of course, Kathy was not going to admit it right away.

"We smell the liquor on your breath!"

"That's not liquor, that's Listerine," Kathy lied.

"It's Listerine trying to camouflage the liquor! Plus, you're doing all these outbursts in church like you have a problem or something!"

"I was just saying hallelujah!"

"Yeah but all your hallelujahs were in all the wrong places! Now you better come clean with us or else!" Toni was an attorney for the Department of Defense, a woman after my own heart. She would get to the bottom of this case even if she had to take it all the way to the Supreme Court!

We come to find out Kathy was in an abusive relationship with her husband, Pastor Mitchell, and she was using alcohol to mask the pain. She could not speak to the older mothers in the church because they were more prone to tell her to just 'Pray for your husband.' She could not speak to any of her peers, or other First Ladies in the church community as this would embarrass her husband and make it worse for her at home. Kathy would eventually need to make a decision that would change the rest of her life.

I received a call in the middle of the night from Kathy crying, "Tasha, can you please come over here?"

"Kathy? Is everything alright? Are you okay?"

"I am okay. I need some advice. I need to talk to you, in person."

"Alright. I-I'm on my way!" I hurriedly threw on some clothes, jumped in my car, and rushed to Kathy's apartment. Apparently, she and Pastor Mitchell had just gotten into an altercation; he left and said he was "going out of town." That is code for his side piece's house down the street! Kathy showed me several items of clothing she kept hidden in the back of her closet that were blood stained from the beatings by her husband over the course of their marriage.

"Why are you keeping these?"

"I don't know, I guess to remind myself of the type of man he really is, even when he's being nice to me."

"Kathy," I hesitated because I am always hesitant about giving people advice about their marriages, but hell, she's the one who called me over here at 3 o'clock in the morning!

"You can't love this man more than you love yourself! You are beautiful, smart, and intelligent! Why would you be putting up with this bullshit from this measly preacher who claims to love God!" Even in my hesitation, the straight truth was always the better way to go.

"But he says he does love God; he just has this temper!"

"So what, does that give him a right to use you as his punching bag? People say they love God all the time, but they do not show it! Love is an action word. How can he say he loves you, yet he beats you? He does not love you, Kathy! Look at all this blood on all these clothes!"

By this time, I was getting extremely emotional as I picked up the garments and threw them back down on the bed. I was really surprised Kathy was acting as confused about this situation as she was. Kathy was tall, thin with big eyes, and had a beautiful smile. Kathy was at least 15 years older than me, but I always felt like I was the big sistah! She put me in the mindset of Olive Oil from the cartoon Popeye, but most importantly, Kathy had a master's degree in Hospital Administration. She had options! So why was she taking this bullshit from this broke ass pastor at this church with 10 members, while they beg for money to pay their rent every month! My goodness!

Not too long afterwards, Kathy left Pastor Mitchell and moved back to Portland, OR, where she worked as a Hospital Administrator. Damn! I had been trying to get my Mama to leave these niggas all my life! I guess the only difference between my mother and the Kathys of the world are their options. It can still be done, but my mother would need to have more willpower to do it. Several years later I was pleased to get a call from Kathy with an update on how well she was doing in Portland. Living her best life!

Whether we are talking about Joyce with her cheating pastor of a husband, or Kathy with her beating pastor of a husband, somebody in the church must start taking a stand for what is right! If not you, then who? If not now, then when? Remember, you have a following also, a platform. The younger women sitting in your church are looking at you. What example are you setting? If you could do it all over again, what would you do differently? If you could remarry, what kind of man would he be?

It is so easy to lose ourselves in a marriage. Let us not be so busy becoming 'we,' that we forget who 'I' was. I had to remind myself, although I am married; I was still an individual who is now a couple, and I needed to figure out how to mesh the two.

Charles and I clearly did not agree on how to handle the church debacle because I needed to stand against the shenanigans, and he felt he needed to *play it safe*. My friend's life was on the line since she had already attempted suicide, so I did not have the luxury of *playing it safe* and refused.

Although Charles said in one breath that he wanted to leave Cleveland Avenue Christian Church, in the next breath he then tells me he has a 14-year-old son who he never told me about.

"What the fuck! A fourteen-year-old son!"

I was thinking maybe he got a girl pregnant and did not know she was pregnant. I was thinking maybe she left college and never told him she was pregnant, so therefore, this is all a surprise to him as it is to me. But no! He knew about the baby, had even gone to the hospital to see the girl after she had the baby, and he even held the baby in his arms. So, for 14 years he never once mentioned this child? Never talked to the child? Never sent the child's Mama any money? No birthdays? No Christmas gifts? What kind of man did I marry?? The list continues to go on. All these question marks. All these, "What the fucks?"

When my heart hurts, my soul hurts, and my spirit feels burdened, so very sad. There's a hole in my heart when my loved ones lie to me and hurt me. Of course, I had many follow-up questions, but Charles could not seem to answer any of them intelligently, or give any acceptable explanation. He did tell me the child's mother had contacted Charles' mother in Baltimore to get his phone number. Instead of giving out his phone number, his sister, Kim, was trying to call him to inform him this lady was trying to reach him. I knew that shit did not feel right! At this point he ended up calling the child's mother who stated she just wanted her son to know his real father. She had recently gone through a divorce from the man who apparently raised Charles' son, D'Angelo. Now that they were divorced, she told D'Angelo who his real father is, and she wanted to reach out to Charles to make sure it was okay if D'Angelo contacts him.

My world was turning upside down. Flipping cartwheels! The marriage I thought I had, that I knew I did not have, but pretended to have, did not even exist. The man I married who I was not even sure I should marry, but married anyway, was not the man that I thought he was, even though I did not know enough about him to make an informed decision. Nothing I thought I knew, or even pretended to know, was coming together for my benefit. This is why you cannot think you know or pretend to know. The best thing to do is acknowledge you know nothing, and it is a constant journey of progressing to knowing something.

"She says she doesn't want any money. She just wants me to get to know my son," Charles said.

Money? He actually thought money was my biggest issue with this situation. He knew my father disowned me and many of my other siblings. He knew everything I had gone through to get to know my father and to develop any type of relationship with him. Yet he thinks this is about money! About child support?

One thing some men do not understand is it is not just about the money. While money is needed to support children, the presence of a father being there is much more important than his money. Money buys shoes, clothes, and food for kids; it helps keep a roof over their heads. Money does not help your son study for his spelling test. Money does not show up to school award ceremonies for the honor roll. Money does not discipline your child and show him love. Money does not show up at football games, cheering the child on. Money does not show your son how to protect himself in a playground scuffle, nor teach him the rules on how to 'try not' to become a victim of police brutality as a black man in America. Fathers do that, not money!

"So you were aware that you had another child and did not think that it was important to mention that to me before we got married?"

"Well, I knew how you felt about dating a man with children, and since I already told you about Corey, I decided not to say anything about my older son."

Ain't this some shit!

"So basically, you told a partial truth, which is a lie?"

"I don't think it was a lie, as much as it is not telling the whole truth."

"Same thing, Charles!" I hated it when people tried to turn shit back on you instead of apologizing with their lying asses!

"Well, I honestly didn't think you would have given me a chance if you knew I had two sons."

"So what! That would have been my option to choose. But you took that option away from me by not telling me the truth! But most importantly, you let your son grow up without a father, and that disgusts me!"

"His mother had moved on and married some other dude who was taking care of D'Angelo, and I didn't want to interfere with that."

Lord, help us all! I just did not get how a man could sit back and let some other dude raise his son when he was more than capable, and not even have a presence in his child's life! I was furious!

Oh, do you remember all that bullshit Charles talked about when I wanted to leave Cleveland Avenue Christian Church? "If everybody who is of the *Light* leaves the church, then there will be nothing but *Darkness* left. If you remove all the good seeds, then how will the other seeds grow?"

It was easier for Charles to NOT take a stand because of the sin in his own life, because of what he was hiding from his own wife! Good seed my ass!

There was no point in me rehashing what was already done; trying to get to the bottom of a story that made no sense to me. I did not know what kind of man I had married. The kind who was not into taking care of his responsibilities! Unbelievable! I had no earthly idea! I felt as stupid as they come!

I eventually forgave Charles for holding this 14 year secret for four years of our marriage. It was the only way I would be able to move on with him. I was determined to have my marriage, this marriage that lived on in my head. Not perfect by any means, but workable, doable. At this point the only successful marriage I had witnessed were my grandparents. I had no idea all they went through, how many times they had to compromise with one another, forgive one another, or turn blind eyes as if something did not happen. Forgive and Forget. What I do know is I am a very strong woman. Whether God made me that way or I became that way through trials and tribulations, really didn't matter. Somehow, I made it to this place of strength and power, and whatever I put my mind to, I was capable of doing. My marriage can survive this if I was able to survive it, and I know I am.

I chose to forgive and stay with Charles because forgiving was my only option at this point. I was still young, and still had so much to learn about myself, about my husband, and about life in general. I wasn't ready to give that up.

Forgiving is a personal choice. Sometimes we forgive for ourselves, not necessarily for the other person. Some people may not understand why I forgave him, or even if I did it for the right reasons. I believed I was fighting a bigger battle of not wanting to be just another statistic. No other marriage in my family, outside of my grandparents, had survived. I was the first to go to a four year university and graduate with a bachelor's degree, to get out of the hood, and was determined to be the first to have a successful marriage. I knew there would be a price to pay, unlike the three Hebrew boys from the Bible, as most people would never come out of the fiery furnace with no burns. I never considered how high a price I might have to pay. I had no idea how much it would cost me. Nor how much I was willing to pay to get the life I felt I deserved.

Chapter 19

THE MARRIAGE

I never worked in chemical engineering again after I left Westinghouse. After we purchased our first home, the real estate agent encouraged me to get my real estate license because he thought I would make a good agent. Primarily because I was extremely thorough in giving him what he needed, and following up with the mortgage lender throughout the transaction. In 1997, I decided to get my license and practice real estate. The first company I joined was America's First Realty. America's First was owned by an African-American broker, Don Croom, who was also a builder of new construction. We ended up finding a house that was being custom built by Don Croom, put a contract on the property, and began to move forward with the completion of the home. This was to be the second home we purchased.

The firm manager's name was Will Thompson. He was instrumental in preparing me for the real world of real estate. Will and I went to all the properties that the firm listed to measure, input into the multiple listing service, and make sure all documents were in place for each property. Will also trained me on how to go over all the important contracts with the clients. I liked him as a person and a mentor. Without his assistance, it would have been more challenging to learn the ropes as quickly as I did.

One day Will called me into the conference room and closed the door. This was not unusual, as normally we are going over contracts in the conference room or talking about properties. As Will opened a binder as if he was in training mode, he then closed the binder and looked at me and smiled. I was trying to figure out what the look was all about, as I had no clue.

Then he says to me, "So, I want to know if you would like to go up to the mountains to do some horseback riding?"

"Are you asking for me and my husband to go with you and your wife, like on a couples trip?"

"I know you like horseback riding because you've mentioned it before, and I want to know if you would like to go up to the mountains with *ME* this weekend? I own a cabin there and we could go horseback riding together."

What the fuck! Is he seriously asking me to go away with him for the weekend? Where did he get an idea like that? Was it something I said or did? Did I somehow inadvertently lead him on to have these thoughts about me? None of it made sense to me. Not one time did I look a certain way, feel a certain way, or feel a certain attraction, even from him. So, for him to have the audacity to ask me to go away with him, I was floored!

"Why would you even ask me something like that?" I was in a state of confusion.

"I just thought maybe you wanted to go with me," he replied dumbfoundedly.

"Without our spouses? I have no idea why you thought you could have the balls to even... Never mind, I don't even know why I'm wasting my breath on you! I'm not about to put up with this shit! I'm gone!"

I hurriedly pushed back my chair, got up, and stormed out of the conference room. I'm nervous, I'm mad, I'm afraid, I'm confused! I went into my office, grabbed my purse, and left the office without a word.

"Mothafucka! Now he's messing with my money!"

I have no idea why people think they can do whatever they want and say whatever they want without any thought of the repercussions. First of all, I do not even know why he thought there was a possibility of a yes. Will looked like somebody's Uncle Tom. He wasn't very articulate. He wasn't really attractive. He did not have much money, and he looked much older than Charles. I am trying to figure out what made him think he could *snag* a woman like me! Bottom line. And a married woman like me at that! I was confused by his actions. 'I'm so done!' I could not wait to get home so I could tell *my husband* what happened at the office today.

I'm not even sure why I was so surprised by Charles' reaction, which was, "Well you need to try to stay there long enough so we can get the construction of the house completed. We don't want Don to renege on us because you stopped working as an agent at his office."

Why am I even surprised? This house is more important to him than his wife's peace of mind at work. This man has just sexually harassed his wife and all he has to say is, "*I think you should stay long enough to make sure the house gets completed.*" Over and over again he repeatedly showed me what type of man I married, because clearly, I had no clue. What is the point of a husband if I end up fighting my own battles when it comes to things like this? Charles had never even been to my office, even though I would go to his office and have lunch with him. I do not think he ever thought what I did for a living was important, even though my first full year in real estate I made just as much money as he did as an Information Technology Consultant. I helped many people through the homebuying process, getting them the proper financing so they were paying less money to purchase than they were to rent!

Charles was definitely developing a habit here. Anything and everything was more important than me, his wife. As long as he did not have to take a stand or ruffle any feathers, he was okay to live his life this way. Oh, but I was not! I am not the one who will let you get away with things just because I do not want to confront the issue. I am the woman who wants to lay it out on the table, get it out in the open so we can move on from it and get over it. Charles and I were two totally different types of people. Every occurrence in our marital journey allowed me to get to know him more as the type of man who does not mesh with the type of woman I am. It was becoming painfully obvious.

I let a couple of weeks pass by before going back into the office. I did not have anything to say to Will, so my training was technically null and void. Once again, I was out here by myself having to figure it out. This wasn't anything new for me, I just thought once I was married I would not have to fight this war alone. Clearly this was not the case. The office was now a very uncomfortable place for me.

When I walked down the hall past Will, I would walk close to the opposite wall so his shoulder could not brush up against mine. This is how much I despised this feeling his suggestive comments gave me. Being the woman I am, I decided to confront Will about the unwanted, unsolicited advance towards me.

"Can I see *YOU* in the conference room for a moment?" Yes, two can play that game! Will met me in the conference room and I said, "Close the door please. The reason why I am even speaking to you at this time is to let you know that I do not appreciate the way you came to me asking me to go away with you for the weekend. I am totally offended at the fact that you thought you had a chance to get me to go with you, and behind both of our spouses' backs. I have no idea what was done or said, or what you thought was done or said to you to make you think that there was an opportunity for me to accept such advances from you. Because I respect the fact that you have a family is the only reason why I would not be reporting this incident of sexual harassment to the Real Estate Board. I would suggest you never say another word to me, and don't even look my way!" I was definitely on fire!

"I apologize if I made you feel uncomfortable," is all he could come up with. It's funny how a man will try to say or do something that doesn't work in his favor, then he wants to apologize for '*if* it made me feel uncomfortable' or here is my all-time favorite: "If I've done anything to offend you, blah, blah, blah, blah...."

"No, let me stop you right there. Do not apologize *if* you made me uncomfortable when you **know** you made me uncomfortable, and you are out of order. But you don't ever have to worry about me being in this office because I won't be staying in an unhealthy work environment. I will be packing my things today and I won't be coming back!"

I stormed out of that building and decided I would just work from home until I found another company to transfer my license to. It was such an uncomfortable position to be in, I was stuck between a rock and a hard place. Attempting to learn the ropes in this newly established real estate business, with no mentor, and trying to deal with the Broker/Builder to get our house completed, without saying *ne'er* a word. I really do surprise myself sometimes. The fact I did not curse Will out was a huge accomplishment!

A couple months later we were doing our walkthrough of the property and needed to choose the lighting, carpet color, and granite countertops for the house. We were in the car with the Broker/Builder, Don, going to the different places to choose the final amenities. Don suggested we stop by the office since Charles had never been there before. Oh Lord! Of all the times, now he wants to stop by the office and introduce Charles to the staff! Jeez! This is going to be interesting. Don proceeded to introduce Charles to the secretary, and then we went to Will's office so he could introduce Charles to him. Obviously Charles already knew who Will was and what he was about because of all that happened a couple of months prior. So, when we got to Will's office, Charles shakes the man's hand, then asks him if he could talk to him for a minute in his office. They both went in and closed the door.

What! I'm shaking in my boots! What is he possibly going to say after a couple of months to this man who harassed his wife? They must have been in that office for 15 or 20 minutes as I paced the floor wondering what was going on in there. Is he giving him a piece of his mind? Is he ripping him a new one? Is he threatening him? Fighting him? What is going on in that office? When Charles came out, he looked rather calm, but then again, he always looked this way. I was finally excited about the possibilities of him confronting this man even though he was two months late! Better late than never, I guess. When we got back in the car, we were waiting for Don to come back out so we could finish the tour of the vendors where we would choose our final selections for the house.

"So what happened Charles? You were in there for about 15 or 20 minutes! Tell me what happened?"

"Nothing," he replied.

"Nothing? What do you mean nothing? What did you say to him?"

"We just talked. That was it."

Talked? That was it? To this day Charles never told me what went on during that 15 to 20 minutes in Will's office. I have no idea why he wouldn't have shared it with me since it was an incident that happened to me. I didn't get it. Now that it finally looked like, or appeared, that he was stepping up, he would not spill the tea, as they say. Eventually, I just let it go and realized Charles is who he is and clearly, I was not about to change that. He was becoming a drain.

I was beginning to realize that more time should have been spent in getting to know who I am and who I was becoming as a woman prior to marrying. There is no way possible I knew enough in my mid-20s to be able to avoid the pitfalls of my marriage. The type of person and the compatibility of a person is extremely important when choosing a mate. Because we are individuals, there is still work and compromise that would be needed in order to make a relationship work. However, being on different ends of the spectrum is like a disaster waiting to happen. We need to be equally yoked, and that does not just mean believing in the same God.

After the Cleveland Avenue Christian Church debacle, Charles and I became members of Evangel Fellowship Church in Greensboro, North Carolina. While Charles played the piano for the main praise teams and choirs, I sang on the praise team and occasionally for the choir. This was our way of being able to spend time together while volunteering for the church. I eventually moved to the Thursday morning Bible study praise team because of flexibility with my real estate business. I had an incident with the drummer, Brother Roy, who would always go to grab my hand in the prayer circle prior to rehearsals. I began to feel uncomfortable with Brother Roy as he held my hand and moved his fingers up and down the inside of my palm. Now I may not know exactly what that means, but I know it's something nasty. My spirit is never comfortable with certain things people do, or perhaps the way they look at me, that stems from some type of malicious thought or act. Several incidents of prayer and him holding my hand caused me to realize he is doing this shit on purpose. Here we go again!

Once again, I went home to tell my husband what happened, and his response was, "Are you sure that's what it means?"

What I am sure of is how it made me feel. With that feeling I know there are ill intentions from the other person. My gut doesn't lie, nor does it lead me astray. Since I realized Charles was not about to have a talk with Brother Roy, or by the time he decided to talk, all would be forgotten, I decided to go to the praise team leader, LaShawn. LaShawn, being a woman, I thought she may understand. She never downplayed my accusations, but she had never dealt with this type of situation before, and was not privy to the next steps. LaShawn told her husband who is an Elder in the church. Well, Elder Williams did not know how to handle this either. When LaShawn came back to me to let me know that they did not know what to do about it, or if they should do anything about it, this is what I said to her.

"I have given you a fair warning and opportunity to have a conversation with this brother on your own. However, since you refuse to, I'm going to tell you what I intend to do. The next time you call for prayer and he runs up beside me and grabs my hand, I'm going to politely interrupt you, call Brother Roy into the back room, and give him the tongue-lashing of his life! This is how I am going to handle it since no one else will. I'm just letting you know ahead of time so that you're not surprised!" These people, I swear!

I honestly don't think people believe me when I say what I'm going to do. There has not been one thing in my life I said I was going to do, that I did not do. Mark my words. If Natasha said it, it is true, and it will come to pass.

Sure enough, at the next praise team rehearsal on a Thursday morning, LaShawn opened up with prayer and asked everyone to join hands. Like clockwork, Brother Roy runs up next to me and grabs my hand. I snatched my hand away from him, turned around towards him, and said, "Can I see you in the back room?"

LaShawn and the other praise team members were appalled I had interrupted prayer, but I did not care. I had already given her fair warning, and now it was up to her to calm the questionable looks from the rest of the team.

Brother Roy followed me into the back room and as I closed the door, I went in on him! I know the other praise team members were wondering what in the world was going on.

"I do not know what your problem is, but when it is time for prayer, you come and grab my hand, then you start moving your fingers up and down in the palm of my hand. Clearly you don't think I know what's going on, but I got news for you, because I know that action means something nasty like you want to have sex. I am warning you right now, the next time LaShawn calls for prayer, do not run up and grab my hand! Do not touch me! Do not even look my way!"

Why do I feel like this has happened to me before? Oh, because it has! People must think I'm naive or I'm too nice to say anything but clearly, they don't know me very well. Or maybe it is just they are accustomed to getting away with this shit since there is no fear of consequences. I can be cool with you and cordial with you, but the moment you cross that line with me, you have crossed over to the other side of Tasha. Please do not mess with her! Because you will regret it!

Of course, Brother Roy was playing the innocent role. What other options did he have? "If I've offended you or anything, that was not my intention blah blah blah blah..."

Yes, I've heard it ALL before.

"I don't want to hear anything you have to say. Just keep your distance, and keep it moving!" I never had any more problems from Roy after that meeting. He's lucky I didn't tell his wife! Oh, she probably would not have believed me anyway, right?

Women have always been subject to sexual harassment whether on the job, at church, at the club, or even in the grocery stores. It does not matter where it happens, the problem is, it continues to happen. Until every woman finds her voice and speaks against it when it happens, men will continue to violate her personal space, and continue to be disrespectful unless they are called out every single time. Sooner or later when they're no longer getting away with it, then it will end. At some point, even those of us who are married, cannot expect the man to protect us. We must always be ready, willing, and able to protect ourselves when the time comes. Oh, and it will.

By the year 2000, I decided we should try to have a baby. We were already six years into the marriage and it was as mediocre as it comes. There was not much excitement other than the church debacle, and let us not forget the son Charles never told me about. We did not have much fun, but we also did not have much drama, so I will take that for what it was worth. At this time in my life, I'm 30 years old, and thought there has to be more to life than what I'm experiencing.

I stopped taking birth control pills, and literally like clockwork, in three months, I was pregnant! I believe Charles was determined to be a better dad to this child than he had been to his other children. Maybe because he really did love me, or maybe because we were married; but either way he was going to be a decent father to this child, and I was going to make sure of it. Even throughout the pregnancy I made him go to every single doctor's appointment. If I must take off work to go to a doctor's appointment for this baby, then you will, too! He was there like clockwork. Never missed an appointment. If the OBGYN says you need to rub her feet every night, he was rubbing my feet every night. He put together her crib, the rocking chair, a changing table, even built shelves for her stuffed animals and hung them on the walls. Charles was definitely on board with this pregnancy. Maybe he was ready to be a father this time.

When it came to naming our child, he was very adamant about which name we would give her. It was his idea to name her Jana, meaning God is Gracious. I was good with 'Jana,' especially since it was a name where people could not tell she was black before she even walked into a room. That would be one less hurdle she would have to tackle!

Charles would get up every morning and make me pancakes as that was what I craved for breakfast when I was pregnant. When the baby was born, he was there to cut the umbilical cord, and was the first one to hold our daughter. He played classical music for her when I was pregnant, to make sure she had a love for music. She does. I would say that Charles was the best father he knew how to be to our daughter. I had to give him that.

I decided to plan a surprise 40th birthday party for Charles. He was not the best husband, but he was not all bad either. So, I decided to go the extra mile to surprise him. I called both of his sons' mothers and told them I wanted to fly their sons up for the weekend for Charles' birthday party. Both moms complied. The oldest son, D'Angelo was 17 at this time, and Corey was about 12 or 13. This would be my first-time meeting D'Angelo as he was kept a secret from me for the first four years of our marriage. I was willing to let bygones be bygones, and be the bigger person *as usual*. Plus, the child is always the innocent party even though their parents can make horrible decisions for their lives. Don't I know it!

The birthday party went off without a hitch! I had plenty of friends lined up to help me with the surprise.

When I met D'Angelo, he was about six foot seven and slinky, with a huge smile. He seemed like a nice kid. For some reason D'Angelo took a liking to me more so than he did his own father. After the rest of the party guests left the house, D'Angelo came to my bedroom and knocked on the door, asking if he could speak to me. Of course, I would oblige.

D'Angelo began to tell me about a time when he was younger, how the next door neighbor had violated him.

"So, I just wanted to share something with you; I was molested by the man that would come to our house and hangout with my stepfather."

"Ok," I responded. He literally just came right out with it as if he knew his secret would be safe with me, or maybe our spirits just automatically connected in that way. "I was also molested as a child by my stepfather."

"I kind of just wanted to talk to someone about it because I feel like I'm having some struggles."

"Do you believe that you are a homosexual?"

"I've never acted on my feelings of homosexuality, but I definitely feel something for other men."

"Well D'Angelo, a lot of times when boys are molested by men, they become attracted to that initial feeling of someone fondling their private parts. This may be somewhat confusing because although the feeling itself is not bad, the way in which it came about is a violation and a crime. Do you understand?"

"That makes sense."

"So how come you're talking to me about this instead of your own father?"

"I thought it would be harder to talk to my father and wanted to talk to someone who would be more open to listening."

Well, of course I could not blame him for that.

This would be a hard pill for Charles to swallow; that his eldest son is a homosexual. Then there's the guilt of a black father who was not in his son's life, that possibly could have changed the course of his life forever. D'Angelo said he had not had sex with another guy, but had an affinity towards men. What could I say? At some point in our lives we all have to figure out who we are, who we want to be, and deal with the reality in between.

He was already 17, and there was probably no turning back from whatever journey he was about to embark on. So I just let him be and encouraged him to be who he is and try to live in his truth.

My relationship with Charles was getting more and more mundane every day. I thought the surprise birthday party would somehow show him I am still in this marriage, and would love to see it through with him. He seemed to be growing more and more distant, and I had no idea how to respond to his behavior. In October 2003, just a couple of months after his 40th birthday party, we moved into separate bedrooms. I remember making our first marriage counseling appointment because I felt there was a strange tug of war between the two of us. I had no idea where it was coming from. I was doing my real estate investment business and I was constantly busy. However, I always took care of my child and always took care of my home. If I had to guess, Charles may have been a little jealous as to some of the moves I was making in real estate without his assistance or permission. I tried to invite him to be a part of this journey with me, but he did not want to have anything to do with it. But that wasn't going to stop me. At this time I had moved him to the guest bedroom just for the sake of peace. I remember putting a sign on the master bedroom door stating, "You cannot sleep here tonight."

Journal Entry October 17th, 2003

Today, Charles and I will go see a marriage counselor. It is very important that we get to the bottom of our marital challenges. It is very difficult when I'm trying to stay in motion, and he refuses to move. I know it is only because I have caught the vision, but what good is it when I have to fight with him to keep it. I am not happy in my marriage right now because it has been such a struggle to be happy. Will it always be this way? No, it cannot! I'm not willing to be unhappy all my life. I choose happiness. Hopefully these counseling sessions will benefit us both. Yes, they will, they have to.

Marriage counseling actually went better than I had expected today. Charles and I even went to lunch together afterwards, like a real date. We had not done that in a long time.

Journal Entry November 18th, 2003

Today our counseling session went well. I cried. I think my biggest fear is actually having to make the hardest decision of my life; either putting up with Charles never changing for the rest of my life, or ending the marriage. Both will be very difficult decisions to make and either way, I lose! He doesn't seem to have a clue and it shows.

Journal Entry November 29th, 2003

This morning I made a very difficult decision. I decided that if my husband could not make me happy, I still have a responsibility to find joy, peace, and happiness in Christ. I have been letting so many things about my marriage and about my husband annoy me, that I actually considered smothering him with a pillow while his loud snores echoed through my head at night. I knew at that time my flesh was building up hatred towards him. I have made up my mind that my husband is probably never going to change. And I have decided at this point to not do anything about it. It's too difficult. It's so draining, it takes too much energy. I have to realize that we are two very different people. We speak totally different languages and what's important to one is not important to the other. I have to accept that this is as good as it gets for me and that's a hard pill to swallow. Charles will never change, just as his mother said his father never changed. Again, my expectations of marriage were way too high, and I guess that is no one's fault but my own.

My happiness did not come within my 10 year marriage to Charles, I had to find that happiness within myself. We rarely took vacations although we could afford to; he was always so concerned about missing church services and "who's going to play piano for the choir?" We rarely went out on dates, never went dancing, or to any concerts or plays, except a couple of gospel concerts. We did however have season passes one year to Carowinds in Charlotte NC, since we both enjoyed roller coasters, but I believe that is one of the only things we may have had in common.

So like most people in this situation, I poured myself into my work. I had a growing real estate brokerage which was thriving, and I got much satisfaction from teaching classes on credit repair, budgeting, how to get out of debt, and purchasing real estate investment properties. I also wrote plays for the church drama department and sang on the Praise Team.

Other than that, we both loved God, except I was not a fanatic about it. I also did not live a life of secrets. We all have secrets though, right? Or shall I say, most of us do!

Journal Entry February 4th, 2004

Today was the worst day of my life! The day I found out that my husband was cheating on me!

I was on my way to take my daughter to daycare when I went to Charles's car to look for my lip-gloss that had fallen out of my purse the day before. We typically switch cars often, depending on who is taking Jana to daycare. As I got into his car, which was a red two seater, Honda del Sol convertible, I looked under the seat because I thought maybe the lip gloss rolled under the passenger side, and I started pulling all this junk from under the seat. I was thinking, wow, he really needs to clean out this car! Lo and behold, I pulled out a box of condoms! Correction, an empty box of condoms! My heart sank into my stomach as I began to wonder who this belonged to. Yes, denial did set in. However, I knew he was ministering to one of the brothers who was a member of the band at the church. Maybe these fell out of his pocket and slid under the seat. Either way, this was something I would have to deal with after I came back from dropping Jana off, then having a hair appointment. Jana was already coming out into the garage to get in the car, so I pushed everything back under the front car seat hoping and praying it was not going to be there when I got back. I then strapped Jana into her car seat in the back of my BMW X5, hands shaking, but trying my hardest to keep my composure.

After I dropped Jana off at Primrose Daycare and went to get my hair done, the ladies in the hair salon were talking about a woman in the church whose husband had been cheating on her. I felt like they already knew my story before I was privy to it. I did not know who they were talking about, but I do know they would probably be talking about me next.

On the way home I cried so hard while having a real conversation with God, and I asked Him to tell me the truth! I deserved to know the truth! It was like I heard the audible voice of God say, "It is what you think it is. It is what you know it is. You do deserve to know the truth. But no matter what happens, you will be alright."

Even though I had just heard the audible voice of God, by the time I got back to the house, there was a part of me hoping I was hallucinating about the empty box of condoms. What if the box is no longer there? How would I have proof I even saw it in the first place? What if Charles has already removed the box? Question after question, after question, ran through my mind just so I would not have to deal with the inevitable.

Charles was working from home on this day, so it was a perfect time to have this extremely challenging conversation. As I went back to his car and dug out the junk from under the passenger seat, that empty box of condoms was staring me in the face! Now I have to deal with this. I quickly grabbed the box and rushed into the house, adrenaline flowing. Charles is sitting in the living room on his computer working.

"What is this?" My voice was trembling as I held up the box to show him that he is cold busted! "What is this?" I re-emphasized, the empty box in my hand.

"I don't know, you tell me," he murmured.

This was not the time nor the place for his cynicism!

"I deserve to know the truth, Charles. I am asking you a question, and I expect an answer. So I'm going to ask you one more time, what is this!"

"Oh, uhh, okay," he said slowly. "Sit down," gesturing me to sit on the ottoman in front of the oversized chair in the family room.

I took a deep breath and sat down on the ottoman. Although I raised my voice at him, I was pretty surprised how calm my spirit was during this confrontation. He began to explain to me he had a one-night stand with a woman he met from the chat room. The chat room? I didn't even know what that was in 2004! I had been married to him for 10 years and was definitely out of the loop as to how people are meeting each other on the internet. Hell, when I got married, there was no internet yet! "How many women?" I didn't even know what questions I should be asking.

"Just one," he offered.

"This empty box of condoms had three condoms."

"We did it multiple times in one night."

Honestly, it did not matter if it was one time or 100 times, the knife in my back could not get any deeper. The wound could not hurt any more than it did at this moment. The pain of betrayal is very real. No amount of 'I'm sorry' could undo what was done to me. The feeling of disrespect and disgust that ran through my soul was indescribable! I have never felt this much pain in my entire life! Oh yeah, that was that father thing! Now I am experiencing it again from my own husband!

I did not curse at him, I did not bust the windows out of his car, or slash his tires. I did not take a bat and damage all of his studio equipment, I did not throw his clothes out onto the driveway and set them afire. Oh, but I thought about it! But then what would be the point? Damaging property, fighting, having the neighbors call the police, him getting arrested, maybe even getting a restraining order. I just didn't see the point. Was it because I didn't see the point in fighting for a marriage that was dreadfully monotonous for 10 years? When people are fighting, what is it they are fighting for? To keep the marriage? To let the marriage go? What is the fight all about? All I know is I had no energy to fight. Whether to fight to stay, or whether to fight to leave; there was nothing left in me.

The only thing I could do was go into the bedroom, slam the door, lie on my bed and curl up in a fetal position and cry. All day long, for hours I cried. All the energy had left my body, and it felt as if my spirit went into hiding. I had never felt so disrespected in my entire life from a man who claimed to love me! When I set out to purposely make this marriage into something I could live with throughout all the communication challenges; then he goes out and cheats on me with some lowlife chatroom hussie! And a white one at that! Not that it would have been any less disrespectful if she was a black woman, but damn, I'm just saying! The only reason why this was coming out now was because I inadvertently found out. Otherwise, he would have been fine to take it to his grave. God has a way of bringing things that are done in the dark into the light, that is for sure, whether you are ready for it or not.

A few hours later Charles knocked on the bedroom door and came in with a letter he wrote me. The letter stated he had lied, that it was not just one woman. That he had multiple partners back to back. He was currently in the process of setting up his fourth encounter with yet another woman he met from the chatroom before he got caught. He also said when he was young he was a peeping Tom. He used to peep through the keyhole of the bathroom when his aunt was taking a bath or shower. He also admitted a male neighbor tried to molest him when he was a boy. He also admitted he had been watching porn through the entire 10-year marriage. The list went on and on, and on, to a point where I knew, without a shadow of doubt, I did not know the man I married. How could I when he never shared any parts of his personal life with me? How in the world did I marry a man I was not even friends with??

I started to recollect all the times I talked about my life growing up, the molestation, seeing so much abuse as a child. I tried to connect with this man who I said I loved, so we could be close, and for 10 years he held back all these things that he had struggled with, painting a perfect picture of his world, acting as if he had no knowledge or could not connect to what I had been through. And yet I knew nothing about him. Nothing!

On a scale of 1 to 10, sex with Charles was a 5 at best. Just because a man has a Boeing 757 doesn't mean he knows how to land it. However, he could have been a 10 to the next woman. Every woman is different. In order for sex to be great with me, I need to actually have a connection with the man. I could have never gotten out of my marriage what I needed because my husband was not authentic or transparent. If I don't know you, how can I love you? How can I make love to you? There was a grave disconnect between Charles and me. I thought I was making a connection with a real person, but instead my connection was with his representative. In other words, there never was a real connection. It was something I know I kept working towards, but could never figure out where the breakdown was. I felt like a complete fool! It is like digging a hole to plant a tree, but never getting the hole deep enough to plant the tree! What was the point!

I had a little more than a handful of sexual experiences before my marriage. I never had an orgasm prior to my marriage, nor through intercourse during my marriage. That experience came many years later. Charles did introduce me to masturbation, which I knew nothing about before him; and he eventually figured out how to make me climax through oral sex. Even though it would take him 30 to 45 minutes to get me there, usually because my mind was always somewhere else instead of taking in the feeling. I always thought there was something wrong with me. Perhaps there was, as I came with my own set of baggage. However, I later learned when you're really into someone, making love really is a beautiful thing. It is a Mind, Body, Soul, and Spiritual experience. Without that chemistry, it's just sex, where the mind would wander off to doing laundry or making that mental grocery list.

The next couple of weeks were a blur and all I can remember is crying and praying a lot, trying to sleep it off. I rarely left the room except when taking my daughter to daycare and picking her up. On top of that, Charles's company was bought out by a Canadian company and they were moving the employees to Canada. The only options were to either move to Canada or be unemployed. Of course, Charles is now without his six-figure income. On top of dealing with his infidelity, now my man is broke! A broke and broken cheater is definitely not a good look at all!

Journal Entry November 28th, 2004

I realized my husband would never be the husband I needed him to be. I had realized that for some years now. I guess I've never done anything about it because of fear. Where would I go? What will I do? I could not live the next 10 or 20 years in emotional bondage. I only have one life to live and after that's over, that's it for me. I cannot teach my daughter what a good relationship is if it doesn't even exist in my own life. I'm tired of pretending that everything is okay when apparently it is not. And I'm tired of trying to live with it when I no longer want to. Why should I? How can I? I'm tired of talking about it, I'm tired of trying to change things I don't control, and I'm tired of pretending my marriage is strong. I am tired of trying to make something into what it is not. I want out of this marriage! I want out of this bondage! I want to enjoy life more; I want my freedom! I want it now! It is too hard trying to talk to Charles, trying to put up with all the crap I hate, from his snoring to his hocking phlegm, to him blowing his nose like an elephant, to him always walking five steps ahead of me, then farting, leaving that gaseous poison in my pathway to strangle my lungs, to him not communicating, to him not connecting with me, to him not knowing how to care for me. I'm tired! Tired of being the teacher and the babysitter. I needed him to grow up years ago and to this day he still cannot make decisions by himself. I hate that! If there is such a thing as a soulmate, I'll spend the rest of my life single until he finds me, but in the meantime, I just want to be free.

The question that I know will come up sooner or later is, "is there someone else?" The answer to that question is yes! Me! There's finally someone else in this equation and that someone is Me. **ME** *will not be overlooked.* **ME** *will not be devalued.* **ME** *will not be humiliated or disrespected.* **ME** *will not do all the work, all the forgiving, all the taking a backseat.* **ME** *will not be cheated on. I am* **ME** *and I will not lose my self-worth, nor my self-respect because someone else decided to flip the script. When I look in the mirror at myself I need to be satisfied with the* **ME** *that I am. And right now I'm not satisfied with tolerating this foolishness from Charles.*

Journal Entry November 29th, 2004

Right now, I am in the process of making some major changes in my life, and many people may be hurt. But for once I must do something for my own happiness, not for Charles's, and not for Jana's. Not for my friends or the church members who looked up to us. Not for Pastor and Sis. Lockett. The only reasons I am still in the marriage are: #1. My daughter, #2. I did not want Charles to self-destruct financially and emotionally. But now, once again, I am at another place in life. I will begin to reevaluate my marriage hopefully for the very last time.

Journal Entry November 30th, 2004

Yesterday I finally told my husband I wanted a separation. He thought it was because of the infidelity, but that was only a part of it. There are too many things I do not like about my marriage and as I told him, the infidelity was only the straw that broke the camel's back. After I told him, and of course he was not very happy, but I on the other hand had a sudden sense of relief. I took a bubble bath, lit some candles, and went to bed. I slept very well, I might add. I feel alive again, less burdensome. It's on now!

Journal Entry December 2nd, 2004

Last night Charles and I met with Pastor and Sis Lockett to discuss our separation. I think the meeting went well and although in their hearts they want us to be together, they also understand the heartache that Charles has taken me through. I recall Sis Lockett saying, "So

Bro Charles, since the infidelity, what have you done or tried to do to get back in Natasha's good graces?"

Charles replied, "Well I know that she wanted me to be able to help her with the bills since I lost my job, so I have been helping her in her business."

Sis Lockett chimed in, "But have you bought her flowers or gifts or written her a love letter or a letter of apology or anything in that way?"

Charles replied, "No."

Sister Lockett just looked at him and shook her head.

Yes, that was the best he could do. Not that flowers or gifts were going to mend the hole in my heart, but where is the effort? Charles had an opportunity to work for an insurance company in his IT field, but he decided not to take that job because he thought it was best to "help me in my real estate business." He actually thought I wanted to look at him every day and teach him how to make money so he can help me pay our bills? Now why would I want that? Not one time did he ask for my opinion, not once.

I feel I will always love Charles and he will always have a place in my heart as my child's father. Well, at least that is what I told myself when I was trying to be politically correct. I decided I will not spend the rest of my life trying to figure him out, trying to mold him into the husband I needed him to be. It's too much work for me and he has made me work way too hard in this marriage already. I need my life back! My peace of mind, and I will get it by any means necessary and that's my final answer!

Chapter 20

THE SEPARATION

L ife as I knew it was about to change. I had changed. I can recall one of the counseling sessions where the Pastor asked Charles what he thought was the problem. Charles said that I was *changing*. He said every time he turned around I was changing. Yes, I *was* changing. If you're not changing, you're not growing. Charles was determined to stay in the same place, where I was determined to define my place, leave my imprint on the world. Who Charles was, and who I was becoming, were extreme opposites and no longer meshed for me. I was no longer the little college girl he had married. I was becoming the woman who was developing inside of me. Growing, flourishing, making moves, yes changing!

I recall in a separate individual counseling session with Pastor Lockett, he kept asking me the following question.

"Sistah Natasha, do you still love your husband?"

"Sure, I still love my husband," I would reply without giving it any thought. It just seemed like the proper thing to say. I mean, how can you be married to someone and then after he cheats on you, you just stop loving him?

"I want you to write down what love means to you. Just one-word answers. I believe you are the force that can save your marriage if that's what you want."

I began to think about what love means to me. "Faithfulness, honesty, dependable, trustworthy, respectful, friendship, communicative, open, fidelity, stability, security." Tears began to roll down my cheeks. "No Pastor, I no longer love my husband." I just had an epiphany!

"No," the Pastor interjected, "I wasn't trying to..."

"I know what you were trying to do, hoping that Charles would have been able to live up to *some* of my definitions of love, what love means to me. But the fact of the matter is Pastor, he no longer qualifies for my love. I no longer love him and probably have not for some time!"

"No, Sistah Natasha! Now, now let's be rational!" Pastor Lockett was known to rub his head often when he got frustrated with the Saints.

"I think I've been very rational under the circumstances, Pastor." I got up from the chair to leave the counseling session. "I'm so sorry we've wasted so much of your time. I'm sure there are plenty of other people who can use your services."

I believe Pastor Lockett had his hands full with other couples who were literally 'fighting' to save their marriages. One sistah shared that during their counseling meeting with the Pastor she was throwing all kinds of books, vases, and lamps from the shelves at her husband! Ramshacking the Pastor's whole office! Rearranging furniture and shit! Crazy! Yes, the Saints were a mess! I was the type to just leave quietly, but once I'm gone, I won't be coming back! Once again, I did not see what the 'fight' was about.

"Sistah Natasha, do not leave just yet, please have a seat. I understand Charles has hurt you and you have every right to choose to walk away from your marriage. While my job is to help keep the family together, it is not my job to force you to stay in an unhappy situation. I would never want to do that."

"Pastor, Charles *really* hurt me! He has disrespected me and it is not something that I feel I can just get over and let go! And then he has this nonchalant attitude as if he can just say he's sorry and I'm just supposed to forgive him and take him back! I'm tired of being the one who always ends up with the short end of the stick! I'm sick of doing all the work and then people shitting on me as if somehow, I deserved it and then all they have to do is say, "I'm sorry" or "I made a mistake," or "I'm not perfect." By now I was crying so hard the Pastor had to hand me a box of tissues and give me a moment to pull it together.

"You will have to find it in your heart to forgive Charles for the pain that he caused you. However, it's strictly up to you if you decide to take him back or not. Since he was the one who was unfaithful to you, according to the scriptures, you do not have to stay in the marriage. But you MUST find a way to forgive him."

"I thought if I forgave him, it means I needed to take him back and stay married to him." Damn the things we hold ourselves hostage to!

"Forgiving Charles releases yourself. You will need to release yourself regardless if you decide to stay in the marriage or not. It's not just about him."

That actually made a lot of sense. I was so busy holding on to the pain Charles caused me that I felt like I needed, not necessarily revenge, but some type of restitution, so he would have to pay for *something*, for what he did to me, but forgiving him would also release me! It would be like when I had to forgive James. "Forgive him, Natasha, so that you can be FREE! Release yourself! This is more about you than it is about him! He may not deserve it, but you sure do!" I had to constantly remind myself to do right by ME!

Although I asked Charles to leave the house during the separation, he never did. I was basically trying to clear my space of his negative energy. He pretended to be looking at places to purchase or lease. Oh, but I knew well enough that no one was going to allow him to buy anything or lease anything without a job, since he had lost his six-figure income. The real estate investment business he was helping me with did not have his name on it. The tax returns for the business, nor the bank statements included his name. So how was he going to prove his income??? Exactly. He wasn't. Instead of remaining Charles' roommate any longer, I decided I would move out of the house and needed to start searching for a place to go. Clearly, he wasn't planning on going anywhere and was hoping for reconciliation, which was never going to happen. Once my mind was made up, it was a wrap!

Now that I'm processing this newly found mental freedom, I started thinking about my next move. What am I going to do when I become single? What is it like to be a grown woman and dating again? Charles and I had a counseling appointment with the Pastor on yet another day. Charles walked in with a letter in his hand. Apparently, he had printed it out from my emails that he had gotten off the server being the computer guy he is. Of course, I had no idea he would be able to retrieve *my* email messages. And these email messages were very explicit writings. I had been practicing how to flirt and how to be sexy. Since I decided to leave the marriage, I figured why not be ready when I get out there again.

I was totally embarrassed though, as the Pastor read the note out loud.

"I can't wait for you to r-r-ub your big strong hands b-b-between my j-juicy thighs and make my p-pussy drench with your m-moist t-tongue..." The Pastor stumbled through the words from the email print out. "Sistah Natasha!" He was flabbergasted!

"Goddammit! That was such a punk-ass move Charles!" I thought, as I kept my poker face on, mean-mugging him of course, while upholding my calm demeanor.

I had convinced the Pastor that it was just harmless flirting. Oh, but I had to do much convincing and it took some doing! Charles was just trying to flip the script on me, as if this was all my fault! I could not understand why Charles was spying on me when he had already fucked up the marriage and he knew damn well I had already asked for a separation. This was his retaliation, to find me doing something wrong! To catch me in the act, like he had been caught! Now he has the Pastor looking at me all sideways!

I never even mentioned to the Pastor the fact I went to talk to Charles the other night where he was sleeping in the guest bedroom, and he had his laptop computer open. Yep! Just as I thought, he was still talking to these stank white hoes in these chat rooms trying to schedule their next rendezvous! 'Beckys' were waiting when he apparently fell asleep during the conversations. Then he had the nerve to tell me God told him that we needed to fast and pray for our marriage. Now ain't this some shit!

I did not go tit for tat with Charles when he tried to bust me out in front of Pastor Lockett. For what, I already had one foot out the door! Technically, I am already gone; mentally, emotionally, and soon physically. I refused to give him any more of my energy!

Like Chrisette Michelle said in her song, *Blame it on me, say it's my fault, say I'm a liar, a cheater, say whatever you want, as long as it's over!"*

Every night when I was in bed asleep, I would hear the garage door of the house opening and closing. What was Charles doing at 2 and 3 o'clock in the morning, going in and out of the garage? I really did not think much of it, until one day he repeated something I said to Lil' Mama when I was on the phone talking to her while in my car. He actually asked about my grandmother one day out of the blue, which was strange. We had been married for 10 years, and he had never once taken time out to talk to Lil' Mama, who was the closest person to me. When she would call, he would say, "hello, how's it going?" and just pass the phone over to me. He was never interested in connecting with anybody. But all of a sudden, he has questions about *my* Grandmother. Hmmm, makes me wonder.

Now that I know he is looking to have something over my head, I'd better be more careful, just to keep the level of drama down, at least until I find another place to land. Once we were done with the counseling session, I drove over to my friend Penny's house and decided to look for a private investigator from the Yellow Pages. Yes, the Yellow Pages were before we had to Google for information. I figured someone would be able to tell me how he might be recording my phone calls when I'm in the car. The private investigator was extremely helpful as he instructed me on where to look for a mic. The mic was wired along the dashboard and there was a recorder under the console near the brake and accelerator.

"That son of a bitch!" I thought.

He is really hard up to try to catch me doing something wrong! I guess he figured if he caught me in any type of indiscretion then we would be even. Now all of a sudden, he's mad? Now I can get a rise out of him! Too little, too late!

Now, why would Charles be going through all this trouble to try to get me to stay with him? What was he going to do, beat me over the head with guilt? I honestly do not think he ever thought I would really leave him. I probably should have left his ass years ago, but I was known to push through the muddy terrains of life. But at this point I was just tired and did not have enough positives to outweigh the negatives. I was now ready to get on that Midnight Train to Georgia, wherever it would take me. I took off my wedding ring and threw it on the bathroom counter. He later took his off and left it on the same counter. Copycat! Getting on my damn nerves!

Three months after our in-house separation, I went to my friends Paula and Darryl's house to let them know I was getting ready to move out. They encouraged me to let them come to the house with me as I packed up my personal belongings. I packed my clothes, my good towels, and my child. Charles did not say *ne'er* a word!

We had recently purchased a condo as an investment property that was to be renovated and resold, but I decided to move into it. I ended up going to a hotel for about three weeks while the condo was being renovated. I basically went from a 3000 square foot custom built home on almost 1½ acres, to a two-bedroom, one bath, 900 square foot condo, and I could not have been happier!

Being in this space by myself, for myself, for my own well-being, meant I was back in control of my own life. No more talking to this man trying to hold a conversation and figure out how to communicate with him when he really doesn't want to talk. No more cleaning up after him, putting up with his stinky farts and loud snoring. No more of any of that! Then for him to turn around and tell me one day, "I don't like the way you fold my socks."

"Then fold your own damn socks! Matter of fact, do your own damn laundry from now on!" You know when your marriage is over because you just don't like anything about the other person anymore. "He even breathes ugly, hell!"

This was the break I needed to keep my sanity. I was happy and I was at peace, and that was all that really mattered.

I was out of the house about two weeks and went to church one Sunday and lo and behold, Charles was there. He was sitting a couple of rows behind me, as I noticed when we were going up to the front to pay our tithes and offerings. I had no idea the lady behind him was actually *with* him. As I was leaving the church the saints pulled me to the side to say, "who is that white heifer bitch with your husband?" Yes, the saints can curse up a storm! No one knew at this time we were even separated, and for him to bring his new girlfriend to our home church was so shady! I can see what he's trying to do, trying to get me into an emotional entanglement. Trying to get me to react to his nonsense. I just put on my poker face and pretended as if it did not affect me. Multiple church members stopped me as I was exiting the church to bring attention to the situation. All I said was, "Charles and I are separated and he is free to date whomever he likes." Of course, they didn't care much about that as much as they did about him bringing her to the church. Her new name was '*that white heifer bitch*' for weeks to come! After our 12-month separation, as required by law in the state of North Carolina, we were divorced. Sometime during that same month, May 2006, Charles was remarried. Yes, to that *white heifer bitch!* I found out later her real name was Julie.

It's surprising to me that Charles would even date a white woman, yet alone marry one. He always spoke of them as if he could not stand them and had no physical attraction towards them whatsoever. As a matter of fact, during our entire marriage he called all white women 'Gertrude'. As if to give them all one name since they were all clearly the same to him. Yet, I came to find out when he was out having his one-night stands, they were all with white women! I know this because I made him call one of them on the phone so I could let her know she was messing with a married man. I honestly didn't care very much at that point; it was just a way for me to let off a little steam.

I can recall one time when it was Charles' week to have Jana, as we shared joint custody, I was at the hair salon getting my hair done. Jana was in the salon with me as she waited for her dad to pick her up. He came in to get her and took her out to the car which was parked in front of the salon. He then came back into the salon and sat down. Adaomma, who was my hair stylist, was like, "What is he doing?" I had no idea what he was doing, but I was wondering why he would take my child out to the car, then come back inside and sit down, not saying a word. Then all of a sudden he stood up and turned around and said to me, "Next time you need a babysitter, you need to call me first instead of letting someone else keep Jana."

What! Where did this come from? First of all, we both have used the same babysitter, Michelle, who also cleaned our home for us for many years. She babysat Jana for us even when we were married. And I happen to know he would call Michelle sometimes when he needed a babysitter. So, this time I called Michelle when I needed a babysitter, and she came over to the house to babysit Jana; and he acts like he has a problem with it? How absurd! Then Charles let something come out of his mouth that took me straight through the roof!

"You sorry-ass excuse of a mother!"

I know I saw his lips moving, but clearly, I did not hear him correctly! All I know is I jumped up out of the salon chair, with cape on and all, leapt into another chair where the dryer was, like Bat Woman, and I was about to jump on his back and start beating him upside his mothafuckin' head, when the Stylist got in between us and stopped me midair! I was still holding Jana's black Barbie dolls in both hands. I guess I was planning on pistol-doll whipping his ass!

"Who the fuck are you calling a sorry-ass excuse of a mother! That's why your black ass is being sued by Julie's husband! I hope he takes every last penny you got!"

Charles looked around slowly and was so embarrassed I knew this piece of information. Not a word was coming out of his mouth now. Boom! I got yo punk-ass now! What you got to say now, punk-ass bitch!

What Charles did not know was I was privy to this information. He had no idea I had met with Les, even before he married Julie, and got the tea on all his shenanigans!

"Oh yeah, you didn't think I knew, did you? Well, I suggest you take your sorry ass back to whatever rock you crawled from under, 'cause clearly you must have bumped your head on something, or you must be on drugs or something, coming in here talking crazy to me! I don't know who you think you are, talking to me like that. You must be out of your goddamn mind!"

Once I lit into yo' ass, it was hard to put out that flame!

I cussed him plum out! On the contrary, Charles and I never used profanity in our house in our entire 10 years of marriage. I guess it was boiling over and time to release the valve!

Charles ran out of that salon with his tail tucked between his legs, his head hung low, lickin' his wounds. Please don't come for me because Tasha Mack will come out on yo' ass! By the time I was done with him he was looking, and most likely feeling, two inches tall.

Mind you, I was doing all this fussing and cussing while standing on top of the hair dryer chair in the salon. I looked around the salon and every woman who was under a hair dryer was now up. Some had purses as a weapon, books they were once reading, one was working on the computer, another had already taken off her shoes where the heels would double as a weapon. After the whole incident had subsided upon Charles' departure, I looked around and saw a posse full of black women, ready to jump in what they thought was going to be a black man beat down! We all laughed so hard as we each told how we planned to participate in the downfall of yet another black man. We were about to beat Charles' ass and then call the ambulance to tell them to come get him. There are certain lines you do not cross, and that day he crossed the mothafuckin' line. I never had this problem from him before, and never plan to have it again. The one thing you cannot mess with is a black mother when it's dealing with her child. Because I would rip you a new one! And don't let there be back up because he was never going to make it out of there alive!

One day I received a call from a friend of mine who says her mother, who works at the courthouse, saw Charles' name come across her desk. Apparently, Charles was being sued by Julie's husband, for Abandonment of Affection. In North Carolina, you can sue anyone you can prove has stolen the affection of your spouse from you. That's how I knew Charles was being sued.

About a week later, after things had calmed down and I had finally moved into my two-bedroom condo, I received a call from a friend of mine expressing her concern about a dream she had.

"Sis, I had this very disturbing dream about you last night."

"Oh really?"

"Yes, I don't know how I feel about telling it to you though."

"Why, what harm is it going to do?"

"Okay so I was somewhere with my husband and we had invited you and your husband."

"Okay... and?"

"But the problem is the husband you were with was not Charles. The man that you were with was clearly somebody that you were totally in love with, but it was not your husband. Are you cheating on your husband?"

After I explained to Tanya, because I know she means well, that my husband was unfaithful to me and I have already moved out of the house, but just never said anything to anyone until I was able to get settled. She was very adamant about this dream and the fact I was the one in love with another man and it looked like I was the one who was cheating with this man.

The only thing I could say to myself was, "God, why are you putting my business all out in these streets?"

Chapter 21

NEW BEGINNINGS

I *will love you anyway, even if you cannot stay*

> *I think you are the one for me, here is where you ought to be*
> *I just want to satisfy you, but you're not mine and I can't deny it*
> *Don't you hear me talkin', baby, love me now or I'll go crazy... Woo-ooo sweet thang...*

As I was driving to the grocery store to pick up a few items, I was jamming to Chaka Khan's song "Sweet Thang," wondering how this next chapter of my life would pan out. I hadn't had many relationships as an adult, seeing that Charles and I got married right after college and I was 10 years deep in marriage and 12 years total with the same man.

But now, my situation presents itself with new opportunities and more options. Hold up, there's only one problem, I was green... meaning inexperienced, naive, gullible, in the way of relationships outside of marriage. 'I don't know nothing about dating out here in these streets!' I'd constantly remind myself. I've had my marital blinders on for so long, and rightfully so, that I probably wouldn't even know when a man was flirting with me. Case in point, by the time I arrived at the Harris Teeter grocery store I was searching for something down one aisle, there was a man down the same aisle who appeared to be looking at me, but I wasn't quite sure. Then when I went down another aisle, there he was again, and then when he caught up with me on the third aisle, he finally walked past me and said, "Hey, you must be following me!" Looking perplexed, I thought to myself, 'Why would he think *I* was following *him*?'

On my way back out to the car, my cell phone rang. It was Terrence.

Answering the phone, "Hey what's up, Terrence?

"Hey, you got a moment?" he asked. Terrence's voice was deep and kind of sexy, but of course I had not noticed that before .

"Sure, let me get in the car right quick because it's cold outside today." I arrived at the car, got in, started the ignition, shut the door, and quickly blasted the heat.

"Ok, I'm here," trying to get settled. "What's going on?"

"Hey, I just wanted to check to see if you needed any materials for your seminar at the church next weekend." I was hosting a 'Clean up Your Credit' seminar at Evangel Fellowship Church.

"Oh no, I'm fine, I have everything already printed out and in binders. It's going to be a really good class I'm sure," by now I was driving back home.

"You speak to people so effortlessly," he said, "and people really seem to connect well with you so I know they will be blessed."

"Ahh, thanks Terrence," I was kind of blushing. "That's truly a compliment coming from you."

Terrence was one of the leaders in our church. I had known him for several years, but not personally. He seemed to be one of the good guys. Evangel Fellowship was a thriving ministry in Greensboro, NC. It was growing fast with many professional African American couples. We worked together to put on events, seminars, plays, etc. Many people are what we call, 'churchy' - so overly religious, they are no earthly good. I, however, did not grow up in the church, so my 'church' experience was more spiritual and about my relationship with God, not about religion.

"Oh, one more thing," I continued, "did we get the notice out to everyone that the meeting is changed from 9 am to 10 am on Saturday?"

"Ahhh, yes, of course, that was already done and all attendees have already confirmed. Matter of fact, all the seats are filled!" Terrence said.

"Oh wow!" I was excited, "That's good news, Terrence. Thanks!"

"Of course," he replied.

After giving it some thought, I asked, "Hey, can I tell you something funny that just happened in the grocery store a few minutes ago?"

He seemed interested in wanting to continue conversing, "Sure!"

I shared the story about the man following me from aisle to aisle in Harris Teeter.

"What? You can't tell when a man is flirting with you!" he seemed so surprised.

"I mean, why should I? I never even paid any attention until now since my marriage is on the rocks!"

"Wait, what? Your marriage is on the rocks? Nooooo!" Terrence seemed genuinely concerned.

"Yeah, it's a sad situation, but it's pretty much over. I'm just waiting for my husband to move out. I really don't want to talk about it though." I knew enough to pull back from this conversation.

"I know what you mean. Relationships can be tough," he seemed so welcoming and easy to talk to.

"Tough is an understatement." I couldn't resist the need to vent. "I mean, I really don't know where it went wrong. I would have never thought in a million years, that Charles would've cheated on me. Our relationship wasn't all bells and whistles, but it was what I would consider stable. I guess?" Taking a deep breath, "I'm sorry, I don't even know why I'm sharing all this with you. I guess because I haven't had anybody that I wanted to talk to about it. It's just too embarrassing!"

Terrence was such a good listener and didn't offer anything negative about the situation. "Well Natasha, what I do know about you from what you share in your classes, you will bounce back like you have done for your entire life. Healing takes time, and I'm sure you'll get there."

"I appreciate the encouragement, Terrence, and didn't mean to bog you down with my drama."

"Honestly, it's my pleasure," he began. "I'm glad you felt comfortable enough to share and glad I was here to help."

"Yeah, I guess I had it bottled up for too long. I needed to vent."

"Not a problem," he reaffirmed.

Terrence and I were volunteer work buddies. We never had any reason to speak about our personal lives to one another. He knew of my husband and knew I was the *"preferred"* church real estate agent and that was the extent of it. Our in-person and telephone conversations were limited to ministry business, real estate, and nothing more.

"Ok, so getting back to you not knowing when a man is flirting with you," Terrence was not ending the conversation.

"Oh so that's where we're going? That's crazy, though, right? I'm a 34 year old woman and I can't tell when a man is flirting with me!" I laughed.

"I would just assume that a woman of your caliber would be more aware..."

"Caliber?" I was trying to tune in. "What do you mean by that?"

"You're beautiful, smart, and determined. When you walk into the room, your presence commands attention. And more than likely the attention of men. Oh, trust me, women are looking too, wanting to be like you, wishing they were you."

Dayuuummmm, it was like that? Or was he just trying to feel my head with some bullshit? "Really?" I don't know if I was a little uncomfortable with where this conversation was going because all of a sudden I got a weird feeling in the pit of my stomach. "Well you're right I am focused and I intentionally wear blinders so that I don't have to see what's going on around me. I feel like it's best that way."

"I understand that," he said. "But what are you going to do when you see a man you like?"

"What do you mean, I'm not gon' do nothing, but wait for him to approach me."

He began laughing, but I didn't see anything funny. "What, what's wrong with what I'm saying?"

"Oh, so you wouldn't approach a man first?"

"Hell, naw! I mean, no sir...not in a million years!"

"Not even if you thought he was nice looking?" he began to push the issue.

"Like I said, not in a million years! That's definitely not my style. I guess I'm just old school." My grandmama didn't raise me like that!"

"Well, it's ok for a woman to go after what she wants, as long as she knows what that is."

"That's just it, I'm not even sure that I know what I want. I've been with one man for so long, I've kind of lost sight of that."

"There are a lot of men out there who pretend to be something that they are not," he began. "That's the biggest challenge from what I hear. So be careful."

"I wish they had a book called *Flirting for Dummies* because I could definitely use a tutorial."

Someone actually wrote that book a few years later.

"Or...." Terrence began.

"Or...what?" I asked.

"Or maybe, I could tutor you. As long as you don't get any ideas!"

"Really, ok...ok, you're gonna tutor me?"

"Yeah, not really tutor, but give you some pointers," he was very matter-of-fact.

"Alright, bet!" I was all in! I was just excited to have any kind of assistance. Being married, it's not like I had any guy friends. The only male friends were from the couples that Charles and I had as friends. Terrence seemed like a good person from working with him over the years so I was willing to give this a try. Plus I didn't want to get my girlfriends and family involved with my marital drama, so this would serve as a pleasant distraction for now.

Meanwhile, back at home, I settled with the thoughts of my marriage being over... I knew the exact moments (there were two moments to be exact) when I had come to this conclusion.

The first moment was when I was in a counseling session with our Pastor and he asked me to write down what love meant to me, and I then realized that Charles no longer qualified for that love. I left that counseling session with a new outlook on life. I felt like chains had me shackled and bound to this marriage because I did not want to look like a failure... to myself, to my family, and especially to my daughter.

The second moment I knew my marriage was over was one day when I was walking past and saw myself in the mirror. I thought to myself, "What kind of woman am I to stay in a marriage that is already unfulfilling? What am I teaching my daughter about finding her happiness if I am unwilling or unable to find mine? Don't I owe it to myself to choose the way I want to live out the rest of my life? Plus, he had the nerve to cheat on me!" Charles' infidelity actually gave me a way out, and I decided to take it. I decided I wanted to explore the next chapter of my life.

Terrence and I continued to talk and text more as I was trying to learn to flirt and trying to deal with this mess at home. I can't remember the exact message that I texted him one day when I sent my first attempt to flirt with him. I then called him.

"Hey," he answered the phone.

"Hello, did you get my text?" I was a little nervous because this was my first try.

He hesitated, "Uh, yeah, I got it. Is this your attempt to send a flirtatious text?"

"Yes, so did you *not* feel like you were being flirted with?" I honestly thought I was doing something.

"Uh, no, not at all!" he stated honestly.

We both just fell out laughing, cracking up! I laughed so hard; my side was hurting. Terrence and I were very open and authentic with one another, just in the way we spoke to each other. I can't ever remember having such light fun with my own husband, that was just not his thing. Terrence and I had become pretty close friends as the months flew by. By now, we began to share more about our relationships from the past, family drama, financial challenges, goals and dreams. We began to share our hearts with one another and it honestly seemed so natural, so organic, so easy. Nothing like what I had with Charles.

Terrence was extremely handsome. He stood about 6'3, dark chocolate, with a salt and peppered shadowed beard, broad shoulders, and well-kept dreads! When he looked at me in the classes we would host every Saturday at the church, his eyes could burn a hole through my soul. Not only was he good-looking, but he was also highly intelligent, articulate, and fun to be around. Regardless of how 'FINE' Terrence was, I never paid him any attention until one day... I did.

I remember going into this saying, "I wonder what it feels like to break the rules?" Everybody was breaking the rules except me. I was known to walk the straight and narrow for the most part. No, I was not perfect, nor was I trying to be, but I saw things clearer in black and white and did not dabble in the gray areas too much in my life. First of all, I was too scared to play with fire and secondly, I just was not a big fan of drama.

What I had going on with Terrence was innocent, well at least that's the way it started. I had to give myself permission to break the rules, flirting with someone while I was still legally married. Separated, but very much married, and still living in the same house together. I guess this is the type of situation that they refer to as being *Complicated*. Even though my marriage was over, and even though I made Charles move to the guest bedroom on the other side of the house, I was already feeling guilty as I was catching feelings for another man. YES, I gave myself permission to break the rules! For once in my life! I had no idea or any further thoughts of where this may lead at this time. I was trying to learn to flirt with him, he *was* flirting with me, and I was welcoming the experience. Not knowing where this journey would lead us long-term, I knew I had something special with Terrence, a friend, a confidant, a new love interest... perhaps?

My relationship with Terrence grew stronger and stronger as we got to know more about one another. There was so much passion, sensitivity, and respect in our relationship that I did not see it coming as it was flowing so seamlessly.

Will I dare say, it just happened? No. That's what most people would say, but no, it did not just happen. I chose it. We chose it. I welcomed it into my life when I needed it the most and then little by little, with every flirt, every phone call, every text, every email... it happened. Not by accident, not haphazardly... it happened on purpose!

Remember that email that Charles gave to Pastor Lockett in one of my counseling sessions? "I can't wait for you to rub your big strong hands between my juicy thighs and make my pussy drench with your moist tongue..." I had finally gotten my flirtatious game up and was receiving rave reviews from Terrence when this email surfaced.

Well, Charles took that same email print out over to Terrence's house to confront him with it. I then received a phone call from Terrence's wife, Nakita. Terrence had a moment to forewarn me that this was happening.

"Hello," I answered the phone nervously already having rehearsed my responses in my head.

"Hello Natasha, this is Nakita, Terrence's wife. Do you have a moment to talk?"

Yes, Terrence was a married man! My guilt with flirting with him was not just because I was still legally married and was still living in the same house with my husband, but it was also because Terrence had a whole wife! On top of that, how could I treat another woman the same way some white heifer-bitches had treated me! It was a damn shame wasn't it? And for once in my life, I was all for *the damn shame*! For now, it was time to play the game that everyone else was playing.

"Hey, Nakita, what can I do for you?" I played it cool.

"So Charles just left my house."

"What! What was he doing at your house?"

"He came over here to show me a letter that apparently he printed from an email where you and Terrence were having conversations."

"What?"

"Yes, Terrence also explained to me that it was harmless flirting and I just wanted to hear your side of the story."

"Yes, it was just harmless flirting and I do apologize for that, as you know Terrence and I work together volunteering at the church. Charles is just mad because I asked him for a separation after I found out that he cheated on me. I'm so sorry that he has dragged you and your husband into this mess just because he's already messed up our marriage."

"Yeah that makes sense. I'm sorry to bother you with this, but I just wanted to make sure everything was good."

"Well I can assure you; everything is good, Nakita. Thanks for calling. Merry Christmas!"

"Merry Christmas to you, too!"

Whew! I hung up that phone so quickly and let go of the breath that I had been holding on to since I first answered the phone! I had never been in a predicament like this before! I actually had somebody's wife confronting me about cheating with her husband because my husband had gone to her house and made some allegations! What the fuck!

I made sure I quickly moved out of that house as from the looks of it, Charles wasn't going anywhere. Charles was unraveling, becoming loose at the hinges and I had no idea what he would try to do next. I'd better get out as soon as possible and that's when I got my friends, Paula and Daryl involved to assist with my move.

After getting a legal separation and staying in a hotel for several weeks, Terrence and I began to have our face to face meetings. He would bring dinner to my hotel and check up on me. Terrence was a shoulder to cry on, a confidant, a friend, and I felt my attraction for him growing stronger and increasing with each meeting. He was just what the doctor ordered as going through a divorce is such a tasking event. Especially since we had our daughter Jana to be concerned about and also 13 rental properties at that time, plus the custom built home that we once shared. Also let's not forget shared bills and bank accounts. We both hired attorneys to whom we paid thousands of dollars to fight each other on our behalf. It was a mess! I was drained mentally, emotionally, physically and let's not forget, financially.

By the time I moved into my newly renovated condo after I had my friend, Paula, work her interior design skills to decorate and furnish it, I finally felt like my new life was beginning. Although I was still going back and forth with Charles about drop off and pickup times to and from Jana's school, doctors' appointments, school activities, rental properties, tenants, etc., I was now in my own place! There's nothing like having your own! I can breathe now! Relax, relate, release! I was finally in my happy place, all by my happy self!

Then my phone rang; it was Terrence. While we had toned down the flirting tremendously as things started to get a little messier than I was equipped for, I still thought about him, often. He was extremely supportive, patient, but unwavering, strong. All the things I needed in a man. But why would I have such thoughts about a man who's not even available, a married man? Then again, my divorce won't be final for another year. Am I prepared for the drama that can follow these thoughts? Not at all!

"Hello," I finally answered the phone.

"Hey, how are you?" he asked in his low sexy voice.

"I'm exhausted. It's been a very long day."

"I understand that. Have you eaten?"

"No, but I'm not really hungry. I think I'm going to turn in early."

"Ok no problem. Get some rest. I'll check up on you tomorrow or in the next couple of days."

"Thanks, Terrence."

"Have a good night."

"You, too."

As I pushed the end button on my cell phone I realized how much I had been thinking about Terrence and how wrong those thoughts were. However, the chemistry and attraction that had grown between us was undeniable. Or was it? Was Terrence just being a nice guy and letting me vent and cry on his shoulders or was I reading more into this than it really was? How could I be sure he had feelings for me? Did I have feelings for him or was I just infatuated because he was everything my ex wasn't?

I picked up my cell phone and called Terrence back. He answered on the first ring.

"Hey, is everything ok over there?"

"Um yes, everything's ok. Although I'm on my way to bed, I want to know if you can come over tomorrow evening to talk?"

"You sure? I can come over now if you need me to."

"No, I'm sure. Jana will be with Charles, so tomorrow works out better."

"Ok, do you need me to bring some dinner?"

"That's sweet, but I'll cook instead."

"Ok, so I'll come over tomorrow around 7pm."

"Then 7pm it is. See you then."

"Goodnight."

I definitely couldn't see him tonight because I needed to get my head together. I needed to make sure I wasn't reading something that was not there. I needed to be sure if these feelings that I was having were real or just a figment of my imagination. I had never felt chemistry like this before, like two magnets pulling each other inward and although I'm doing my best to pull back for the sake of both of our situations, the force is overpowering. Or is this all just in my head? I needed to find out. But for now, I need rest.

The next evening, all went as planned. Terrence came over, we had dinner and we talked and laughed and had a good time.

"What is this?" I finally asked.

"What do you mean?"

"I mean, what are we doing?"

Terrence grabbed my hand across the kitchen table, "We're allowing to be what was meant to be."

I felt that funny feeling in the pit of my stomach again. "But you're a married man, so these feelings are not right."

"Technically, you're right, but there's no doubt that they are real feelings. Several years ago when I first saw you at the church I knew you were something special."

"So you had eyes for me years ago?"

"Yes, but of course I would have never infringed on your relationship with Charles, but then recently when we began working together, it just took my crush to a whole new level."

"Wow, I had no idea."

"Right, I'd never give you any reason to suspect that I had a crush on you. But now sitting across from you, holding your hands and looking into those beautiful eyes, draws me into you. You have a hold on me, on my heart."

Along with the feeling in my stomach came a tingling feeling that my vagina had not felt in many years! What the fuck! Moisture with no penetration!

"You know how everyone thinks that we've already done something? I mean Charles told Pastor Lockett and Nakita about the flirtatious comments in the email, and who knows if she has told any of her friends. Needless to say, they already assume we broke the rules. They already think we had a sexual affair."

Dang! I knew Charles' mind could run wild with it, but at that point I really didn't care. I did not know that Pastor Lockett and Nakita actually thought we had a sexual affair. But I was beginning to understand that emotional affairs are just as dangerous or more tumultuous because when the heart is involved... beware!

"Well technically we broke the rules when we started flirting with each other."

"I know, but that's more like a misdemeanor, not a felony. But what if we actually *broke* the rules?"

I had never broken the rules before. Well maybe some small infractions when I was in high school and college, but never in adulthood. I honestly wanted to know what all the hype was about with breaking the rules. Why did most people want to do it and like to do it? Although I was never a "monkey see-monkey do" type person, I was extremely intrigued with the opportunity to break the rules. Not with just anyone, but with a person that I already admired and respected and connected with.

Then it happened! Terrence pulled my hands toward him as we both stood up from the kitchen table. "What if we broke the rules together?" He grabbed my face with one hand and we kissed passionately, turning my body against the kitchen wall and stretching my arms toward the ceiling.

"Yes, I'd love to break the rules with you!" I said in a breathy whisper.

He grabbed me with his strong arms and wrapped them around my body tightly and I continued to melt like butter in his presence. As I felt his nature rise between my legs I took my right hand and grabbed his big dick letting him know that I wanted to feel all of him, every freakin' inch of him. My pussy was calling his name and he knew it! He passionately kissed my neck and down to my breast while he unbuttoned my blouse with his teeth. I then unbuckled his belt and let his pants fall to the kitchen floor. As he stepped out of his pants, still kissing me and pulling my long hair, we stumbled down the hall into my master bedroom.

"Are you sure this is what you want?" he asked gazing into my eyes while dropping those drawers!

I stopped for a moment to catch my breath from panting, looked down at his dick which was standing up at attention, dropped down to my knees and stroked my tongue up and down his penis; but just a few times, not to spoil him too early.

"What do you think?" was my answer.

He grabbed me and picked me up and let me straddle his body as we pounced on the bed and made love, for the first time. Round 1, round 2, round 3! I had never felt this close to a man before this point in my life, not even my husband of 10 years. What Terrence possessed was the ability to connect with me. To see me! We had the best after sex pillow talk ever! We shared so much with one another and became so comfortable and close within the following months. Terrence and I had fallen deeply in love very quickly.

It was like a whirlwind effect. I had broken the rules with someone who made my heart sputter and my pussy juicy! And most importantly, Terrence and I had a genuine love and respect for one another. We knew exactly who we were and what we had until one day I decided that it wasn't enough.

Before I knew it, my relationship with Terrence had spun into a full blown love affair! Although we would meet at my condo, we would also have dinner at restaurants, and sometimes meet at hotels. We have gone skydiving and done other fun things together. When having an affair, the rush and adrenaline comes from the thought of getting caught or just having close calls. If someone sees us, then we'd have to come up with a story on the spot, thereby testing our ability to be spontaneous. Even having to sneak in phone calls at night when he couldn't get away to come and see me. If either one of us had trouble sleeping, Terrence would tell his wife he needed to run out to the store, just to have a conversation with me in the car. Terrence and I were always there for one another, through the good and the bad, through the ups and downs. The precious nature and purity of the relationship should not go unnoticed, but the fact that I was totally in love with and sleeping with another woman's husband was a total atrocity! The fact that I was living the life of someone that I knew I was not, and enjoying every minute of it was quite perplexing for a woman like me with strong morals and values. What a dilemma!

For about the first six months of the affair, I enjoyed it wholeheartedly. Maybe not initially, since it's not who I am, but eventually I leaned into it and it became a part of my everyday life. Sneaking around, ducking and diving, taking chances, telling lies on top of lies! The sin! It was something about the sin that kept making me want more of the sin! Case in point, one Sunday, I was already seated in the pew when Terrence and Nakita entered the church and sat right beside me. Meaning he sat beside me and she was on the other side of him. He sat beside me on purpose to send a very important message to his wife, the Pastor, and the church. "Clearly if they had something going on, he would not be sitting next to her with his wife on the other side of him." It was brilliant, yet risqué.

Every time the Pastor would state, "Look at your neighbor and say, neighbor, it's so good to see you." He'd always turn to look at me first. I'd then play along and cross my legs to show him some skin as I only wore dresses to church. With pointed toes in my stilettos, oscillating my leg back and forth, I watched him as he watched me. I'd then pull my cell phone out of my purse and text him, "Meet me at the condo after church. I have something special in store for you."

Whew! I'd sit in church all hot and bothered until I could get him back to my condo to do ungodly things to him! And he, of course, would be more than happy to return the favor!

Everything we did was hot and sexy and fun and exciting and spontaneous and organic! While we were afraid of getting caught, that fear clearly did not outweigh the adrenaline that ran through our veins, which made it all worthwhile.

Then one day, there was a shift. I went to one of my real estate client's weddings at the church. I sat in the back of the church while I thought about my torrid love affair with Terrence. As I listened to the couple recite their vows, I dissected those vows, I honored those vows and at one point had much respect for those vows. I began to rethink what I was doing in my life versus what I really wanted. My client was now a wife, it is the highest position of the land, in my opinion. I was once a wife, now a mistress! Me? A mistress? Those two words did not even go together in my mind. The wife is the first lady; the mistress is nothing but the side chick!

"What have I done?" I asked myself the much needed question. I created a love affair based on a fantasy that I wanted to live out simply because I was hurt by someone else. I'm wife material! I'm nobody's mistress! The mistress doesn't reserve the right to Christmas, Thanksgivings, and family reunions. No date nights and couples' retreats. Those rights only belong to the wife. The mistress is kept a secret. Yes she gets the unadulterated fun and uninhibited sexy part of who he is, but she can never have all of him. And that just wasn't enough for me. I'm an "all or nothing" type of woman!

When I arrived home from the wedding, I knew what had to be done. I knew I would have to break things off with Terrence, for good this time. Yes, I had tried to break up with him multiple times before, but I struggled between letting go of the friend when breaking up with the boyfriend. I tried to keep my friendship with him, which was very precious to me, but we kept sucking each other back into the affair and there was seemingly no end to this rollercoaster ride. I knew it would be difficult to let him go, as my love for him was pure and kind and precious, but I also knew what I had to do. Since I didn't want to risk saying my goodbyes face to face, I left the message on a digital recorder and texted him that it would be under the mat outside my condo door. I was not in a position to talk to him. That's how I broke up with Terrence, for good. I knew it was time to move on and it was time for him to give his marriage the attention that it needed and deserved since he had decided to stay in the marriage.

Leaving my friend was the single hardest thing I had to do after my separation from Charles, but my divorce was about to be finalized and I was about to be free. How can I be free when I'm too busy being entangled with a married man!

Do I have any regrets? Yes and no. Yes I regretted that I loved up and loved on another woman's husband. And no, I do not regret the experience from the type of relationship that I learned could actually exist. To love your best friend is a blessing, except it cannot be another woman's husband! Lesson learned. Check.

Chapter 22

GOOD OLE' PAW PAW

My father and I had not spoken in about a year and Jana's elementary school was celebrating Grandparents' Day.

"Mommy, where is my Paw Paw? All the kids at school talk about their Paw Paw for Grandparents' Day. How come I don't ever see my Paw Paw?"

I started to tell her that her Paw Paw was dead, but then I'd have to eventually tell her the truth later that evil doesn't die that easily. So I decided to take the high road, as a good parent, and let her call my father on the phone. They would talk on the phone once every other week for a few weeks and then I heard Jana say, "When are you going to come see me?"

Oh hell! I was hoping for sure these telephone calls would be enough for her. How long does this Grandparents' Day shit last at her school anyway?

"Mommy, can we go see Paw Paw? Please! Please!" Kids were always begging for something. Like me when I was a kid, she had no idea what she was getting herself into!

"Let me see what I can do, Jana." I grabbed the phone from her, took a deep breath, swallowed my pride, put everything aside that I felt about this man for the sake of my child, and asked him the question, "Are you planning to be in town next weekend?"

"Y-yeah, y-yeah, we'll b-b-be h-here," he stuttered. Surprisingly, he seemed a bit excited that I would be asking.

"Ok, I will see if I can get a flight for Jana and me to fly out to Nashville."

"W-W-Will you n-n-need a ride f-f-from the airport?"

"No, we will rent a car. Is it ok that we stay at your house the first night and the last night? I will drive to Memphis to see my Auntie Nita and Lil' Mama and spend Mother's Day with them."

"Oh, o-okay! T-that s-s-sounds good then."

"Alright, I'll text you the confirmation."

I was not at all excited about seeing my father, but it had been a while and maybe there was a slight chance that things were different now with the new wife, Alyssia.

Yes, Floyd had married Alyssia (a girl in her 20s who was 30 years younger than him!) in the same month that his divorce from Lois was final! They actually got married in the house that Lois helped buy! Nothing in the house had changed. Same furniture, same decor, same wallpaper, same everything. Damn, he probably didn't even flip the mattress that he and Lois slept on! What woman would move into a house that the man owned with a previous woman and not want to redecorate and change some things? Clearly a young one who didn't know any better! Which is probably why he chose her in the first place. She was young, inexperienced, and didn't have much, yes the perfect target!

The afternoon that we arrived, Jana was so excited that they had a fish tank with some beautiful fish. Orange, blue, red. She could not take her eyes off those fish.

"Ms. Alyssia, can I please feed the fish? Can I? Please, please?"

"Yes, Jana, I will show you how to feed the fish, but you have to wait a little while longer until it's feeding time."

A couple of minutes passed and Jana asked again. "Ms. Alyssia, is it time to feed the fish yet?"

"Not yet, Jana."

"How much longer, Ms. Alyssia?"

"Maybe 20 more minutes."

A few more minutes passed because of course Jana didn't know the difference between 20 minutes and 2 minutes. "Ms. Alyssia, has it been 20 minutes yet?"

"No Jana, not yet."

I felt sorry for Alyssia because my child was beginning to wear her down. "Jana, don't keep asking Ms. Alyssia about feeding the fish. When it's time for the fish to eat, she will let you feed them."

"I know, mommy, but they are so beautiful and they look ready to eat to me. Don't they look ready to eat to you, Ms. Alyssia?"

"Ok, Jana, you win, let me show you how to feed the fish," Alyssia had given in.

"Yayyy!" Jana jumped up and down as she was happy to finally be able to feed the fish and I was happy that she could stop begging the poor girl about it. After Jana finished the feeding, my father came through the back door into the kitchen.

"D-did somebody j-just feed the f-fish?" You would have thought somebody drank the last of the almond milk and put the empty carton back in the refrigerator.

"Yes, I let Jana feed the fish a little early," Alyssia said, trying to keep the situation calm.

"You k-k-know you're not t-t-to feed the fish b-before 4'oclock, their feeding t-time!" my father said in a more stern voice than before.

Jana's eyes began to weld up with tears, "I didn't mean to get you in trouble, Ms. Alyssia!"

I had to put a stop to this! "Daddy, why is it such a big deal? The fish are supposed to eat at 4pm, it's 10 minutes to 4! So what? You come in here hollering at your wife in front of my child making her feel like she's done something wrong. Damn! Is it gon' kill the fish to eat 10 minutes early?"

Ooooh, if looks could kill! He looked at me and rolled his eyes and walked out the back door. What was it with this guy? I mean, Jana is a kid. Don't come in here making my baby cry for no reason because it will be a major problem! If he wanted to holler at his wife, do that shit after we leave or when we go to bed at night like he used to do to Lois back in the day! But don't bring that shit in front of my child and make her feel guilty for asking to feed the damn fish early! He reminded me why I couldn't stand his ass, why we didn't get along, why I didn't have my child around him, and why I had stopped talking to him in the first place. You can't teach old dogs new tricks!

Floyd pretty much kept his distance the remainder of my stay. I tried to befriend Alyssia while I was there. But unlike Lois, there just wasn't much of a connection. She didn't have any friends, she didn't have any hobbies, she didn't like to do anything except go to work, come home, and go to bed by 5:30 in the afternoon. The girl was still in her 20s acting like a 60 year old!

As I assisted her in cleaning up the kitchen after dinner, I had been putting the dishes in the dishwasher when she stopped me. "Oh no, Tasha, we can't use the dishwasher."

"Oh really, why not?"

"Because Floyd says the dishwasher wastes too much water."

So in other words, she's the dishwasher.

"Well, they do have the new dishwashers out now that are water savers. Maybe he can buy you one of those."

Shiiiit! Let me hurry up and help this girl get these dishes out of this dishwasher before this man comes in here fussing at her again. He's gon' really blow a gasket next time!

Later on that evening, I was upstairs in the office with Alyssia and my younger brother, Jay (who is close to Alyssia's age).

"Hey, Alyssia, I need to print out my boarding pass. Can you log me into the computer?"

"Oh, I don't have the login information to the computer."

"Oh so you never use the computer?"

"Yes, but I just have to get Floyd to log in for me any time I want to use it."

Then Jay says, "I have the login information. I'll login for you."

How does my brother have the login information to the home computer and he doesn't even live there, but my father's wife has to ask permission to use the computer? Unbelievable!

Late in the middle of the night I heard noises. Knocks and bumps against the wall. Wait? Is that another dream? My mother? Lois? Alyssia? Damn! I'm not coming back here. Jana's just gonna have to get over it!

The next morning, when Jana and I were preparing to leave to drive to Memphis to see Lil' Mama and Auntie Nita, Alyssia came to the guest bedroom.

"Hey, good morning, we are on our way to Memphis now. Where is Daddy as he is supposed to tell me the easiest route to get there."

"Uhm, he left early and has already gone to the gym."

"Oh, so he just left without saying goodbye?"

"Well, I can show you how to get to the highway."

I'm not surprised at my father's actions. A typical temper tantrum thrower! He's been known to act out like a two-year-old when things don't go his way. Meaning when I stood up against him for Alyssia about letting Jana feed the fish. Really it wasn't about Alyssia, as much as it was about my child. If anyone does anything that goes against what he wants, then that person is basically in the doghouse with him.

Alyssia's directions sucked but I eventually found my way to the highway and then to Memphis. The next morning when I awoke and checked my voicemail messages, I realized I had missed a call from a blocked number at 2am in the morning. It was from Floyd.

"I-I do n-n-not a-appreciate you c-coming into my h-house like you own the p-place when you h-have not paid one d-damn bill u-u-p in here. You h-h-ave dis-d-disrespected me and you have d-d-isrespected my w-w-ife acting j-just like a l-little b-b-bitch. Therefore, y-you are n-no l-longer welcome in m-my house since you had the the-th-the audacity to s-say something n-n-egative about my d-dishwasher. So I-I-I-I don't care w-where you sleep when you r-r-eturn to Nashville. You can s-sleep in your c-car or you can s-sleep on the streets f-f-f-or all I-I-I care but your b-b-ougie ass is n-n-ot w-w-elcome here with me and my w-w-ife. P-Plus you're just j-j-ealous because she's y-younger and p-p-prettier than y-you anyway. Y-you a-a-asshole!"

So my punk-ass father just called me in the middle of the mothafuckin' night and blocked his number so I wouldn't know that it was him and left this bitch-ass message on my voicemail because he wasn't man enough to say it to my goddamn face! Plus with all that damn stuttering, it took him five minutes to leave a fuckin' two minute message! And to add insult to injury, shiiittt, his wife couldn't light a candle to my pretty ass! But how absurd it is for a father to say that about his own daughter. Loud and wrong as usual! I'm so done with him! This was definitely the last straw! No man has ever called me outta my goddamn name, except my father.

What a shame! What a mothafuckin' shame! I was livid! I was hurt that my own father would speak to me and about me in that way. So what, I stood up to him! I was going to keep standing up for myself and for my daughter and if he didn't like it, then FUCK him! And to think that I begged God for his ass to be in my life. This was the true meaning of getting the short end of the mothafuckin' stick. He was the worst man I ever met! The man that I loved the most at one time is also the one who ended up disappointing me the most. I had no idea he would be so evil until I had my own personal experience with him. An experience that will unfortunately forever be embedded into my soul. Good ole' Paw Paw was nothing but a little bitch baby!

Chapter 23

MARKET CRASH AND BURN

A fter my affair with Terrence was officially over, I poured the majority of my time and energy into my real estate investment business. My business was flourishing as I added more agents and full time employees to the business. I purchased my next home, for Jana and me, which was beautifully decorated by my friend Paula and set up to look like the replica of a model in my new home subdivision. My daughter was doing well with the transition of her parents being divorced after some bumps and hurdles, and we were living our best life!

I could afford to buy my child and myself anything we wanted! We enjoyed many spa days of pampering, dinners at the finest restaurants, traveling, weekends at the beach, along with whatever materialistic things our hearts desired. We were also big givers. Giving to our church and other charities, paying people's mortgages through our church or other non-profit organizations without them knowing who the funds came from was an exercise we practiced. For Christmas, we would adopt families through the Salvation Army, and Jana would pick out all the girl toys her heart desired and we would wrap them together and deliver them to the Salvation Army to be delivered to our adopted families. I am and always have been a firm believer of "to whom much is given, much is required." I didn't mind giving of myself and giving what I had. When I figured out how to pay off my debt, I was trying to teach everybody else how to pay off theirs. When I treated myself to a spa day at the Grandover Hotel and Spa, I made sure I treated one of my girlfriends, a client, a church member, or even real estate colleague to enjoy the day with me. I was never going to be stingy with what God had blessed me with. I was always willing to share the knowledge that I achieved, and also the fruits of my labor.

When Pastor Lockett came to bless my new home he was amazed! "Sistah Natasha, I had no idea that I would be walking into this beautiful place. I mean I knew it would be nice, but I was expecting maybe a condo or townhome." It's no secret that after a divorce, people don't expect for the woman to do as well without the husband. I'm not going to lie, I had something to prove, not to anyone else, but to myself. After my divorce was over and I allowed time for the dust to clear, it was time for me to get my hustle on and that's exactly what I did!

I was paying for many real estate seminars that taught me how to become an expert in the area of Short Sales and Pre-Foreclosures throughout the Tri-City area in 2006 and 2007. At this time, I was considered the Short Sale Queen as other investors would send me their deals since their knowledge base was only in purchasing foreclosures at the courthouse steps. Whereas I was getting the deal before the property went to foreclosure. Yes, there was a lot of money invested to gain the knowledge I had and I did take many risks to reach that point. Every time an investment is made there is a risk. Some things worked, some things didn't. If no risk is taken, there will never be anything to gain. Everything I learned and gained was worth the risk. My business was expanding as I also was purchasing properties to renovate and sell for profit.

My love life at that point was also in a good place. I dated a wonderful man for about a year and a half who wanted to marry me, but I just did not want to marry again this soon. Sometimes it really is about timing. I started dating him shortly after my divorce was finalized, and I felt like I needed more experience with dating as an adult woman before I settled down with the next guy I fell in love with.

Penny and I leased an office space together in High Point, NC. Penny was a real estate broker and also turned investor like myself. She was also my road dog as we both frequented all the Ron Legrand short sale seminars in Las Vegas as we grew our businesses. We were definitely expanding as I had already hired multiple agents under my brokerage, and we both shared a full time assistant and receptionist. We had a corner of the real estate market that promoted First Time Home Buyers, and we also mastered the investor's side of the industry.

Then one day, it happened! All the Homebuyer Programs suddenly disappeared overnight. Interest rates went up and like a domino effect we were in a recession! Things were changing rapidly, businesses were closing, people were being laid off, tenants could no longer pay their rents, no one was able to buy any houses, everything was at a standstill.

Mind you, in the beginning, I was thinking this was going to blow over in several months. I had the experience of growing up poor and never having anything, but back then we couldn't tell the difference if the economy was doing well or not because we were still going to be on welfare! But as an adult, this was my first time experiencing a recession and I had no idea of the domino effect that it would have on my life and the rest of the world!

One Saturday in December of 2007, one of my agents called me to give me the news. "Penny is not at the office!"

"What do you mean, Penny is not at the office?"

"I mean, she's not here. She's gone."

"So, maybe she didn't go into the office today."

"No Natasha, her office and her assistant's office is cleared out. All of her plaques and pictures are off the walls and her name tag is gone. Everything is completely gone!"

What the fuck! I immediately tried to call Penny but the call kept going straight to voicemail. Did that heifer block me? I even tried emailing her with no reply.

Basically, Penny hung in there with me for several months after the recession had begun, but she was not able to pay her share of the office expenses so I was paying everything. It was nothing for us to cover one another from time to time but only until the next closing was to take place. However, this time was different. After the market had dried up, there were no more closings in the pipeline. No more business in sight, except for a few investment properties trickling in. My saving grace was that I had no debt (except the new house I had recently purchased), and I had enough money saved up for at least the next year. My grandmother had taught me that. But now since Penny has stuck me with all the bills, that money won't last that long! Jesus!

After tightening my purse straps, the bleeding still did not stop. I had a two year lease on the commercial property that I shared with Penny (who had disappeared on me!) I assume she went back to doing hair in the hair salon. We were only one year into the lease and I had to break the lease to downsize. At this point I was still slightly hopeful that I could keep the business afloat if I just cut my expenses. Unfortunately, the management had not allowed our businesses to guarantee the lease; we had to be personally liable for it, so that meant they had gotten a 40k judgment against us. Well, there goes my good credit!

I couldn't worry about that at the moment when I was just trying to keep my business afloat through such a tumultuous time. I downsized into a much smaller unit thinking I would be able to handle that, but was only able to stay afloat for several months and had to break another lease. Although it was a shorter term, it was another 17k judgment against me! Now I would just need to work from my home office and my agents would need to do the same from their kitchen tables just as we did back in the day.

As things continued to get worse financially, I depleted funds from my checking, savings, retirement, and Jana's 529 college savings account (thank God that baby didn't want to go to college!) to try to hold on to the real estate properties that I owned, including my primary residence. About seven of the investment properties were vacant because either the tenants vacated because they had job losses and could no longer pay the rent, or I had to evict them for non-payment of rent. I carried the mortgages for as long as I could and worked with the lenders as long as humanly possible until they were foreclosed on. The remaining six properties were either sold to the tenants who still had income or to other investors at deep discounts. There was not much profit involved, if any, as by now most properties were "upside-down" in equity, meaning I owed more on them than they were now worth. And to think, at some point, my equity position on these investments was almost a million dollars! Damn! How fast things can change!

Let's not forget my primary residence. I had worked on multiple loan modifications with my lender and every time they would approve the modification of the new loan amount I still couldn't afford to pay it because I was not making any money consistently. The money I would make from a random closing here or there I would need to save for food, gas, and utilities. Even that money had become scarce when I first received a pink notice from Duke Power Energy and I plum forgot that I received the notice. It's funny when you know you don't have the money to pay people, you tend to forget about the bills that need to be paid!

One day I came home from showing houses (yes, just because no one was closing on houses, doesn't mean I wasn't still out there trying to work), I walked into the kitchen and opened the refrigerator and the light was off. Damn is the refrigerator broken? I flipped the kitchen light switch and the light didn't come on. Damn, does the circuit breaker need to be flipped off and back on? I walked to the living room and tried to turn on the

TV. Goddammit! The power is off! Shit! I hurriedly grabbed my cell phone and called Duke Power Energy to see if there was a power outage in the area. There was not. They kindly reminded me of the pink notice that was mailed out to me 10 days ago which was a disconnection notice. Shit! I had forgotten all about that because I didn't have the money to pay for it. I was hoping I would have this new client under contract by now, but nothing's happening. Duke Power informed me that I would have to pay a reconnection fee on top of the late payment in order to get my power restored. Well, if I didn't have the money to pay the balance due, why do they think I had the money to pay a reconnection fee on top of that? Stupid!

This was so embarrassing! Not too long ago, I was at the top of my game, making money hand over fist. I wasn't wealthy, but I definitely lived in the land of plenty. I saved my money, I sowed into the lives of many other people, I supported my church and other charities and nonprofits; I was kind to people. I understood the world was in economic distress, but honestly, I thought God would have protected me. I thought He would have covered me to be able to at least handle the financial responsibilities of my own household, but no! Everything around me was crumbling and it was taking a mental and physical toll on my well-being.

I fell to my knees in the middle of my living room floor and screamed to the top of my lungs. "God why am I going through this! Why are you allowing this to happen to me? After all I've been through! After all my hard work and diligence! After all I've done to help your people! All the seeds I've sown! Why God! Why are you not there for me! Why are you leaving me out here with nothing!"

I've never felt so deserted by God in my entire life! I sobbed until there were no more tears left in me and then I realized the time. It was already noon and I'd need to figure out how to get these lights back on before Jana got home from school. I went through all my purses and wallets in my closets to see if there were any dollar bills that I had missed before. There weren't. I went through every drawer and jewelry box. Nope, only costume jewelry was left. I had already hocked the real jewelry months ago for some other bills. I headed to Jana's room and although this was my last resort, I had to empty my baby's piggy bank. I cried profusely as I shook out all the coins that her piggy bank held and counted them one by one. I began to separate the pennies from the nickels from the dimes and counted up $147. The electricity bill was $111 plus a $30 reconnection fee. I gathered all the coins in a plastic grocery bag and rushed to the Harris Teeter grocery store and dumped the coins in the change machine. I was able to pay the utility bill through their Customer Care Service at Harris Teeter and was told the service should be restored within the hour.

Jana arrived home from school, but the power was not on yet, so I told her that we would go to get her favorite food which was Chick-fil-A chicken nuggets.

"Mommy, why aren't you eating anything?"

"I'm not hungry baby."

"You sure? I can share my chicken nuggets with you."

"Yes, I'm sure. You go ahead and enjoy your food."

As a mom, I definitely tried to protect my daughter from the harsh reality of my situation. It didn't matter if I was hungry or not. My job was to make sure my child had food to eat and to keep things as normal as possible for her. She had been accustomed to eating at the finest restaurants, frequenting plays and the ballet, sleepovers in nice hotels, spa days, etc. But at this point when Jana had a sleepover for her ninth birthday, my friend Paula and I ordered chicken nuggets and had to paint the girls' nails and toes ourselves and do their facials. I overheard a conversation between Jana and one of her little friends, Amber.

Amber: "So we're not going to the spa for your birthday like we used to?"

Jana: "My Mommy's money is funny, so don't even ask!"

Yes, her Mommy's money was funny. It was so funny it was non-existent. I honestly didn't know what I was going to do about it. One day I received a call from a friend of mine, Michelle. Michelle was also a real estate agent and real estate investor and was in a similar predicament.

"Hey girl, you need to go ahead and apply for food stamps."

"Food stamps! Ain't that the same as welfare?"

"Well, it is a part of the welfare program."

"I'm not getting on no welfare!" I was offended! Everyone who knows me knows I have worked my entire life to not be a product of my environment, not be on welfare, not be another statistic. The feeling that it gave me just thinking that this is where I was in life was nauseating! I was sick on the stomach! Repulsed!

"Oh no! I will not be applying for nobody's food stamps!

"So what are you going to tell your child the next time she's hungry and you're not able to feed her?"

Damn! Michelle had a very valid point. Albeit a difficult pill to swallow, I would have to lay the little bit of pride I had left to the side and do what I needed to do. Hell, I already had to rob my baby's piggy bank to get the utilities back on. This would just add to the list of humbling experiences. As if I hadn't already had enough.

"Ok, Michelle," I sucked it up, "Tell me what I need to do."

"The place opens at 8 but you need to be there no later than 7:30 because the line gets long."

"What? We can't apply online?"

"No, not in Guilford County, you can't."

More embarrassment, I thought. What if one of the church members sees me? Just over a year ago, I was one of the highest tithes and offering givers in the church. What if one of my clients sees me? I had worked with a lot of buyers and sellers in the city. What about one of my tenants? Hell, I guess I needed to stop worrying about them and start worrying about me and my child.

"Ok, are they going to need to know what kind of house I live in and what kind of car I drive?"

"No, they only need to know that you haven't had any income in the last three months."

"Well hell, I haven't had any income in the last 9 or 10 months! I'm already on the verge of losing my home and thank God the car is already paid off!"

I did what Michelle had advised me to do. Whatever I needed to do to get approximately $300 of food into my household per month so that I would not have to worry about how my child was going to eat would be a huge burden off my shoulders. Even if it was a government handout, I guess I was now the person in need of the government handout, like old times.

As usual, I arrived 30 minutes earlier than Michelle had suggested to the Social Services office. And just like she said there were already people forming the line. It was a cold winter day so you could see the people wrapped up in their huge winter coats, hats, and gloves. I was cold natured so I made sure I would sit in the heated car for as long as possible with my hot chocolate. I wasn't planning on letting the line get too long though. I would have to time it, when I would get out of the car and join the line with the other food stamp applicants.

I was careful to park my BMW x5 towards the back of the parking lot. As far away from the building as possible, but yet close enough to where I could see the line forming.

I didn't want anybody judging me or my situation. Thank God I had paid the car off two years after Charles and I purchased it. It would probably be repossessed by now if I hadn't. It was paid off after I flipped my second investment property. After I flipped my first property, I paid off my student loans. I knew exactly what to do with money when I had it. I just never imagined in a million years there would be a time when I wouldn't have it.

I needed to give myself a pep talk before entering this building. "Ok Tasha, this is not *who* you are. This is only *where* you are. This is only a temporary situation. You have a lot to offer the world. The economy may be bad right now, but it will turn around soon. Your business will thrive again soon. This is only temporary."

No matter how much I tried to make myself believe what I was telling myself, I still did not feel any better about what I had to do. Then I reminded myself, "Your child has to eat, doesn't she?" After that it just didn't matter how I felt about the situation. I got out of the car, stood in line with my head held high along with the others until they unlocked the door to the building, sat in the lobby until they called my number and had my interview. I had my poker face on the entire time to make it through, but about 10 days later I received a link card in the mail and was able to purchase food items every month for six months. Although I felt a sense of relief and humiliation at the same time, I would reapply every six months for the next couple of years. At least food was one less thing I would have to worry about!

There were other serious matters at hand, as one day I looked out the window of my home and the Sheriff's car was in the driveway!

"Shit! Now what! Are they coming to arrest me?" I thought. I was thinking maybe they could arrest me and drag me off to debtor's prison or something. I honestly didn't know! I decided to go outside before my neighbors had a chance to be nosey and draw their own conclusions.

"Yes, officer, how may I help you?" I asked nervously.

"Are you Natasha Starghill?"

"Yes."

"Do you own the property at Toby Ct with a -uh Charles Starghill?" the Sheriff asked, looking down at the paper he held in his hand.

"Actually, I do not. But I used to own it with my ex."

"So your ex-husband is Charles Starghill?"

"Correct."

"And he owns the property on Toby Ct.?"

"Correct."

"Does he also live on Toby Ct.?"

"To my knowledge, yes, he still lives there."

"Has he ever resided at this address with you?"

"No, he has not."

"Are you sure about that?"

"Positive."

"Well ma'am, I'm sorry for disturbing you today. You enjoy the rest of your evening."

"You do the same, Sheriff."

I stood in the driveway and watched him pull off and ran in the house and locked the door. I could finally let go of the breath I had been holding while talking to the Sheriff! I had never had a Sheriff come to my house before. Again, not as an adult. This shit was driving me crazy. But it was good to know Charles was struggling as much as I was. I'm just saying, it's good to know it wasn't just me! It looks like the Sheriff was trying to track him down to serve him foreclosure papers on the custom built house that we once owned together. I thought the Sheriff was coming to serve me. Oh, but that was just a prelude to the kiss! A couple weeks later, that same Sheriff showed up in my driveway and I already knew what it was about. It was almost like robbing a bank and just walking out of the bank after getting caught. 'Just come out with your hands up and drop to your knees so they can handcuff you and drag you off to debtors prison!'

The next time when I saw the Sheriff again I wasn't surprised. He explained to me why he was there and had me sign the papers stating that I received them. As I signed them, I just began to cry. If I lose my home, where will my daughter and I live? Will we be homeless? Will we have to go on the section 8 list and wait for three years just to get a voucher that puts us to live in the projects? Hell, I'm already receiving food stamps! What will become of us? If I moved out, I wouldn't even be able to get an apartment without a security deposit, first month's rent and stable income. On top of that, no one would hire me! I am a woman with a Chemical Engineering degree who has been an entrepreneur for 15 years and I could not buy an interview even if I could afford it! The few interviews I did have an opportunity to go on, even when I attempted to 'dumb down', the hiring managers seemed to be intimidated by me. Even when I felt the interview went really well,

I would get the rejection email. Some people would let me know they did not want to hire me because I was overqualified for the job. Others feared that once my business was back up and running I would leave them to go back to real estate. No one would cut me a break even if they had a job available. I was shit out of luck! Nothing was going in my favor. God was no longer blessing me!

I was growing more and more disappointed with God as one event spiraled into the next. I felt like God abandoned me when I needed him the most. I had no protection, no covering, no back up plan, no one to lean on, and was now about to lose the roof over my head. And then someone was ringing my doorbell, again. I'm sure it was someone serving me with papers for a credit card gone into collections or another judgment. I guess it'll end up in the pile with the others! I snatched the manilla folder from the Processor who served me, scribbled my name on his pad and began to look through the mail as I walked into the kitchen.

What the fuck! Darrell and Susan Harvey were suing me for fraud! Oh hell naw!

Darrell and Susan Harvey were a couple of my private investors. I had done business with them for about three years. They would loan me money to purchase investment properties. I would pay them monthly interest on the money loaned and then return their seed money to them once the property was renovated and sold and then we would do it all over again.

The Harveys had made about 35k in interest in three years from doing these transactions with me. Now you know damn well they couldn't make that kind of interest from a CD, which is the avenue they were previously using. They were loaning out approximately $75k-$100k at one time. The last home that was purchased with some of their funds was just months before the market crash. The property needed a total gut and renovation which cost another $85k to gut and $150k to renovate. The total gut was completed with other private funds and my own personal funds. Unfortunately, with the quick decline in value of the neighborhood, it was no longer possible for me to renovate the house and sell for a profit. Before the market crash I stood to profit over $150k after expenses. At this point, the house could not be renovated because it would be a total waste of money. The real estate market was really bad! The value of this property was about 50% less than what it would have been had the market not crashed. We were all in a pickle, we all had to lick our wounds, we all took a lot of losses.

But not the Harveys! They wanted to try to sue me for their losses instead. I don't know where they thought they were going to get the money. Like Lil' Mama used to say, you can't get blood from a turnip! I visited the Harveys at their home to try to reason with them about the market and the value of the home. I also explained to them my financial situation and how I could not continue to pay them interest on the loan because I just did not have any income. Hell, I was even on the verge of losing my own home at this time. They didn't want to hear it. They only wanted what they wanted.

The Harveys even went as far as filing a complaint against me with the Greensboro Police Department claiming criminal activity of fraud. Those bitches tried to have me arrested! They claimed I stole their money!

I received a call from the Police Department. "Ms. Starghill, we need you to come down to the station."

The station? What the fuck? I had never been to a police station in my life! I didn't even know where the police station was located! I then brought in proof of a copy of every cashiers' check for the past three years of us doing business together showing they made money by doing business with me. Also, they hired me as their real estate agent for three transactions and used me as a consultant for their rental properties. I had email proof of every transaction that we completed together and every conversation where they reached out to me for advice. Because the evidence presented showed that each transaction represented the Harveys invested their money and received a return on each investment until we got to the last investment right before the market crash, the Harveys felt like they shouldn't have to take the loss, so they wanted to sue me for criminal activity. The evidence also showed that we were in a mutually agreed upon business relationship and that I in no way tried to take advantage of them, as that's what they were claiming. As long as the Harveys were making money from all my hard work and endeavors, they were happy; the moment they were no longer making money, they were being taken advantage of. People! The Detective dismissed it and said there was no basis for their claim and they did not have a case.

"I demand to speak to your superior!" Darrell Harvey went storming into the police station.

"I am the Superior!" stated the Detective who was the Supervisor of the Fraud unit.

He tried to go over her head because she was a black woman, but little did he know, there was no other head higher than hers in that department, so she had the final say. She had to have that joker escorted from the station before he was arrested!

There was no reasoning with the Harveys, so after they went through every attorney in town trying to find representation for a civil lawsuit, they finally dug up some attorney from under a rock who had many slaps on the wrists by the North Carolina State Bar. They had me served right at the three year mark which was the statute of limitation. Damn! They couldn't get me on criminal charges, but now they were trying to get me on civil charges! Now I have to deal with this shit! And I don't have any money to hire an attorney!

I only had 21 days to respond with an answer, and I don't know much about the law. I reached out to my real estate closing attorney, Konrad Fish, to see if he could assist. Since Konrad was a party to the real estate transaction, his malpractice insurance attorney informed him that he could not assist and to cease all communications with me. I was instructed to visit the malpractice insurance attorney's office in which that attorney referred me to another attorney who was a friend of his and owed him a 'favor'.

"Here, call this guy, Attorney Thomas Johnson, Jr., also known as TJ. He owes me a favor. He will work with you." He scribbled the name and number on a sheet of paper.

"Ok, did Konrad let you know that I am unable to pay this attorney for his legal services?"

"Yes, Konnie told me and I have already spoken to TJ and everything is good."

"Ok, good, thanks so much for your help!" I hurried back to my car so I could call Thomas Johnson and schedule an appointment to meet.

"Yes, can you come this evening after my last appointment at 6pm? I'm located downtown on Gray St."

"No problem. I'll be there!"

It was truly a blessing to know someone, who knew someone, who knew someone, especially when you need an attorney. When I arrived at Attorney Johnson's office and gave him a copy of the summons that I was served from the Harveys, we went right to work on the discovery. There were many law books out on his desk and we researched many cases. We worked on the answer to the complaint at least until 10pm. "Hey let's pick this back up tomorrow morning. Why don't we meet at Harpers Restaurant in Friendly Shopping Center and grab some breakfast at about 7:30am and then we'll go from there."

"Ok no problem. I'll see you there."

I was just happy that God was putting some people in position to help me finally! Maybe this would put an end to the drama with the Harveys and give me some relief. Finally, God was answering my prayers. Finally, he was hearing my cries and listening to me again. He and I had been on the outs since this market crash. The struggle was real!

I met Attorney Johnson for breakfast and I was trying to talk about the case, but he was constantly trying to talk about my personal life and my family life. I really wasn't here for small talk but since he was doing me a favor, I was at least trying to be nice and courteous.

"So why don't we go back to your place first?"

Did this monthafucka just flip the script on me!

"Go back to my place for what? All the law books are at your office, not at my house."

"Well I just figured we could swing by your place for a while and then we can head back to the office."

Unbelievable! This nigga thought that I was going to pay him in ASS! Please! He would NEVER be able to afford this pussy!

"Are you crazy!" I looked at him with the most evil look I could conjure up!

"Well, you didn't really think my services were free, did you?"

This nasty, offensive, vulgar, manipulative, disgusting, foul, bastard!

"Fuck you Thomas!" I got up so quickly from the table and knocked the chair down. I walked out of that restaurant so fast as tears welled up in my eyes.

'Can't trust none of these mothafuckas!' I thought.

I sat in the car in the parking lot just crying and praying to God to give me some direction. I was at my wits end! I was exhausted! My head was pounding, my energy level was low. My tolerance was at zero! I was shocked and appalled! Even professionals were acting worse than thugs in the streets! Pretending to be kind, claiming to be a Christian, just to turn around and stab me in the back. Trying to manipulate me and take advantage of my situation. One thing he needed to know about Natasha is there is a girl from the hood by the name of Tasha that lived inside of me. I will give my last breath to hold on to the last shred of dignity that I have! I refused to sell my soul to the devil! He was not getting no ass from me, regardless of how bleak my predicament was! Not today! Not ever!

Hell, I couldn't even focus on reporting Thomas Johnson's stank ass to the North Carolina State Bar for harassment and misconduct. I had to find another attorney really quick as my time was running out to answer this complaint on this lawsuit. I then called another attorney, Monica, who I had completed some real estate transactions with and told her the situation. She asked me who I was working with and I just began to cry all over again.

"He insinuated that I give him sex as payment."

"Who did that to you?"

"Thomas Johnson."

"Yeah, I'm so sorry that he did that to you. This is not the first time I've heard of him doing this to women. This has come back to me several times."

"It's a damn shame and until we all get together and bring his ass down, he's going to continue to get away with it."

"I know and you're right, it is a shame that he keeps preying on women who needs his help and taking advantage of their situation."

"Well look, I don't even have time to spend on him right now. Can you assist me or do you know of an attorney who can help me file an answer for this lawsuit?"

"Actually, I would love to help you, but in the event it goes to trial you will need a litigation attorney. Come by my office today and I will make the referral. I will call the attorney first and let him know your story so that you won't have to keep reliving it and he will take good care of you."

I was trying to hold back the tears, but they just came bursting out.

"Natasha, what's the matter?"

"It's nothing. It's just that I've heard that before. That's what the last attorney said about TJ and look what I ended up with! An asshole! He knows I'm on a deadline and he just tried to take advantage of me!"

"Listen, I can assure you from one black woman to another, this attorney will do right by you and if for some reason I am mistaken, you let me know and I will handle him myself! You hear me?"

"I hear you, Monica."

"Don't worry, you're going to get through this. I'll see you in a bit."

"Ok thanks. I'm on my way."

I didn't have any choice but to take another chance. What options did I have? Thank God Monica was right! The attorney she referred to me was everything that she said he would be. He was a true Christian. Not just in word, but in deed. He was also very smart and knew the law. He cared much about his clients' well-being and about bringing them justice. After going through mediation with the Harveys we were right back at square one which is I didn't have the money to continue to pay them interest on the funds borrowed that was lost in the decrease of the value of the property due to the market crash. I had offered to quit claim deed the property over to them over a year ago, but they didn't want the property. At the end of the mediation, I ended up doing a quit claim deed to them. Jeesh! They refused to believe that I was in dire need like the rest of the world, and that couldn't have been further from the truth. If you want money from me, you may as well get in line with everybody else!

It's funny how people will turn on you with the quickness when things don't go their way. As long as they're making money off you, all is gravy. Otherwise, you're a fraud and a criminal!

After this lawsuit was dismissed, my attorney advised me to go ahead and file bankruptcy. I let him know that I felt bad that I was not able to pay him for all the hard work he had done and maybe I would be able to pay him back later when the market turned around. He told me that he would not be able to accept any payments from me after I filed bankruptcy and that would be my best course of action. I had to borrow $1800 from a friend in order to file for bankruptcy. This was the true meaning of broke, busted, and disgusted!

Had I known better, I would have filed bankruptcy much earlier and saved my money. That's what my white friends told me I should have done. But no! Black people have been taught you need to use every penny you have to try to save what you have, but at the end of the day, I did that and lost it all anyway. Lesson learned.

Even greater than the financial losses, when the market crash first began, I lost one of my favorite aunts, Auntie Terri, to a surgery gone bad. Auntie Terri was the one who helped me to find James on the prisoner website so that I could go to confront him. She is also the one who was going to beat Rusty's ass for taking my money and lying and said he bought new tires for my car. Well Auntie Terri had a hysterectomy in 2008. She was having complications for months when the surgeon had to put her back under to see what the problem was. When he opened her back up a part of her ovary was left inside of her and it infected all of her other organs. She immediately went into a coma and then died.

I found an attorney in New York who was open to looking into a malpractice lawsuit, but Auntie Terri's fairly new husband of three years, Damon, (I really didn't know him that well), decided that he wanted to go with a local attorney. Although we told him not to use a local attorney to sue a local medical doctor in the same town. Of course, he didn't listen! That attorney gave him the run around until the statute of limitation ran out. There was nothing we could do without Damon's permission since he was the surviving spouse. Therefore, I feel my aunt's death was in vain.

Eighteen months later in 2010, Lil' Mama died. Jana and I cried all day. Lil' Mama was my heart. Not only was I losing a grandmother, I was losing my mother and my friend. I was losing my confidant. When I was a child, she was my safe place, my home. Lil' Mama had a kidney infection from the dialysis and just had a successful surgery and was taken back to the nursing home. She died the next day in her sleep. I think she was just tired. Tired of this world and all its ailments. I didn't blame her for wanting to transition. But I still miss my Lil' Mama dearly.

During this time I was dealing with my own ailments. Outside of financial struggles, foreclosures, lawsuits, and bankruptcy, I was also having medical issues. One month my cycle came on and never went off. I was bleeding every day for months. I would visit my medical practitioner and report this problem and was told that it was just a hormone imbalance. For 18 months my doctor prescribed a different birth control pill under the auspices of irregular hormones. However, the blood kept coming down!

Sometimes the flow would be similar to a regular period, sometimes there would be spotting, but other times there was gushing like a waterfall to the point where I would have to wear a tampon and two super duper maxi pads!

I recall a time I was meeting a friend for lunch for about an hour and a half and the blood bled through my clothes. I didn't even notice it until I got out of my car and looked back at the seat! How embarrassing! I was losing so much blood every day.

My head was constantly hurting, pounding. So bad, one day, I decided to drive myself to the Urgent Care. Once they took my blood pressure and stated my blood pressure was so high that I shouldn't even be walking let alone driving, they immediately called the ambulance to take me to the Emergency Room. That's when I found out that the constant blood loss had caused me to have high blood pressure.

I was so sick of this! I felt like the woman with the issue of blood! For 18 months I was bleeding, my head was hurting, and I was drained, emotionally and physically. I wasn't even speaking to God at this time as we were not on good terms. I literally had nothing going for myself! I felt like Job from the old testament in the Bible. What more can you take from me, God? I have nothing else to give! Or how about Jesus on the cross, "Why has thou forsaken me?" I felt alone and in such a dark and lonely place. Even God wasn't stopping by to visit me anymore.

After my primary physician finally got a bright idea to refer me to my OBGYN, since she could not figure out what was going on with my body, I was relieved. By the way, I had to borrow money from someone to catch up on the payments on my insurance premium just to be able to see the doctor.

Do you recall the Sheriff that served my foreclosure papers? Sheriff Jerry was his name. Jerry later came back to my house and left a card on my door encouraging me to keep my head up. He was genuinely trying to lift my spirits and I must say it was a very nice gesture. Well in that card, Jerry asked me out to dinner with him and left his number to call. I eventually called him and we hung out for a few months. Jerry was the 'someone' that paid up my insurance premiums for me. He wanted to seriously date me, but I honestly wasn't feeling him in that way and so it didn't go anywhere. Plus, I had way too much going on and could not add another thing to my plate!

When I walked into Dr. Stringer's office, a black male doctor and my OBGYN when I was pregnant with Jana, and told him my symptoms, he said, "It sounds like you have fibroids. We are going to do an ultrasound just to be sure, but I'm pretty certain."

Sure enough, he was right. I had multiple fibroids but also polyps that attached themselves to the fibroids that punctured my uterus that was causing the bleeding.

So I've been bleeding for 18 goddamn months because that white heifer bitch PCP doctor of mine doesn't know what she's doing in regard to a black woman's body, and then I walk into the black doctor's office and tell him my symptoms, and he knows exactly what's wrong with me! I was so pissed! This bitch has caused me to have high blood pressure! Giving me a different birth control pill talking about it's just hormonal! Practicing medicine on me, wasting my $25 copay, which I don't have to spare. I was fiery mad! This shit had me pissed the fuck off!

"Statistics show every 1 out of 4 women of African American descent have fibroids," Dr. Stringer shared with me. Damn! I wish I had known that before I got them. I wish I had known to be aware of them, so when my PCP was busy practicing medicine on me, I could have at least informed her since she clearly did not know these statistics about African American descent women. Now, unfortunately, her other black female patients would have to go through the same thing!

Dr. Stringer quickly scheduled the surgery to remove the polyps, even though there was a chance they could grow back. My only other option was to have a partial hysterectomy. But that's what killed my Auntie Terri! Nah, I can't deal with that shit right now. No surgery for me!

Chapter 24

LUCKY #7

It was 2009 and not much was going right in my life, but at least I was still here, and since the bank had not yet foreclosed on my home, I decided to plan a Sibling Reunion with all of my father's children. This would be the very first time that all eight of us were under the same roof at the same time! Right here in my home in Colfax, NC! This would go down in history! A memory that we would never forget!

The order of age is Lewis, me, Ron, Lisa, Tabula, Kenyatta, Tony, and then Jay. Lewis and I had the same mother and same father. All the other siblings had different mothers. Ron, Lisa, Tabula, and I were all born in the year 1971; Kenyatta was born in February 1972. In essence, our father, Floyd, had five children within a 13 month time span by five different baby mamas! I guess he was trying to break some kind of world record or something! Tony was born seven years later, and Jay six years after Tony. Of all these women, Floyd had only married Kenyatta's mother and they only stayed together for a short period of a few months. He did propose to Tabula's mother, but she gave him his ring back once she realized there was no way that she could be married to such a shallow, narcissist as my father. Ron's mother even shared a story of when she was pregnant with Ron, Floyd tried to convince her to drink turpentine in order to terminate her pregnancy. If she did, he promised to marry her. Thank God Ron's mother did not follow through with it!

Through it all, we each have had our own experiences and our own journeys with Floyd, some good, some bad, and a whole lot of ugly. And now, for the first time, by whatever mountains we had to climb to get here, we made it! We had an entire weekend planned of eating, drinking, laughing, crying, and getting to know one another all over again or in some cases, getting to know each other for the first time.

Then Floyd started blowing up Lewis' phone.

"Are y'all sitting over there talking about me? How come Tasha didn't invite me?"

First of all, I had not spoken to my father in a year, so why would I ever invite him to my home or anywhere else for that matter?

There is one good thing that came out of knowing my father and that is gaining all my siblings! After the Sibling Reunion I wrote in to the Dr. Phil Show to share our story of how we all decided to come together in spite of our father not trying to bring us together. Lo and behold, Dr. Phil's producer's called me to talk about possibly having us on the show.

"The catch, Natasha, is we would want to get your father on the show, too."

"Well, that would be impossible. He's never going to go on your show."

"You don't think he would want to tell his side of the story. Well, let us try to call him anyway. This is our job; this is what we do."

"Ok, but I'm warning you right now. He is a piece of work."

About 20 minutes later Dr. Phil's producer called me back.

"Well, Natasha, you were right, after spending 20 minutes trying to convince him, your father never would give any direct answers to being on the show. He just kept stating his baby girl needed help and kept asking if we could get you some mental help because he was just not sure of your state of mind. You were right, Natasha, he is definitely a piece of work!"

"I told you; he would never show his face on national television because he would never be willing to tell the truth. That's why most of us don't fool with him now."

"Well, unfortunately, for this segment, we won't be able to do the show without him. I'm sorry."

"I understand. Thank you for trying."

My father's ass is the one that should be in a mental hospital going around here impersonating a human being!

Shortly thereafter, I received a call from my younger brother Tony.

"Tasha Mac! What's up?"

"Pretty Tony, what they call him!"

This was our brother-sister ritual when we first got on the phone with each other. "Hey, I have something to tell you. I think we may have another brother here in Nashville."

"Oh, really?" clearly I wasn't surprised.

"Yeah, I was just thinking about how wonderful it was that all of my siblings were together for a sibling reunion and that made me think of this kid that I met about 15 years ago when we were in high school."

"15 years ago, Tony? How come you're just now telling me this?"

"Because I never really had any proof."

"So tell me what happened 15 years ago."

"I remember our school was having a skate party with another school. After the party, this lady came up to me out of the blue and asked me if my dad's name was Floyd Murrell. I told her that it was, then she introduced me to this guy and said he was my brother and his name was Antuan."

"Are you serious!"

"Dead serious, Sis! As soon as they left, I called Daddy from my cellphone to tell him what had just happened and he was like, "What did you say her name was again? No, that name doesn't ring a bell." I was only about 16 years old at the time. Shoot, I'm 31 now, so that was about 15 years ago!"

"Wow! That is so interesting! Tabula always said she bet we have some more siblings out there; it just took time for them to surface. I wonder if he still lives in Nashville. Do you remember his last name, Tony?"

"I believe his last name is Foxx. Yeah, it was Antuan or Tuan Foxx."

"Ok I wonder if we can get together and swing by the area high schools and look through some yearbooks when I'm in town in a few months for Jay's wedding?"

"That sounds good because it can only be one of two schools that he could have attended. Matter of fact I'll check Facebook and put out some fillers to see if anybody knows of him."

"Ok great! Just keep me posted so we can try to get to the bottom of it."

"Will do, sis!"

"Love you, Pretty Tony!"

"Love you too, Tasha Mac!"

Later that same day Tony already had a response from someone on Facebook whose grandmother lived next door to Antuan's mother. She told Tony she would stop by her grandmother's house and get Antuan's phone number from his mother. As promised, the informant delivered, and we were able to speak to our newly found brother later that evening on a conference call. Tony, Ron, Tabula, and I were on that call to welcome him into the family!

I reached out to Antuan the next day to apologize on behalf of Floyd for all the things that did not happen that should have happened in regard to him being acknowledged by our father. It pains me to see yet another black man whose father was not in his life, but in this case, little did he know, Floyd had done him a huge favor.

"I actually met Floyd about seven years ago when I was 25 years old."

"Oh really? Where did you meet him?"

"My mother told me that he worked for the Fire Department and I called around until I found him and we met for lunch. He told me they had a blood test that came back negative, but my mother says otherwise."

Antuan was born in 1976 when a blood test was the only way to tell if, "You are the father!" in the voice of Maury Povich. However, Ms. Pam, Antuan's mom says Floyd is lying about that blood test, but she doesn't remember the results giving a definitive answer.

"Tasha, I'm telling you Floyd is lying because I hadn't been with nobody else! But I wasn't gon' beg him to be a father to my baby. Antuan deserved better than that!" Ms. Pam was a straight shooter; a lot like me. That's why it was hard to imagine her hooking up with my father as she would have had to put up with a whole lot of bullshit. I guess she was young and inexperienced like the rest of the women in his life.

"What happened with the blood test situation?"

"All I know is, they had me waiting in the lobby up at Juvenile court and Floyd walked in with his firefighter's uniform and headed straight to the back where the workers were. I assumed he was taking the blood test, but then they called me in and took me a different way into some other rooms to have the blood drawn from Antuan. The letter I got in the mail wasn't clear what the results were as if they couldn't read the results. I don't know. I didn't really understand it. When I spoke to Floyd again, he said that his letter said that the results were negative and showed that he was not the father. He made it clear to me that he didn't want nothing to do with helping me raise our baby."

"I am so sorry Ms. Pam, that you had to go through this. Is it possible you can go get a copy of the blood test?"

"I sure can!"

"I just want to see what the blood test says since you actually had one done. I think it's only fair to Antuan to help him get to the bottom of this mystery and at least put it to rest."

Ms. Pam went to Juvenile Court to get a copy of the file, but discovered that the file had been sealed. Now why would Floyd have the file sealed? Ms. Pam had to set a court date so that the judge could unseal the file just so she could have access to a blood test that belonged to her as she was the mother of the child. She sent a copy of the file to me.

"Ms. Pam, this blood test says it's inconclusive. It does not say *negative*."

"See, there! I told you! I knew Floyd was lying! He just didn't want nothin' to do with my son. He ain't no good!"

I already knew everything Ms. Pam was saying was true. I just didn't understand why my father had caused so much havoc in the lives of so many people.

"Ok I think I'm going to suggest that Antuan take a DNA test with one of the siblings so that we can move forward. Just so we can have proof that he's our brother. I don't doubt you for one second, Ms. Pam, but right now, it's your word against Floyd's."

"That's a good idea, Tasha, because that DNA test can only come back with one result, positive!"

I researched some testing centers in Nashville and had Tony and Antuan schedule an appointment to take a DNA test. I also had Jay go with them to videotape it and document it. In the back of my mind, I knew there would come a time that we may actually need proof that a DNA test was done, so a neutral third party, Jay, was there to witness.

In a nutshell, the DNA test came back that Tony and Antuan are brothers through the matching Y-chromosome lineage. Of course, Ms. Pam was telling the truth, confirming once again, 'cause I ain't been with nobody else!' Now Antuan was the new Lucky #7 in the group of siblings. He now fell in seventh place, bumping Tony to eighth place. The majority of us were excited to have found a new brother. Hell, why not? The more the merrier!

We were all the definition of bastard children. All except Kenyatta. But while most of us were also fatherless children, no one could ever accuse us of being brotherless and sisterless. I had 10 brothers and sisters total! My mother has four children and my father has nine children (that we know of so far).

When Antuan came along, I'd definitely say I was a little protective. As the big sister, I wanted to make sure he became acclimated to the siblings and formed individual bonds with them. I knew everyone wouldn't be receptive and he would not have a relationship with everyone, hell I don't have a relationship with all 10 of my own siblings. Sometimes people just don't mesh and it's understandable to not have much in common with some people. Such is life!

I continued to develop and maintain strong bonds with my siblings. Well, at least most of them. As a matter of fact, my sister Tabula applied for us to be on The Family Feud, and shortly after we had all gotten together in Nashville for Tony's wedding in February 2022, the Producer called us to ask us to film the show in April. It was Tabula, Tony, Jay, Kenyatta, and myself. We auditioned in 2021, but were asked to be the first family of the new season in 2022. We were able to play two games and had the experience of a lifetime meeting Steve Harvey! Being on the Family Feud actually brought us closer together as siblings, we had so much fun, encouraging each other and being there for one another. No, we did not win, but we cleared the board twice and we looked good doing it!

Chapter 25

ANNULLED

At the beginning of 2011 I was tired! Tired of fighting to keep the last remaining possessions that I still owned, tired of fighting period. I was especially tired of fighting to keep the $350k house that I resided in and had come to the conclusion that I needed to make a change. Hell at this point, I just needed to get this burden off my shoulders.

I started dating a guy named Kevin. We met on an online dating site called BlackPeopl eMeet.com. Kevin was from New Jersey and was a Capricorn. He possessed many earthly qualities like myself, being born in January. He seemed to be grounded and knew what he wanted from life. He was pretty consistent and lived by a routine. He also seemed to be stable. Hmmmm, stability. I remember what that was like, but it's been some years!

Kevin had been living and working in Houston, TX so we developed a long distance relationship. He would come to visit me in North Carolina from time to time, but because of his work schedule, I was never able to visit him in Houston. He worked on the weekends and was off on Tuesdays and Wednesdays. Since Jana went to school in Colfax, NC from my house, I was never able to be out of town during the week, so he visited me instead.

My and Kevin's relationship was smooth for the most part as we talked and video chatted with each other daily and enjoyed our time when we had our visits. Even when the polyps came back and I was having the bleeding situation again from the fibroids, like the woman with the issue of blood, I had to have another surgery. Kevin paid my $500 insurance deductible and was there for my surgery. I know $500 is not a lot of money, but when I struggled to do the bare minimum, $500 was like 10k! As life kept happening, I found myself in need of someone I could depend on for a change. Someone that I could lean on! Instead of it always being the other way around.

About six months into the relationship, Kevin asked me to marry him out of the blue.

"Will you marry me?"

"What?" I really didn't see it coming.

"You and Jana can move to Houston. It's not that expensive to live here. People who make $35k a year can live decently here. Once you get settled, you can get your real estate license and start selling real estate. The real estate market is still booming here. You won't have any problems getting your business up and running."

Before I knew it, I blurted out, "Yes! Yes!"

"Yes? Do you mean it?"

"Yes, I mean it!"

"I love you!"

"I love you, too!"

Everything Kevin was saying to me made perfectly good sense. I had recently filed bankruptcy, so I didn't have any debt to worry about. I would deed my house back to the bank instead of letting it go to foreclosure. This way I would have more control over my exit plan versus letting the bank force me to move. I would have to sell all of my furnishings and belongings in the house, but at least this would give me some savings and money to travel with to Houston, TX. I honestly didn't have much time to think about the wedding or the marriage as much as I was just thinking about how much I knew I needed to get my ass out of North Carolina. Clearly, my time here had expired and my favor had run out. After the market crashed there was no light at the end of the tunnel for me here. I had hung in there for several years and was at my wits end! My only exit strategy was to bounce. I believed I could make things work with Kevin in Houston, TX so I decided to go for it!

Kevin did all the planning as I focused on the logistics of getting everything sold out of the house.

"We can go to Vegas and get married. We will need to plan it to where we won't bring Jana to Houston until we actually have our new apartment. Then we can register her for school."

"Ok, I can drive Jana to Atlanta and she can visit our cousins for a couple of weeks. She would love that! Then once we get the new apartment set up, we can fly her to Houston in time for school."

Everything worked out according to plan. Jana and I left North Carolina. Everything we owned was either shipped via Greyhound or packed in the trunk of my BMW x5. I was finally leaving this place and never turning back! Jana and I drove to our cousins' house in Atlanta, GA. I stayed a couple of nights, then Kevin flew down and we drove the Beamer to Houston.

I was excited to start my new life with Kevin. Excited to begin again. I wasn't a stranger to starting over, so this wouldn't be any different. It was just good to have a partner to do it with. To at least have someone to bounce things off and where we can assist each other. I promised myself to keep an open mind and try to go with the flow as this was the very first time I was visiting Houston.

Once we arrived at Kevin's apartment, it was nice on the outside. It definitely wasn't in the hood, so that was a plus. As we entered the apartment I began to look around and I noticed there was no furniture.

"How long did you say you lived here?"

"Just about six months. The lease is almost up; that's why I have secured us another apartment in the Spring ISD school district so Jana can go to a decent school.

The other apartment won't be ready for another two weeks so after we return from getting married in Vegas, we will stay in a hotel until we move in. See I have everything already planned out. Everything is taken care of!"

It was good to know that Kevin had taken care of all the details. It was definitely a far cry from what I had been accustomed to. 'If you want something done, you have to do it yourself!' When I was married to Charles I was handling the details of every move, every trip, everything we did. Or else it didn't get done.

Then he hit me with this, "I hope you're not too bougie to sleep on the floor."

Wait! What? Did he just say, sleep on the floor? "What do you mean, sleep on the floor?" As I trailed Kevin into the bedroom, I saw a bean bag, a pillow, and a blanket on the floor. Is this his mothafuckin' bed! Oh hell naw! He hopes I'm not too bougie! I might be broke, but baby it does not mean I'm not bougie! Deep breaths, Tasha, deep breaths. If you turn back now, where would you go? What will you do? You have nothing left! You have no options. You can still make this work. It's not perfect, so what. You've lived in imperfect situations all your life. You can handle this. You are strong! You are resilient! You have the power to change your circumstances. You're here now, so what are you going to do? I exhaled, and I laid my bougie ass right down on that floor and got me a good night's rest!

The only thing Kevin had in his apartment was some towels. He did not have a chair or sofa to sit on, a bed to sleep in, nor dishes, or pots and pans to cook with. He ate fast food for every meal and only had the plastic wear from McDonalds. Even when we did our video calls, it would be when he was getting off work getting ready for bed so it looked like he was already laying down. I had no idea he was propped up on the floor with the help of a bean bed!

There were numerous times when I told myself to run as fast as you can, but then reality would set in and remind me I had no place to run, so sticking this out was my only option.

The hotel in Vegas was nice as we stayed at the MGM. I was able to meet Kevin's parents, who were also very lovely people. My brother, Tony, and his girlfriend, Asahi, came from Nashville and my cousin Allan Murrell who resides in Las Vegas were all there to witness the nuptials.

Kevin never officially proposed with the ring that is, until the night before the wedding. I was in the bathroom taking a shower before bedtime and when I got out, he had rose petals and Hershey's kisses on the floor. He put the ring on my finger, but it was dark and I was not able to see the ring until morning. I was, however, able to feel the faint irritable itching of my ring finger in the middle of the night. I recall Kevin telling me when we verbally got engaged over the video chat.

"I'm just going to get us some rings for now, but then I'm going to replace yours in a year." Ok, but damn, where did he get this ring from, the Cracker Jack box? This motherfucka was beginning to itch my finger something terrible! I reminded myself once again, "You're here now Tasha, where are you going to go? What are your other options?" Stay focused.

The day of the wedding Kevin was actually upset with me. "You punched me in my mouth last night!"

"What! I don't remember hitting you. Why would I do that?" I do remember being awakened by some loud, scary, monstrous, bearlike sounds, and I thought I sat up and laid back down. Come to find out, it was him snoring! I have never heard such loud snoring in my entire life to date. He can snore the roof off an entire building! It was just that loud!

"I know you did, because my lip is busted!"

"I am so sorry. I had no idea I had done that in my sleep!" I promise, I don't recall hitting him in the mouth. I must've been completely unconscious! Or maybe it was because my damn finger was itching so bad I had to do something with my fist!

Anyway, we got married and I forced a smile on my face as I delved into the land of the unknown. It was much worse than when I married Charles. I was just young and unknowledgeable then, but now I was much older, wiser, but very much in a predicament that caused me to have to make some decisions I may not have made otherwise. But I'm also a survivor, and we tend to be able to figure it out despite our circumstances.

Once we arrived back to Houston, Kevin had already had our reservations at the hotel. Actually at the Motel 6 or the Super 8, one of them, I don't think there's much difference. I wasn't trippin' though. Let's just make the best of it, and once I get my real estate license, I will help to turn this situation around. Kevin was taking care of everything financially, although it seemed to be pretty tight, he was still doing it and I appreciated that and was not going to complain.

The room that we were staying in for the next 10 days at the Super 8 motel smelled like cigarette smoke although they say, "no smoking allowed". After Kevin left for work, I went and spoke to management to see if I could move our belongings to another room that reeked of less smoke. My allergies were very sensitive in Houston, TX and cigarette smoke is not a smell I can stomach without getting a headache. When Kevin got off work, I told him that I moved us to another room and gave him the new room number.

"I hope you didn't go in there acting all bougie and giving those people a hard time complaining about how bad the room smelled."

First of all, this was a clear indication that Kevin did not know me at all. While I went to speak to the management about the room, I know how to talk to the service people to get my needs met. I have never disrespected or demeaned any service person in my life, and I am a damn good tipper!

"Now why would you immediately assume that?"

"Well I know how you bougie women can be." Clearly we were working with a different definition because to me bougie is aspiring to have or desire things of quality, class, standard, and be willing to work for it. To most people bougie is pretending to be someone that you're not, while pretending to have something that you don't have, all while turning up your nose and looking down on others as if they are less than. I don't think Kevin had any idea of the type of woman that he married, and I clearly had no idea of the man that I married either!

Of course, right before I arrived in Houston, Kevin informed me that his car was in the shop and instead of spending more money to get it fixed, he was just going to wait until I moved to Houston and then once we got settled, he would buy us a new car. In the meantime, he would be ok to walk to the Park & Ride and take the bus to work downtown. When I arrived in town, I would drive him to the Park & Ride every day and pick him up so that he didn't have to walk.

After we got into our new apartment, he had already ordered furniture from one of those 90 day same as cash stores. He timed it just right so that it could be delivered the same day we moved out of the hotel. If he didn't pay that furniture off within 90 days, the interest rate was something crazy like 1000%!

"That's because I don't have any credit."

I've been in the real estate industry long enough to know most times when people say they don't have any credit, it just means they don't have any new credit because no credit card company is offering them any credit. Usually there's some old bad credit sitting in collections for years still waiting to be paid. Most people think after 10 years that old credit will just fall off but to their surprise, it doesn't because the companies will sell bad debt to another company to keep the account alive. Bad debt is a big business.

We were able to get a sofa, our bed, and Jana's bed before Jana arrived in Houston. I remember Kevin wanted to do the fatherly duties and take Jana school supply shopping to pick up her school supplies. I thought that was a very sweet gesture, so they went to Walmart. When they returned there was some conflict about a backpack.

"Jana, a backpack is a backpack. It holds books," Kevin was telling Jana. "I already have a backpack that you can carry to school."

"But I don't want a big, black ugly man's backpack. I want a Hello Kitty backpack. I'm a girl, not a boy!"

Kevin went to the room and brought out his big, black, leather manly backpack. What little girl going to the 5th grade is going to carry that thing on her back to school? He's got to be kidding! See this is what happens when you're with a man who has never had children. "Kevin, no, that's not going to work for her. How much is the Hello Kitty backpack?"

"It was $15! $15 for a kid's backpack? Mine only cost $20 and it's still in good shape. I'm not spending that kind of money on a backpack!"

"That's ok, you don't have to. Come on Jana, let's go back to Walmart."

Jana and I left and went back to Walmart. "Mommy, I also tried to tell Kevin the pencils that he bought are not good ones because we need the mechanical pencils in the fifth grade. The ones he bought won't even sharpen well with the pencil sharpener." So we added mechanical pencils to the list. The nerve of him to try to deprive my child of her Hello Kitty backpack knowing she's going to be the new kid in school in a foreign place. Hell the damn thing was only $15!

Kevin had spent less than $20 total on school supplies and refused to buy my baby a decent backpack and pencils. Was $20 more going to break the bank? If so, why would he have me move to Houston if he knew he could not handle taking care of these things. I was taking care of all the groceries because I still had money on my link card, the food stamp card from my last approval from North Carolina. I was still paying my own phone bill and car insurance on the only car that we had. He was paying for the roof over our heads, of course, but even that was short lived!

I never had a good night's rest when I lived with Kevin because he snored like a grizzly bear! It was like in the cartoon The Flintstones when Fred went camping with Barney and he was asleep under the tent and began to snore. He was snoring so hard that every time he inhaled, he sucked in all this air and when he exhaled and pushed it out, he also almost pushed himself right off the cliff! Other than my very first night in Houston when I had to sleep on the floor at Kevin's apartment, but that's only because I was so exhausted from the long 12 hour drive from Atlanta to Houston. When I brought up this snoring issue to Kevin, he just said, "Well, I'm the only one working right now, you can sleep during the day!" He finally agreed to do a sleep study for sleep apnea but his insurance would not cover the CPAP and he could not afford to buy one. I felt it was unfair as I was looking for a job every day while waiting to apply for my Texas Real Estate License since I had to be a resident for 90 days before I could even apply to sit for the state exam. So, just because I'm not working right now, I don't deserve to get any rest at night like normal people? This is some bullshit!

The last straw was when I went to pick Kevin up from the Park and Ride and I told him we would need to stop for gas.

"Do you think $10 will hold you over until I get paid next Friday?"

First of all, in 2011, gas in Houston was $5.50/gal and I was driving a BMW x5! What was $10 gon' do but move the needle 1 notch! I never drove the vehicle but to take Jana to and from school (as we lived too close for her to ride the bus and too far for her to walk), take Kevin to and from the Park and Ride, and make occasional trips to Walmart which was only a block away.

"I guess, it will have to hold us over if that's all you got."

Once we got back home I told Kevin, "I really can't do this anymore. I don't think we can be together."

"What are you saying, you want a divorce?"

"That's exactly what I'm saying. I can't sleep and you can't even afford to put gas in the car!"

"Ok, no problem, if that's what you want. I'm not going to beg nobody to stay married to me. I'll print the annulment papers out tomorrow at work and we can fill them out when I get home tomorrow."

"Ok, cool."

And just like that after a short six weeks, our marriage was over! Annulled!

Kevin had been married before, but had it annulled. I can't remember what happened with his first marriage. I guess he was no stranger to annulments. The very next day after Kevin left for work, I called Charles to let him know.

"Charles, please don't ask me any questions but I need you to send me a plane ticket for Jana so that she can come live with you in North Carolina for a while. It is not going to work out with Kevin."

Trust me. I knew Charles wasn't going to ask me any questions at all. "Ok, no problem. I'll send you a ticket today to have her at the airport tomorrow."

I finally snatched that cheap ass ring off my finger and threw it on the bathroom counter. Ain't this some shit! There's a green ring around my finger! My damn finger looks infected!

I began to roam through Kevin's things as I knew I should have done more research on him prior to marrying him, but again, I was the one in a predicament and 'beggars can't be choosy'.

Kevin told me he takes a trip out of the country every year and we were going to do the same thing. I found his passport in the top drawer that showed one stamp on his passport in the past 10 years!

Then I found that big, black leather bag. The backpack that he tried to convince Jana to carry to school. It had copies of his tax returns. Kevin told me he was in IT, Information Technology. This is the same field Charles was in so I know they made good money. However, Kevin was not in IT, his role was Help Desk, which income wise is a far cry from IT. With a lot of overtime he was able to clear 57k but his base pay was 35k. Then I remembered his statement, "People making 35k can live a decent life." Maybe a decent life with no furniture and no money for gas for the car! His company had already stopped offering overtime.

The last thing I found was a receipt from eBay. The receipt was for a cubic zirconia engagement ring/wedding band set and a man's wedding band. My ring cost a whopping $29.99 and his ring cost $19.99. No wonder my goddamn finger felt like it was about to fall off!

I just dropped to the floor and screamed, "God why? Why is this happening to me?" But God wouldn't even allow one tear to drop from my eyes, so then I just started laughing. I knew I had not done my due diligence with Kevin; I only dated him for eight months and long distance at that, I never even had a chance to visit his home to see how he was accustomed to living. I never challenged him on anything he was telling me, I just wanted it to be true, I needed it to be true. To be a broke man was one thing but to be a lying broke man was another whole thing! Kevin made sure he did not tell flat out lies, most of his lies were by omission, which are still lies, and he was still being dishonest! And had the audacity to call me bougie when he was clearly trying to be somebody that he's not. Men like Kevin always want what they can't have; women who are out of their league.

Of all the trials and tribulations I had been through, losing my business, my real estate properties, my money, my home, being sued, losing my loved ones, and failing health, this trial had the most impact on my heart as a mother because I had to do something that I had never had to do before, and that was to send my daughter away because I did not have a roof over our heads and I had no idea how I was going to take care of her, or even myself for that matter. Yeah, I know Charles was her father and thank God he was stable enough to come through and step up and take Jana, but that was my baby! After 32 hours of labor, that baby belonged to me! This was the single lowest point of my life. That little girl was the reason I worked so hard, I tried so hard, I took so many risks, so that she could have a better life, more opportunities, better life experiences! And now for her own safety and well-being, I had to send her back to her father. Back to a place where she had her own room and her own friends in the neighborhood. Back to her place of comfort and familiarity. I cried my eyes out after I put her on that plane. Of course, I wore my poker face around her, so she was none the wiser. While I'm out here in these streets trying to figure out where I'm going to go, how I'm going to live and what I'm going to do just to survive.

I attended Lakewood Church one Sunday and Joseph Prince, from Singapore, was the guest speaker. The lady who sat next to me, Ann, had driven up from Lake Charles, Louisiana, that morning with one of her friends just to hear Joseph Prince speak. When it was time for prayer, Ann, a perfect stranger, grabbed my hand and began to prophesy. "God told me to tell you that it may look like you made a mistake, but you didn't. You are right where you are supposed to be. Don't be discouraged by the way things look right now. Everything you touch is going to prosper!"

I cried so hard! From the looks of it, my life was in shambles, total despair. But when Ann spoke a word of hope into my life, I couldn't help but to hold on to those words. Ann didn't know me from Adam. I hadn't told her anything about my situation. She had just asked me my name before she spoke life into my suffering heart. Maybe I was too close to it to see what God was going to do next. I decided to stop trying to figure out God's timing and just start focusing on my future.

I knew I couldn't stay with Kevin because I would have been miserable. The few things I know I needed in life were air, water, and peace. Peace! I would do anything for it! It took me a couple weeks to find a room to rent after going to view several places from Craigslist. I ended up renting a room for $500 from an older Jamaican woman named Ms. Louise. She lived in Spring, TX which was about 10 minutes from where I lived with Kevin, so I was semi familiar with the area.

Ms. Louise lived in a nice area where there were mature trees and overgrown bushes. It was an older home with older furnishings. But the room was fully furnished with a bed and mattress from the 70's! I believe the mattress also had bed bugs, as I itched all through the night, so I had to literally lay pillows on top of the mattress and sleep on top of them. She also had a multitude of cockroaches in her house, you know the ones that come rushing out every time you turn the bathroom light on? It was a rough time, but I hung in there with Ms. Louise for six months until I became licensed and started making money in real estate, and then I got a job in the mortgage industry.

After less than 18 months I flew down to North Carolina and moved Jana back to Houston. We had a very nice apartment on the north side and she was in a good school. There were many ups and downs in life as the real estate market continued to oscillate and things continued to change. I was a full time real estate agent the entire time Jana was with me so I could have the flexibility to be at home when she got home and to help her with whatever homework or projects she needed to be assisted. There were good financial times and there were bad financial times, and I rode whatever wave was to come.

After Jana graduated from high school, she moved back to North Carolina with her father. I was happy to see her go as a young adult because now I could work on what I wanted to do in life. I had already raised her, taught her everything I knew, gave her every part of who I am, and it was now time for her to experience life out from under my wings. It was time for her to spread her own wings. Charles and I had an agreement that since she didn't want to go to college, he would take her in after high school until she could figure out her life. Jana left Charles after six months and has been doing well living by herself and taking care of herself running her own business! I am such the proud Mama Bear! Anytime a 20 year old child can live on her own and not ask her parents for a dime, we should be singing Hallelujah!

After Jana moved back to North Carolina, I was able to land a job paying $17 an hour plus bonuses in the mortgage servicing industry. Once I got there and figured out how to capitalize on those bonuses, I made over six figures in the first year and every year thereafter, even during the Pandemic! Also during the Pandemic I paid off all the debt I had amassed when the market was down when Jana was in high school. The tide was finally turning back my way and I was now looking at life through a much clearer lens. I will always remember the words from the stranger from Lake Charles, LA, "Everything you touch will prosper."

God never puts more on you than you can bear. I used to hate that scripture because I couldn't understand why God was allowing so many bad things to happen to so many good people. It's hard to focus on that part when I am in the situation. But when I look back on the situation, there were some things I had to learn about myself, and there are some things that I also learned about God. My relationship with myself became stronger and my relationship with God became broader. Considering at some points in my life I was rolling my eyes and not even speaking to him anymore! But then I realized, and even though I hate to sound cliche, that my setback really was a setup. A setup for something greater! God was pushing me out of mediocrity and setting me up for my purpose in life! If you apply heat and pressure to lumps of coal, you eventually get black diamonds. I am those lumps of coal, and I am also Black Diamonds!

Chapter 26

MY FOREVER LOVE

L ife for me has gotten progressively easier. After I was debt free and could just focus on saving my money and working on my inner peace, there was still a lack in the love department. While I never had a problem getting asked out on dates, the dating pool was full of a bunch of dried up old playas playing the same old games. I was already 49 years old and starting over for what seemed to be the umpteenth time. I could write a book about the games that people play and the tricks of the trade and maybe I will one day! As I had been saying for years, "Ain't nothing out here in these streets!" This saying still remains true. I'd constantly remind myself that when I find that rare gem, that needle in the haystack, I'd know it when I experience it. I was sure of it!

I decided to take time out for myself. To purge myself if you will. I had been through enough in my life and was getting way too old to be wasting anymore precious time. While I would still go on dates, I was also practicing celibacy. This allowed me to tune into the guy's worthiness. If he was worthy of my time. Yes, I was going to judge it, I was going to judge him because I get to choose who and what I wanted and needed for my life.

I never wasted too much time going out multiple times with a guy. If I didn't like him or wasn't feeling his energy on the first date, then I would not agree to a second date. There would be no need for that. Most guys I met were from online dating, mainly because that is the only place to meet people in this day and age. There were so many times when I'd be out to lunch or dinner with a friend or even alone, and there would be a nice looking guy eating dinner alone and the only thing he's doing is looking down on his phone swiping left or right. Hell, he had a better chance of finding a woman on a dating app than he did in real life because he was never going to look up from that phone to see what was right in front of him!

While I had several online relationships over time, at this point only one lasted longer than a year. Hell, even the marriage to Kevin was over in six weeks! Most of my online dating encounters were epic failures, some were fortunate to just be friends, but every last one of them was a huge learning experience that prepared me for the next one.

"You only need one of them to be the right one for you, Natasha." I'd constantly remind myself. "Keep your standards high, as lowering them has proven to be a disaster, stay open but keep a watchful eye, and if you're not feeling him, keep it moving to the next! It only takes one!"

On July 11, 2020, a guy by the name of Eugene Baymon reached out to me on a site called Plenty of Fish, aka POF. My very first conversation with Eugene was pretty unique. All the things they say you shouldn't talk about in the first conversation, we talked about! We talked about our past marriages and he even shared with me how he was served divorce papers at a family cookout that his ex-wife wanted to have. While he's in the backyard barbecuing, the wife and her family were sitting around eating and drinking and laughing and having a merry time. One of her family members comes out to the backyard and says, "Hey Eugene, someone at the front door needs to speak to you." It was the processor serving him his divorce papers! Damn! And I thought my shit was fucked up. It was good to know that someone else had been through some shit and had survived it and realized he was better off without it!

Eugene graduated from Jackson State University with a degree in Biology. He also retired from the United States Armed Forces as a Lt. Colonel, and was seemingly very intelligent with a hint of ADHD (Attention Deficit Hyperactivity Disorder). I'm normally attracted to the articulate guy, whether educated or not. It may just be the region where he grew up, a small town called Belzoni, MS., located in the Mississippi Delta. It did not take long for me to notice that Eugene's grammar would be considered "subpar" as he was the king of splitting verbs, adverbs, adjectives, and prepositional phrases! And ooooh yes, he was country! I mean that deep down in the Delta, Mississippi country! Multiple times I've contemplated correcting Eugene on his grammar. Then one day I heard God say, "He's gotten this far without you correcting him, why would he need you to correct him now?" Yes, I'm learning to keep my two cents to myself!

There's something extremely genuine and unpretentious about Eugene. It definitely makes him unique. Head and shoulders above the rest. Triple split verbs, double negatives, and all! There's no value you can put on the purity of a man's heart... priceless.

Eugene had very open communication with me from the beginning. I never had to try hard in order to get him to open up and talk about himself, his life, his upbringing, and what he felt about it. He was an open book, just like I am. Genuine and extremely authentic.

Eugene asked me to meet him for dinner on a Sunday night, July 19, 2020. However, he wanted to make sure that we continued our conversations leading up to that point. We ended up talking every night, texting throughout the workday, and meeting at 6:30 PM in City Centre in Houston, TX at a Mexican restaurant called Cyclone Anaya's for dinner and drinks.

Of course, Eugene was already inside the restaurant, had a table near a window and was already settled. I liked that! The man should always get to the spot first and be waiting on the woman, never the other way around.

As I walked into the restaurant and saw Eugene walking towards the door, both wearing masks as we met in the middle of the Pandemic, we said hello to each other and gave each other a hug. All I could feel was a hard chest and big muscular arms. I was not expecting Eugene to have this steel body of muscles! I was pleasantly surprised to say the least. He directed me to our table and pulled out my chair for me. A gentleman I see! I like it! Chivalry is not dead! Thank God it's still alive!

We both sat down at the table and took off our masks. To my right there was a bouquet of flowers on the table. Hmmmmm, thoughtful too, I see!

"Thank you so much for the flowers!" I picked them up and inhaled the fresh scent of roses.

"Beautiful flowers for a beautiful woman."

As Eugene looked over his glasses at me, pulled off his mask, and started smiling, I thought, "Wow I'm definitely interested in this brother! Country and all!"

Eugene was 6 feet tall, big arms and chest, chocolate, bald, bearded, intelligent, and had a nice smile! The smile was definitely the icing on the cake. This was an amazing start!

The first thought I had of Eugene was that he looked much better than his pictures. We met online and had about a week of written conversations on the dating site prior to exchanging numbers. All of Eugene's pictures were in a very casual setting, work, cycling, in front of a state billboard. He also had all selfies that he attempted to take except not at the right angles. He never smiled in any of his pictures, which led me to think he may have missing teeth, gold teeth, or a flat out gold grill. Trust me this has happened to me before, so I was leaving nothing up to chance. I would have to examine those teeth later. However, since I know a lot of men don't smile in their pictures, I was not going to make that a big deal, at least not yet.

We talked about anything and everything under the sun. From past relationships, to family, to children, to work experiences. We laughed until we almost cried! And Eugene being from the Delta and all, could care less about the people at the other side of the restaurant hearing his loud, boisterous laughter across the room. After a couple hours, I needed to go to the restroom. Of course I knew he would be watching me as I walked away, so I was very careful not to slip, trip, or bump into anything. On my way back, I realized we had already been there for over two hours. I told Eugene, "I only fed the meter for two hours because I didn't think we would be here so long."

Eugene stated, "If you have a ticket when I walk you to the car, I will definitely take care of that for you. No worries."

Stepping in and stepping up, huh! That manliness is so sexy to me. He was definitely checking my boxes! Check! Check! Check! It's not about what he was saying, but it was more about the fact that his words aligned with his actions. That night on the first date as he walked me to my car, I mentioned to him that I was in the process of planning my 50th birthday party and was looking for a venue. He suggested that I should let him know when I decide where I wanted to have it and how much it would cost so that he can contribute. Of course, I've been around long enough to know that men say whatever they think you want to hear in the beginning because they believe you may be willing to "give them some" but they have absolutely no intentions on following through. But not Eugene. A couple months had passed and we were still dating and just as he said he ended up paying about ⅓ of the total costs of my venue. I went all out, too! It was top of the line red carpet baby! My family members and friends came down to Houston to celebrate with me. We had the stretch limo, photographer, videographer, all you can eat and all you can drink! We were dancing our butts off like it was 1999!

After the first date, I texted Eugene to let him know I made it home safely and he texted me back the next morning:

"Good morning Natasha! Beautiful, let me tell you about this woman that I met yesterday. I have a new definition of "soul food". She is inspiring, jazzy, motivated, ride or die. She wears a halo; not perfect, but perfect for me. She is down to earth, but can swing out with the best of them. She loves her family and embraces their imperfections. Beautiful understands that God has blessed her as a beacon of light for her family. I am going to see if I can fit in too! Ain't no need for all of those good qualities going up North! I have to call you and tell you more, but she is hot food for my soul! In the words of James Evans of Good Times, 'When I say hot, damn it! I mean hot!'"

The following day I was not feeling too well. I had a sinus headache. Eugene offered to have whatever I needed delivered to my apartment and then also had crab cakes delivered from Ruth's Chris Steakhouse for dinner. This man was being extremely attentive and was definitely a pleaser.

Eugene asked for the second date on Friday July 24th, at Papa's Steakhouse. He wanted to know if I was comfortable enough for him to pick me up. Hell, he already had my address from having food delivered earlier that week. Since the Steakhouse was not too far from my apartment, I agreed that he could pick me up, but he was to meet me in front of the leasing office. I drove my car down from the four story garage to meet him. As I parked, I called him to ask what color his vehicle was.

He stated, "Look around, I'm already here." To my surprise, as I looked around I spotted this beautiful shiny, black Range Rover and he was standing on the outside.

"Ok, I see you!" I thought as I flashed a smile at him. He walked up to me and helped me into the vehicle, as it was tall and a little challenging to step up into it. Luckily, I was wearing a short dress, so he got to see ALL my legs! I wore a blue flowery dress with sheer sleeves and some nude pumps. Eugene stood tall and firm with his colorful Robert Graham button down shirt, with jeans and some nice, shined shoes. He was definitely handsome, and this Range Rover made him look even sexier! It started to rain on our way to the restaurant. I asked if he had an umbrella in the car and he did not. "Oh, but I will stop at a store to pick one up," he said. By the time we approached the restaurant, the rain had ceased, so he didn't have to pick up an umbrella after all. I'm sensing his thoughtful nature!

He valet parked the truck and we walked into the restaurant, masks and all. We talked about everything, ordered our ribeye steaks along with some cocktails and shared the creamed spinach. I was definitely liking him, but life has taught me to be cautious. Most guys will put their best foot forward in the beginning, but will he flip the script? I didn't know. Only time will tell. One thing I did know is the script had been flipped before. "Don't get in your head, Natasha. Baby steps. Enjoy the moment."

I got up to go to the Ladies' room and after I came back, Eugene went to the Men's room. I turned around to watch him walk away and noticed he had a limp in his walk. I thought, "Oh Lord! It looked like he was walking on hot coals. I got an old man on my hands. Or at least he walks like one! It's always something!"

I never mentioned his "old man limp" to him, as I am practicing, 'keeping my mouth shut' and living in the moment. Later, Eugene would tell me that he recently found out that he had a degenerative hip, and he cycles 10-20 miles a day and does water exercises at the gym to loosen the muscles in that area to avoid having hip surgery. Wow! That's dedication! I felt badly about focusing on this "old man limp" and I'm glad I never brought it up to him and even happier that I didn't allow something so minor to deter m e.

As we walked back to the vehicle, Eugene grabbed me around the waist, pulled me into him, and we had our very first kiss. I wasn't surprised about the kiss as I knew by the look in his eyes that he was going to kiss me. The kiss was good, but I figured he may have been nervous or anxious because he really pressed his face to mine just a little bit harder than what I'm accustomed to. I mean, were our skulls kissing or our lips? Stay focused, Natasha! I could later teach him what I like as far as kissing goes. Stop making a big deal out of nothing!

On the next date, Eugene requested that I meet him at his house so that we could ride to brunch together. He had a nice single level brick home in a very nice neighborhood. After giving me a tour of the home, which was beautifully decorated especially for a man, we sat on the reclining sofa for conversation. This was our first 'make out session'. This was also an opportunity for me to show Eugene what I like in the way of kissing. I asked him to close his eyes and to follow my lead. Of course, he did! Kissing doesn't have to be strong and hard and fast in order to be passionate. I believe when you take your time with the person and savor each taste of the lips, this is passion. At least it is to me.

I knew that I was taking a risk with Eugene. Not all men were capable of taking instruction from a woman they liked. However, being almost 50 years old has taught me to let the man know how you like things done so you can get it the way you like it. If not, you may very well go your entire life kissing a man in a way that does not turn you on! I'm way too old for that!

Eugene also gave me more flowers; I love the thoughtfulness of flowers. It's something about a man who gives flowers. No, they are not going to last longer than 7-10 days, but it's the thought in the moment that counts. There was a room in his home that had a wine cabinet where he housed different types of wines to cool. He buys bottles of wine and then ages them for some years. As we were talking about the different wines, we ended up making out on the floor in this wine room.

He came behind me and began gently rubbing his face on the back of my neck. He then started kissing my neck. He twirled me around with his strong arms and kissed me passionately, caressing my body as his hands oscillated up and down the middle of my back. I have no idea how we ended on the floor, but we were just kissing, grinding, rubbing, and being close to one another. Yes, I was still celibate, but only for the moment.

Eugene was pouring it on rather thick. I mean that country, down in the Delta Mississippi thick, like molasses thick! Messaging me about how perfect I am for him and how blessed he is to have the opportunity to get to know me, how beautiful I am and how he just wants to see more of me. It was a lot for me to receive, so much, so soon. I ended up asking him to slow down and let's allow for a more natural progression.

I definitely knew I liked Eugene and he was pulling out all the stops to show me that he liked me. I just wanted us to take our time to make sure we were getting what we thought we were getting. Relationships take time to develop and there is no need to rush when we can just take our time and enjoy each moment.

One day I asked Eugene if he liked pizza and I would bring my favorite pizza, Blaze Pizza, over to his house for dinner. He absolutely loved the pizza and ate it all in one setting! Good thing I bought two pizzas! Eugene provided the salad and wine. We listened to some R&B oldies and sang slow jams to each other. Eugene can NOT sing or dance, but he is so comfortable in his skin, no one would ever know. We were singing loud and wrong and were merely enjoying one another's company. No holds barred!

After dinner, Eugene suggested we play pool. He actually has a pool table in the room designated for a dining room. Most bachelors will not find a need for a dining room, but a pool table room, absolutely!

I informed him that I did not know how to play pool and he suggested that he could teach me. I agreed to give it a shot. For some reason he thought that I was going to catch on pretty quickly and we would play a full game of pool, keeping score and all. However, once he realized in reality that I couldn't even hit the ball and we would need to start from scratch, then he changed his mind and said we would just work on hitting the ball. At some point, he hung up the pool stick and came over to me to hug me. He just held me, without a word. No kissing, no fondling, just music playing in the background. I could hear his heartbeat as my ear pressed against his broad chest. It was such a tender moment. Slowly, a tear ran down my cheek. And I began to melt like butter in his arms. Suddenly I felt...shall I dare say... safe, comforted, and secure. I felt home. I had no idea why I was crying. Was I tipsy with wine? I inwardly laughed at myself as I brushed that tear away before he was able to see it and start asking questions. In that moment, I realized it was a safe place to be vulnerable, to let go of that breath I had been holding my entire life. It was a safe place to finally exhale.

Early mornings I have what I call my "morning glory" rooftop experience. Usually 4-5 times a week. Morning glory is simply listening to my gospel music first thing in the morning while exercising/walking approximately a mile and a half on the rooftop of my apartment building. It's a great view, no-one's there that early, and I also have an opportunity to get a little exercise in. Spending time with God first thing in the morning has proven to be an awakening experience and helps me to focus on the rest of my day, by putting God first.

I was on a five day juice cleanse, just trying to detox. Since Eugene loves to eat and drink, same as I, I had to let him know that I would not be able to see him during my detox. He seemed to have understood.

Days later Eugene asked to come over to my apartment just to see me for a while, even though we had a date scheduled for the next night, I happily obliged. When he arrived at my apartment he came in, kissed me on the lips and had his hands behind his back as if hiding something. First of all I am a sucker for surprises! I had no idea what he was up to. There was a square black box in his hand of medium size. He set the black box on the table and said, "This is for you. I was going to wait until our one-month anniversary, but it came in the mail today and I couldn't wait to give it to you." I looked at the box and there was a picture of a cell phone on the front cover. He suggested I open the box which I did and there were some wireless earbuds. What! He bought me those wireless earbuds after a conversation that we had a couple of weeks prior that the Apple earbuds that I currently had always hurt my ears and I had to plug them into my cell phone in order to use them.

How thoughtful is that? A man who actually listens in general and tries to make my life better than it was before even without me asking! He's definitely a gem. A diamond in the rough. A needle in the haystack. I may have actually found my Prince Charming after all!

Oh Lord! I didn't think we would be exchanging gifts for our one-month anniversary! And even though I know he is not expecting a gift, however, I am not one to disappoint. When Eugene left my apartment that evening I hurried to Amazon.com to try to find him a gift that I could have via prime delivery in one business day. I remember Eugene stating that he smokes a certain type of cigar. I found that cigar online and paid for it to be rushed overnight. I also found a cigar holder on Amazon.com and requested they gift wrap it and ship it overnight. Both gifts came in time for the anniversary. Whew! That was a close call!

On our one-month anniversary, I suggested to Eugene that we not go out, but I would cook our anniversary dinner. I went to Whole Foods and picked up some salmon burgers and made some roasted garlic asparagus. I had a variety of appetizers, chips and salsa, and a cheese and fruit tray.

It was nice and relaxing and I wore my black and white leopard skin sundress from White House Black Market, showing all the cleavage. Eugene looks at me with such awe! Whether I have on a sexy dress or pajama pants and a T-shirt. He definitely sees the beauty within me. Not just the outward beauty that I may have been blessed with. No, he actually sees me.

My life with Eugene has been all that I imagined it would be, all that I imagined it should be. We celebrated his cousin's wedding in Chicago, my 50th birthday party with family and friends in Houston, his son's White Coat Ceremony as he is now an Emergency Room doctor at Brigham and Women's Hospital in Boston, MA, my friend's wedding in Cabo, and even went to visit his family in Belzoni, MS.

After about 15 months of dating, Eugene and I purchased a beautiful home together, and the following month, he asked me to marry him! Of course, he proposed on one knee right there in the jewelry store and we went back to Cyclone Anaya's in City Centre where we first met to celebrate. This is where the connection first began! We will be married in Jamaica in July 2023!

I've always prayed that my partner would be my best friend. Who doesn't want a lover who is also their best friend? A person who can communicate and is amicable about working things out. A person who is a man of his word and is consistent in his endeavors. The person I can work with, have fun with, and enjoy life with. The person I can support and be supported by. The person where the physical attraction matches the intimacy and spiritual connection. The person I can grow with and experience life with. I had to kiss a lot of frogs to get to the Prince, my Prince Charming, but I finally found my person, my safe place, my home. My forever love is Eugene Baymon!

Chapter 27

TRIBUTE TO LIL' MAMA

There are plenty of women in the world whom I could say have paved the way such as Oprah Winfrey, Kamala Harris, Michelle Obama, Angela Bassett, Viola Davis, and so many others. But it was you and only you, Lil' Mama, whose shoulders I stood on, to become the woman that I am today.

You were there when my father and his parents would not even acknowledge me. You were there when my own mother could not take care of me. When I didn't have food to eat, you fed me. When I didn't have a place to live, you sheltered me. When I was sick, you nurtured me back to health. When I was afraid, you were my safe place. When I was sad, you let me cry on your shoulders and wrapped your loving arms around me. You comforted me and helped me to stay in a peaceful state of mind. You raised me as your child. You loved me unconditionally.

You have taught me so much about life. As I watched you work serving food in the hospital cafeteria, I never understood how you were able to feed all us grandkids with two fish and five loaves of bread. Plus we were always able to come back for seconds! Jesus was not the only one working miracles with food! Also, when Lil' Daddy was dying of cancer, I watched as you loved him and cared for him until he took his last breath, while never missing a beat taking care of the rest of the family. Although we did not grow up in the church, the love that you exemplified, taught me about the love of God. When you showed me love, you showed me God, and for that I am eternally grateful.

My only regret is that I was not able to do more for you before you transitioned. When you died, I was so heartbroken because I lost my mother and my best friend. I still think about you often and I have nothing but amazing memories of you and the time we spent together because you were an amazing grandmother and I love you dearly.

I owe you my life. Everything that I am is because of you. Everything that I have ever aspired to be is because you actually made me believe that it could come true. Your presence in my life has made all the difference in the world! I pray that I have made you proud as I stand in my truth, just the way you taught me to do. The truth is sometimes a hard pill to swallow, but also necessary for healing. I hope this book will help other people, especially women, to understand that life can sometimes be difficult, but if they can just hold on to the dream that God put in their hearts, that dream will come to pass. It is impossible for God to lie!

I stand on your shoulders, Lil' Mama! It is because of you I am strong, courageous, persistent, diligent, a survivor, loving, compassionate, loyal, faithful, generous, kind-hearted, genuine, transparent, of good character, a mother, a friend, and a sister. Because of you, I Am Woman!

Made in the USA
Columbia, SC
13 May 2023

33f2e4d2-0a22-43ab-980a-4f1ccb4f24a2R01